Life Application Bible Studies
JOHN

APPLICATION® BIBLE STUDIES

Part 1:
Complete text of John with study notes and features from the
Life Application Study Bible

Part 2:
Thirteen lessons for individual or group study

Study questions written and edited by

Rev. Ed Trenner
Rev. David R. Veerman
Dr. James C. Galvin
Dr. Bruce B. Barton

New Living
Translation

Tyndale House Publishers, Inc.
Carol Stream, Illinois

CONTENTS

A NOTE TO READERS

The *Holy Bible*, New Living Translation, was first published in 1996. It quickly became one of the most popular Bible translations in the English-speaking world. While the NLT's influence was rapidly growing, the Bible Translation Committee determined that an additional investment in scholarly review and text refinement could make it even better. So shortly after its initial publication, the committee began an eight-year process with the purpose of increasing the level of the NLT's precision without sacrificing its easy-to-understand quality. This second-generation text was completed in 2004 and is reflected in this edition of the New Living Translation. An additional update with minor changes was subsequently introduced in 2007.

The goal of any Bible translation is to convey the meaning and content of the ancient Hebrew, Aramaic, and Greek texts as accurately as possible to contemporary readers. The challenge for our translators was to create a text that would communicate as clearly and powerfully to today's readers as the original texts did to readers and listeners in the ancient biblical world. The resulting translation is easy to read and understand, while also accurately communicating the meaning and content of the original biblical texts. The NLT is a general-purpose text especially good for study, devotional reading, and reading aloud in worship services.

We believe that the New Living Translation—which combines the latest biblical scholarship with a clear, dynamic writing style—will communicate God's word powerfully to all who read it. We publish it with the prayer that God will use it to speak his timeless truth to the church and the world in a fresh, new way.

The Publishers
October 2007

INTRODUCTION TO THE
NEW LIVING TRANSLATION

Translation Philosophy and Methodology

English Bible translations tend to be governed by one of two general translation theories. The first theory has been called "formal-equivalence," "literal," or "word-for-word" translation. According to this theory, the translator attempts to render each word of the original language into English and seeks to preserve the original syntax and sentence structure as much as possible in translation. The second theory has been called "dynamic-equivalence," "functional-equivalence," or "thought-for-thought" translation. The goal of this translation theory is to produce in English the closest natural equivalent of the message expressed by the original-language text, both in meaning and in style.

Both of these translation theories have their strengths. A formal-equivalence translation preserves aspects of the original text—including ancient idioms, term consistency, and original-language syntax—that are valuable for scholars and professional study. It allows a reader to trace formal elements of the original-language text through the English translation. A dynamic-equivalence translation, on the other hand, focuses on translating the message of the original-language text. It ensures that the meaning of the text is readily apparent to the contemporary reader. This allows the message to come through with immediacy, without requiring the reader to struggle with foreign idioms and awkward syntax. It also facilitates serious study of the text's message and clarity in both devotional and public reading.

The pure application of either of these translation philosophies would create translations at opposite ends of the translation spectrum. But in reality, all translations contain a mixture of these two philosophies. A purely formal-equivalence translation would be unintelligible in English, and a purely dynamic-equivalence translation would risk being unfaithful to the original. That is why translations shaped by dynamic-equivalence theory are usually quite literal when the original text is relatively clear, and the translations shaped by formal-equivalence theory are sometimes quite dynamic when the original text is obscure.

The translators of the New Living Translation set out to render the message of the original texts of Scripture into clear, contemporary English. As they did so, they kept the concerns of both formal-equivalence and dynamic-equivalence in mind. On the one hand, they translated as simply and literally as possible when that approach yielded an accurate, clear, and natural English text. Many words and phrases were rendered literally and consistently into English, preserving essential literary and rhetorical devices, ancient metaphors, and word choices that give structure to the text and provide echoes of meaning from one passage to the next.

On the other hand, the translators rendered the message more dynamically when the literal rendering was hard to understand, was misleading, or yielded archaic or foreign wording. They clarified difficult metaphors and terms to aid in the reader's understanding. The translators first struggled with the meaning of the words and phrases in the ancient context; then they rendered the message into clear, natural English. Their goal was to be both faithful to the ancient texts and eminently readable. The result is a translation that is both exegetically accurate and idiomatically powerful.

Translation Process and Team

To produce an accurate translation of the Bible into contemporary English, the translation team needed the skills necessary to enter into the thought patterns of the ancient authors and then to render their ideas, connotations, and effects into clear, contemporary English.

To begin this process, qualified biblical scholars were needed to interpret the meaning of the original text and to check it against our base English translation. In order to guard against personal and theological biases, the scholars needed to represent a diverse group of evangelicals who would employ the best exegetical tools. Then to work alongside the scholars, skilled English stylists were needed to shape the text into clear, contemporary English.

With these concerns in mind, the Bible Translation Committee recruited teams of scholars that represented a broad spectrum of denominations, theological perspectives, and backgrounds within the worldwide evangelical community. Each book of the Bible was assigned to three different scholars with proven expertise in the book or group of books to be reviewed. Each of these scholars made a thorough review of a base translation and submitted suggested revisions to the appropriate Senior Translator. The Senior Translator then reviewed and summarized these suggestions and proposed a first-draft revision of the base text. This draft served as the basis for several additional phases of exegetical and stylistic committee review. Then the Bible Translation Committee jointly reviewed and approved every verse of the final translation.

Throughout the translation and editing process, the Senior Translators and their scholar teams were given a chance to review the editing done by the team of stylists. This ensured that exegetical errors would not be introduced late in the process and that the entire Bible Translation Committee was happy with the final result. By choosing a team of qualified scholars and skilled stylists and by setting up a process that allowed their interaction throughout the process, the New Living Translation has been refined to preserve the essential formal elements of the original biblical texts, while also creating a clear, understandable English text.

The New Living Translation was first published in 1996. Shortly after its initial publication, the Bible Translation Committee began a process of further committee review and translation refinement. The purpose of this continued revision was to increase the level of precision without sacrificing the text's easy-to-understand quality. This second-edition text was completed in 2004, and an additional update with minor changes was subsequently introduced in 2007. This printing of the New Living Translation reflects the updated 2007 text.

Written to Be Read Aloud
It is evident in Scripture that the biblical documents were written to be read aloud, often in public worship (see Nehemiah 8; Luke 4:16-20; 1 Timothy 4:13; Revelation 1:3). It is still the case today that more people will hear the Bible read aloud in church than are likely to read it for themselves. Therefore, a new translation must communicate with clarity and power when it is read publicly. Clarity was a primary goal for the NLT translators, not only to facilitate private reading and understanding, but also to ensure that it would be excellent for public reading and make an immediate and powerful impact on any listener.

The Texts behind the New Living Translation
The Old Testament translators used the Masoretic Text of the Hebrew Bible as represented in *Biblia Hebraica Stuttgartensia* (1977), with its extensive system of textual notes; this is an update of Rudolf Kittel's *Biblia Hebraica* (Stuttgart, 1937). The translators also further compared the Dead Sea Scrolls, the Septuagint and other Greek manuscripts, the Samaritan Pentateuch, the Syriac Peshitta, the Latin Vulgate, and any other versions or manuscripts that shed light on the meaning of difficult passages.

The New Testament translators used the two standard editions of the Greek New Testament: the *Greek New Testament*, published by the United Bible Societies (UBS, fourth revised edition, 1993), and *Novum Testamentum Graece*, edited by Nestle and Aland (NA, twenty-seventh edition, 1993). These two editions, which have the same text but differ in punctuation and textual notes, represent, for the most part, the best in modern textual scholarship. However, in cases where strong textual or other scholarly evidence supported the decision, the translators sometimes chose to differ from the UBS and NA Greek texts and followed variant readings found in other ancient witnesses. Significant textual variants of this sort are always noted in the textual notes of the New Living Translation.

Translation Issues
The translators have made a conscious effort to provide a text that can be easily understood by the typical reader of modern English. To this end, we sought to use only vocabulary and

language structures in common use today. We avoided using language likely to become quickly dated or that reflects only a narrow subdialect of English, with the goal of making the New Living Translation as broadly useful and timeless as possible.

But our concern for readability goes beyond the concerns of vocabulary and sentence structure. We are also concerned about historical and cultural barriers to understanding the Bible, and we have sought to translate terms shrouded in history and culture in ways that can be immediately understood. To this end:

- We have converted ancient weights and measures (for example, "ephah" [a unit of dry volume] or "cubit" [a unit of length]) to modern English (American) equivalents, since the ancient measures are not generally meaningful to today's readers. Then in the textual footnotes we offer the literal Hebrew, Aramaic, or Greek measures, along with modern metric equivalents.
- Instead of translating ancient currency values literally, we have expressed them in common terms that communicate the message. For example, in the Old Testament, "ten shekels of silver" becomes "ten pieces of silver" to convey the intended message. In the New Testament, we have often translated the "denarius" as "the normal daily wage" to facilitate understanding. Then a footnote offers: "Greek *a denarius,* the payment for a full day's wage." In general, we give a clear English rendering and then state the literal Hebrew, Aramaic, or Greek in a textual footnote.
- Since the names of Hebrew months are unknown to most contemporary readers, and since the Hebrew lunar calendar fluctuates from year to year in relation to the solar calendar used today, we have looked for clear ways to communicate the time of year the Hebrew months (such as Abib) refer to. When an expanded or interpretive rendering is given in the text, a textual note gives the literal rendering. Where it is possible to define a specific ancient date in terms of our modern calendar, we use modern dates in the text. A textual footnote then gives the literal Hebrew date and states the rationale for our rendering. For example, Ezra 6:15 pinpoints the date when the postexilic Temple was completed in Jerusalem: "the third day of the month Adar." This was during the sixth year of King Darius's reign (that is, 515 B.C.). We have translated that date as March 12, with a footnote giving the Hebrew and identifying the year as 515 B.C.
- Since ancient references to the time of day differ from our modern methods of denoting time, we have used renderings that are instantly understandable to the modern reader. Accordingly, we have rendered specific times of day by using approximate equivalents in terms of our common "o'clock" system. On occasion, translations such as "at dawn the next morning" or "as the sun was setting" have been used when the biblical reference is more general.
- When the meaning of a proper name (or a wordplay inherent in a proper name) is relevant to the message of the text, its meaning is often illuminated with a textual footnote. For example, in Exodus 2:10 the text reads: "The princess named him Moses, for she explained, 'I lifted him out of the water.' " The accompanying footnote reads: "*Moses* sounds like a Hebrew term that means 'to lift out.' "

  Sometimes, when the actual meaning of a name is clear, that meaning is included in parentheses within the text itself. For example, the text at Genesis 16:11 reads: "You are to name him Ishmael *(which means 'God hears'),* for the LORD has heard your cry of distress." Since the original hearers and readers would have instantly understood the meaning of the name "Ishmael," we have provided modern readers with the same information so they can experience the text in a similar way.
- Many words and phrases carry a great deal of cultural meaning that was obvious to the original readers but needs explanation in our own culture. For example, the phrase "they beat their breasts" (Luke 23:48) in ancient times meant that people were very upset, often in mourning. In our translation we chose to translate this phrase dynamically for clarity: "They went home *in deep sorrow.*" Then we included a footnote with the literal Greek, which reads: "Greek *went home beating their breasts.*" In other similar cases, however, we have sometimes chosen to illuminate the existing literal expression to make it immediately understandable. For example, here we might have expanded the literal Greek phrase to read: "They went home

beating their breasts *in sorrow."* If we had done this, we would not have included a textual footnote, since the literal Greek clearly appears in translation.

- Metaphorical language is sometimes difficult for contemporary readers to understand, so at times we have chosen to translate or illuminate the meaning of a metaphor. For example, the ancient poet writes, "Your neck is *like* the tower of David" (Song of Songs 4:4). We have rendered it "Your neck is *as beautiful as* the tower of David" to clarify the intended positive meaning of the simile. Another example comes in Ecclesiastes 12:3, which can be literally rendered: "Remember him . . . when the grinding women cease because they are few, and the women who look through the windows see dimly." We have rendered it: "Remember him before your teeth—your few remaining servants—stop grinding; and before your eyes—the women looking through the windows—see dimly." We clarified such metaphors only when we believed a typical reader might be confused by the literal text.

- When the content of the original language text is poetic in character, we have rendered it in English poetic form. We sought to break lines in ways that clarify and highlight the relationships between phrases of the text. Hebrew poetry often uses parallelism, a literary form where a second phrase (or in some instances a third or fourth) echoes the initial phrase in some way. In Hebrew parallelism, the subsequent parallel phrases continue, while also furthering and sharpening, the thought expressed in the initial line or phrase. Whenever possible, we sought to represent these parallel phrases in natural poetic English.

- The Greek term *hoi Ioudaioi* is literally translated "the Jews" in many English translations. In the Gospel of John, however, this term doesn't always refer to the Jewish people generally. In some contexts, it refers more particularly to the Jewish religious leaders. We have attempted to capture the meaning in these different contexts by using terms such as "the people" (with a footnote: Greek *the Jewish people*) or "the religious leaders," where appropriate.

- One challenge we faced was how to translate accurately the ancient biblical text that was originally written in a context where male-oriented terms were used to refer to humanity generally. We needed to respect the nature of the ancient context while also trying to make the translation clear to a modern audience that tends to read male-oriented language as applying only to males. Often the original text, though using masculine nouns and pronouns, clearly intends that the message be applied to both men and women. A typical example is found in the New Testament letters, where the believers are called "brothers" (*adelphoi*). Yet it is clear from the content of these letters that they were addressed to all the believers—male and female. Thus, we have usually translated this Greek word as "brothers and sisters" in order to represent the historical situation more accurately.

  We have also been sensitive to passages where the text applies generally to human beings or to the human condition. In some instances we have used plural pronouns (they, them) in place of the masculine singular (he, him). For example, a traditional rendering of Proverbs 22:6 is: "Train up a child in the way he should go, and when he is old he will not turn from it." We have rendered it: "Direct your children onto the right path, and when they are older, they will not leave it." At times, we have also replaced third person pronouns with the second person to ensure clarity. A traditional rendering of Proverbs 26:27 is: "He who digs a pit will fall into it, and he who rolls a stone, it will come back on him." We have rendered it: "If you set a trap for others, you will get caught in it yourself. If you roll a boulder down on others, it will crush you instead."

  We should emphasize, however, that all masculine nouns and pronouns used to represent God (for example, "Father") have been maintained without exception. All decisions of this kind have been driven by the concern to reflect accurately the intended meaning of the original texts of Scripture.

Lexical Consistency in Terminology
For the sake of clarity, we have translated certain original-language terms consistently, especially within synoptic passages and for commonly repeated rhetorical phrases, and within

certain word categories such as divine names and non-theological technical terminology (e.g., liturgical, legal, cultural, zoological, and botanical terms). For theological terms, we have allowed a greater semantic range of acceptable English words or phrases for a single Hebrew or Greek word. We have avoided some theological terms that are not readily understood by many modern readers. For example, we avoided using words such as "justification" and "sanctification," which are carryovers from Latin translations. In place of these words, we have provided renderings such as "made right with God" and "made holy."

The Spelling of Proper Names

Many individuals in the Bible, especially the Old Testament, are known by more than one name (e.g., Uzziah/Azariah). For the sake of clarity, we have tried to use a single spelling for any one individual, footnoting the literal spelling whenever we differ from it. This is especially helpful in delineating the kings of Israel and Judah. King Joash/Jehoash of Israel has been consistently called Jehoash, while King Joash/Jehoash of Judah is called Joash. A similar distinction has been used to distinguish between Joram/Jehoram of Israel and Joram/Jehoram of Judah. All such decisions were made with the goal of clarifying the text for the reader. When the ancient biblical writers clearly had a theological purpose in their choice of a variant name (e.g., Esh-baal/Ishbosheth), the different names have been maintained with an explanatory footnote.

For the names Jacob and Israel, which are used interchangeably for both the individual patriarch and the nation, we generally render it "Israel" when it refers to the nation and "Jacob" when it refers to the individual. When our rendering of the name differs from the underlying Hebrew text, we provide a textual footnote, which includes this explanation: "The names 'Jacob' and 'Israel' are often interchanged throughout the Old Testament, referring sometimes to the individual patriarch and sometimes to the nation."

The Rendering of Divine Names

All appearances of *'el, 'elohim,* or *'eloah* have been translated "God," except where the context demands the translation "god(s)." We have generally rendered the tetragrammaton (*YHWH*) consistently as "the LORD," utilizing a form with small capitals that is common among English translations. This will distinguish it from the name *'adonai,* which we render "Lord." When *'adonai* and *YHWH* appear together, we have rendered it "Sovereign LORD." This also distinguishes *'adonai YHWH* from cases where *YHWH* appears with *'elohim,* which is rendered "LORD God." When *YH* (the short form of *YHWH*) and *YHWH* appear together, we have rendered it "LORD GOD." When *YHWH* appears with the term *tseba'oth,* we have rendered it "LORD of Heaven's Armies" to translate the meaning of the name. In a few cases, we have utilized the transliteration, *Yahweh,* when the personal character of the name is being invoked in contrast to another divine name or the name of some other god (for example, see Exodus 3:15; 6:2-3).

In the New Testament, the Greek word *christos* has been translated as "Messiah" when the context assumes a Jewish audience. When a Gentile audience can be assumed, *christos* has been translated as "Christ." The Greek word *kurios* is consistently translated "Lord," except that it is translated "LORD" wherever the New Testament text explicitly quotes from the Old Testament, and the text there has it in small capitals.

Textual Footnotes

The New Living Translation provides several kinds of textual footnotes, all designated in the text with an asterisk:

- When for the sake of clarity the NLT renders a difficult or potentially confusing phrase dynamically, we generally give the literal rendering in a textual footnote. This allows the reader to see the literal source of our dynamic rendering and how our translation relates to other more literal translations. These notes are prefaced with "Hebrew," "Aramaic," or "Greek," identifying the language of the underlying source text. For example, in Acts 2:42 we translated the literal "breaking of bread" (from the Greek) as "the Lord's Supper" to clarify that this verse refers to the ceremonial practice of the church rather than just an ordinary meal. Then we attached a footnote to "the Lord's Supper," which reads: "Greek *the breaking of bread.*"

- Textual footnotes are also used to show alternative renderings, prefaced with the word "Or." These normally occur for passages where an aspect of the meaning is debated. On occasion, we also provide notes on words or phrases that represent a departure from long-standing tradition. These notes are prefaced with "Traditionally rendered." For example, the footnote to the translation "serious skin disease" at Leviticus 13:2 says: "Traditionally rendered *leprosy.* The Hebrew word used throughout this passage is used to describe various skin diseases."

- When our translators follow a textual variant that differs significantly from our standard Hebrew or Greek texts (listed earlier), we document that difference with a footnote. We also footnote cases when the NLT excludes a passage that is included in the Greek text known as the *Textus Receptus* (and familiar to readers through its translation in the King James Version). In such cases, we offer a translation of the excluded text in a footnote, even though it is generally recognized as a later addition to the Greek text and not part of the original Greek New Testament.

- All Old Testament passages that are quoted in the New Testament are identified by a textual footnote at the New Testament location. When the New Testament clearly quotes from the Greek translation of the Old Testament, and when it differs significantly in wording from the Hebrew text, we also place a textual footnote at the Old Testament location. This note includes a rendering of the Greek version, along with a cross-reference to the New Testament passage(s) where it is cited (for example, see notes on Proverbs 3:12; Psalms 8:2; 53:3).

- Some textual footnotes provide cultural and historical information on places, things, and people in the Bible that are probably obscure to modern readers. Such notes should aid the reader in understanding the message of the text. For example, in Acts 12:1, "King Herod" is named in this translation as "King Herod Agrippa" and is identified in a footnote as being "the nephew of Herod Antipas and a grandson of Herod the Great."

- When the meaning of a proper name (or a wordplay inherent in a proper name) is relevant to the meaning of the text, it is either illuminated with a textual footnote or included within parentheses in the text itself. For example, the footnote concerning the name "Eve" at Genesis 3:20 reads: "*Eve* sounds like a Hebrew term that means 'to give life.' " This wordplay in the Hebrew illuminates the meaning of the text, which goes on to say that Eve "would be the mother of all who live."

As WE SUBMIT this translation for publication, we recognize that any translation of the Scriptures is subject to limitations and imperfections. Anyone who has attempted to communicate the richness of God's Word into another language will realize it is impossible to make a perfect translation. Recognizing these limitations, we sought God's guidance and wisdom throughout this project. Now we pray that he will accept our efforts and use this translation for the benefit of the church and of all people.

We pray that the New Living Translation will overcome some of the barriers of history, culture, and language that have kept people from reading and understanding God's Word. We hope that readers unfamiliar with the Bible will find the words clear and easy to understand and that readers well versed in the Scriptures will gain a fresh perspective. We pray that readers will gain insight and wisdom for living, but most of all that they will meet the God of the Bible and be forever changed by knowing him.

The Bible Translation Committee
October 2007

WHY THE
LIFE APPLICATION STUDY BIBLE
IS UNIQUE

Have you ever opened your Bible and asked the following:

- What does this passage really mean?
- How does it apply to my life?
- Why does some of the Bible seem irrelevant?
- What do these ancient cultures have to do with today?
- I love God; why can't I understand what he is saying to me through his word?
- What's going on in the lives of these Bible people?

Many Christians do not read the Bible regularly. Why? Because in the pressures of daily living they cannot find a connection between the timeless principles of Scripture and the ever-present problems of day-by-day living.

God urges us to apply his word (Isaiah 42:23; 1 Corinthians 10:11; 2 Thessalonians 3:4), but too often we stop at accumulating Bible knowledge. This is why the *Life Application Study Bible* was developed—to show how to put into practice what we have learned.

Applying God's word is a vital part of one's relationship with God; it is the evidence that we are obeying him. The difficulty in applying the Bible is not with the Bible itself, but with the reader's inability to bridge the gap between the past and present, the conceptual and practical. When we don't or can't do this, spiritual dryness, shallowness, and indifference are the results.

The words of Scripture itself cry out to us, "But don't just listen to God's word. You must do what it says. Otherwise, you are only fooling yourselves" (James 1:22). The *Life Application Study Bible* helps us to obey God's word. Developed by an interdenominational team of pastors, scholars, family counselors, and a national organization dedicated to promoting God's word and spreading the gospel, the *Life Application Study Bible* took many years to complete. All the work was reviewed by several renowned theologians under the directorship of Dr. Kenneth Kantzer.

The *Life Application Study Bible* does what a good resource Bible should: It helps you understand the context of a passage, gives important background and historical information, explains difficult words and phrases, and helps you see the interrelationship of Scripture. But it does much more. The *Life Application Study Bible* goes deeper into God's word, helping you discover the timeless truth being communicated, see the relevance for your life, and make a personal application. While some study Bibles attempt application, over 75 percent of this Bible is application oriented. The notes answer the questions "So what?" and "What does this passage mean to me, my family, my friends, my job, my neighborhood, my church, my country?"

Imagine reading a familiar passage of Scripture and gaining fresh insight, as if it were the first time you had ever read it. How much richer your life would be if you left each Bible reading with a new perspective and a small change for the better. A small change every day adds up to a changed life—and that is the very purpose of Scripture.

WHAT IS APPLICATION?

The best way to define application is to first determine what it is *not*. Application is *not* just accumulating knowledge. Accumulating knowledge helps us discover and understand facts and concepts, but it stops there. History is filled with philosophers who knew what the Bible said but failed to apply it to their lives, keeping them from believing and changing. Many think that understanding is the end goal of Bible study, but it is really only the beginning.

Application is *not* just illustration. Illustration only tells us how someone else handled a similar situation. While we may empathize with that person, we still have little direction for our personal situation.

Application is *not* just making a passage "relevant." Making the Bible relevant only helps us to see that the same lessons that were true in Bible times are true today; it does not show us how to apply them to the problems and pressures of our individual lives.

What, then, is application? Application begins by knowing and understanding God's word and its timeless truths. *But you cannot stop there.* If you do, God's word may not change your life, and it may become dull, difficult, tedious, and tiring. A good application focuses the truth of God's word, shows the reader what to do about what is being read, and motivates the reader to respond to what God is teaching. All three are essential to application.

Application is putting into practice what we already know (see Mark 4:24 and Hebrews 5:14) and answering the question "So what?" by confronting us with the right questions and motivating us to take action (see 1 John 2:5-6 and James 2:26). Application is deeply personal—unique for each individual. It makes a relevant truth a personal truth and involves developing a strategy and action plan to live your life in harmony with the Bible. It is the biblical "how to" of life.

You may ask, "How can your application notes be relevant to my life?" Each application note has three parts: (1) an *explanation*, which ties the note directly to the Scripture passage and sets up the truth that is being taught; (2) the *bridge*, which explains the timeless truth and makes it relevant for today; (3) the *application*, which shows you how to take the timeless truth and apply it to your personal situation. No note, by itself, can apply Scripture directly to your life. It can only teach, direct, lead, guide, inspire, recommend, and urge. It can give you the resources and direction you need to apply the Bible, but only you can take these resources and put them into practice.

A good note, therefore should not only give you knowledge and understanding but point you to application. Before you buy any kind of resource study Bible, you should evaluate the notes and ask the following questions: (1) Does the note contain enough information to help me understand the point of the Scripture passage? (2) Does the note assume I know more than I do? (3) Does the note avoid denominational bias? (4) Do the notes touch most of life's experiences? (5) Does the note help me apply God's word?

FEATURES OF THE
LIFE APPLICATION STUDY BIBLE

NOTES
In addition to providing the reader with many application notes, the *Life Application Study Bible* also offers several kinds of explanatory notes, which help the reader understand culture, history, context, difficult-to-understand passages, background, places, theological concepts, and the relationship of various passages in Scripture to other passages.

BOOK INTRODUCTIONS
Each book introduction is divided into several easy-to-find parts:

Timeline. A guide that puts the Bible book into its historical setting. It lists the key events and the dates when they occurred.

Vital Statistics. A list of straight facts about the book—those pieces of information you need to know at a glance.

Overview. A summary of the book with general lessons and applications that can be learned from the book as a whole.

Blueprint. The outline of the book. It is printed in easy-to-understand language and is designed for easy memorization. To the right of each main heading is a key lesson that is taught in that particular section.

Megathemes. A section that gives the main themes of the Bible book, explains their significance, and then tells you why they are still important for us today.

Map. If included, this shows the key places found in that book and retells the story of the book from a geographical point of view.

OUTLINE
The *Life Application Study Bible* has a new, custom-made outline that was designed specifically from an application point of view. Several unique features should be noted:

1. To avoid confusion and to aid memory work, the book outline has only three levels for headings. Main outline heads are marked with a capital letter. Subheads are marked by a number. Minor explanatory heads have no letter or number.

2. Each main outline head marked by a letter also has a brief paragraph below it summarizing the Bible text and offering a general application.

3. Parallel passages are listed where they apply.

PERSONALITY PROFILES
Among the unique features of this Bible are the profiles of key Bible people, including their strengths and weaknesses, greatest accomplishments and mistakes, and key lessons from their lives.

MAPS

The *Life Application Study Bible* has a thorough and comprehensive Bible atlas built right into the book. There are two kinds of maps: a book-introduction map, telling the story of the book, and thumbnail maps in the notes, plotting most geographic movements.

CHARTS AND DIAGRAMS

Many charts and diagrams are included to help the reader better visualize difficult concepts or relationships. Most charts not only present the needed information but show the significance of the information as well.

CROSS-REFERENCES

An updated, exhaustive cross-reference system in the margins of the Bible text helps the reader find related passages quickly.

TEXTUAL NOTES

Directly related to the text of the New Living Translation, the textual notes provide explanations on certain wording in the translation, alternate translations, and information about readings in the ancient manuscripts.

HIGHLIGHTED NOTES

In each Bible study lesson, you will be asked to read specific notes as part of your preparation. These notes have each been highlighted by a bullet (•) so that you can find them easily.

JOHN

KEY PLACES IN JOHN

ITUREA

LEBANON

PHOENICIA

TRACONITIS

SYRIA

N

GALILEE

Mediterranean
Sea

Capernaum · Bethsaida
· Cana
Tiberias· *Sea of Galilee*

Nazareth·

Bethany·
(east of the
Jordan)

DECAPOLIS
(Region of Ten Towns)

ISRAEL

SAMARIA · Aenon
Salim·

Jordan River

·Sychar

Mount Gerizim +

· Arimathea

PEREA

Ephraim·

JORDAN

Jerusalem · + Mount of Olives
Bethphage· · Bethany
Bethlehem·

Dead Sea

JUDEA

IDUMEA

0   20 Mi.
0   20 Km.

The broken lines (— · —) indicate modern boundaries.

John's story begins as John the Baptist ministers near Bethany east of the Jordan (1:28ff). Jesus also begins his ministry, talking to some of the men who would later become his 12 disciples. Jesus' ministry in Galilee began with a visit to a wedding in Cana (2:1ff). Then he went to Capernaum, which became his new home (2:12). He journeyed to Jerusalem for the special festivals (2:13) and there met with Nicodemus, a religious leader (3:1ff). When Jesus left Judea, he traveled through Samaria and ministered to the Samaritans (4:1ff). Jesus did miracles in Galilee (4:46ff) and in Judea and Jerusalem (5:1ff). We follow him as he fed 5,000 near Bethsaida beside the Sea of Galilee (Sea of Tiberias) (6:1ff), walked on the water to his frightened disciples (6:16ff), preached through Galilee (7:1), returned to Jerusalem (7:2ff), preached beyond the Jordan in Perea (10:40), raised Lazarus from the dead in Bethany (11:1ff), and finally entered Jerusalem for the last time to celebrate the Passover with his disciples and give them key teachings about what was to come and how they should act. His last hours before his crucifixion were spent in the city (13:1ff), in a grove of olive trees (the Garden of Gethsemane) (18:1ff), and finally in various buildings in Jerusalem during his trial (18:12ff). He would be crucified, but he would rise again as he had promised.

JOHN

Herod the Great begins to rule 37 B.C.		Jesus is born 6/5 B.C.	Escape to Egypt 5/4 B.C.	Herod the Great dies 4 B.C.	Return to Nazareth 4/3 B.C.	Judea becomes a Roman province A.D. 6

VITAL STATISTICS

PURPOSE:
To prove conclusively that Jesus is the Son of God and that all who believe in him will have eternal life

AUTHOR:
John the apostle, son of Zebedee, brother of James, called a "Son of Thunder"

ORIGINAL AUDIENCE:
New Christians and searching non-Christians

DATE WRITTEN:
Probably A.D. 85–90

SETTING:
Written after the destruction of Jerusalem in A.D. 70 and before John's exile to the island of Patmos

KEY VERSES:
"The disciples saw Jesus do many other miraculous signs in addition to the ones recorded in this book. But these are written so that you may continue to believe that Jesus is the Messiah, the Son of God, and that by believing in him you will have life by the power of his name" (20:30, 31).

KEY PEOPLE:
Jesus, John the Baptist, the disciples, Mary, Martha, Lazarus, Jesus' mother, Pilate, Mary Magdalene

KEY PLACES:
Judean countryside, Samaria, Galilee, Bethany, Jerusalem

SPECIAL FEATURES:
Of the eight miracles recorded, six are unique (among the Gospels) to John, as is the "Upper Room Discourse" (chapters 14–17). Over 90 percent of John is unique to his Gospel—John does not contain a genealogy or any record of Jesus' birth, childhood, temptation, transfiguration, appointment of the disciples, nor any account of Jesus' parables, ascension, or great commission.

HE SPOKE, and galaxies whirled into place, stars burned the heavens, and planets began orbiting their suns—words of awesome, unlimited, unleashed power. He spoke again, and the waters and lands were filled with plants and creatures, running, swimming, growing, and multiplying—words of animating, breathing, pulsing life. Again he spoke, and man and woman were formed, thinking, speaking, and loving—words of personal and creative glory. Eternal, infinite, unlimited—he was, is, and always will be the Maker and Lord of all that exists.

And then he came in the flesh to a speck in the universe called planet Earth. The mighty Creator became a part of the creation, limited by time and space and susceptible to aging, sickness, and death. But love propelled him, and so he came to rescue and save those who were lost and to give them the gift of eternity. He is the Word; he is Jesus, the Messiah.

It is this truth that the apostle John brings to us in this book. John's Gospel is not a life of Christ; it is a powerful argument for the incarnation, a conclusive demonstration that Jesus was, and is, the very heaven-sent Son of God and the only source of eternal life.

John discloses Jesus' identity with his very first words, "In the beginning the Word already existed. The Word was with God, and the Word was God. He existed in the beginning with God" (1:1, 2); and the rest of the book continues the theme. John, the eyewitness, chose eight of Jesus' miracles (or miraculous signs, as he calls them) to reveal his divine/human nature and his life-giving mission. These signs are (1) turning water to wine (2:1–11), (2) healing the official's son (4:46–54), (3) healing the lame man at the pool of Bethesda (5:1–9), (4) feeding the 5,000 with just a few loaves and fish (6:1–14), (5) walking on the water (6:15–21), (6) restoring sight to the blind man (9:1–41), (7) raising Lazarus from the dead (11:1–44), and, after the Resurrection, (8) giving the disciples an overwhelming catch of fish (21:1–14).

In every chapter Jesus' deity is revealed. And Jesus' true identity is underscored through the titles he is given—the Word, the only Son, Lamb of God, Son of God, true bread, life, resurrection, vine. And the formula is "I am." When Jesus uses this phrase, he affirms his preexistence and eternal deity. Jesus says, *I am* the bread of life (6:35); *I am* the light of the world (8:12; 9:5); *I am* the gate (10:7); *I am* the good shepherd (10:11, 14); *I am* the resurrection and the life (11:25); *I am* the way, the truth, and the life (14:6); and *I am* the true vine (15:1).

The greatest sign, of course, is the Resurrection, and John provides a stirring eyewitness account of finding the empty tomb. Then he records various post-Resurrection appearances by Jesus.

John, the devoted follower of Christ, has given us a personal and powerful look at Jesus Christ, the eternal Son of God. As you read his story, commit yourself to believe in and follow him.

THE BLUEPRINT

A. BIRTH AND PREPARATION OF JESUS, THE SON OF GOD (1:1—2:12)

John makes it clear that Jesus is not just a man; he is the eternal Son of God. He is the light of the world because he offers this gift of eternal life to all people. How blind and foolish to call Jesus nothing more than an unusually good man or moral teacher. Yet we sometimes act as if this were true when we casually toss around his words and go about living our own way. If Jesus is the eternal Son of God, we should pay attention to his divine identity and life-giving message.

B. MESSAGE AND MINISTRY OF JESUS, THE SON OF GOD (2:13—12:50)
1. Jesus encounters belief and unbelief from the people
2. Jesus encounters conflict with the religious leaders
3. Jesus encounters crucial events in Jerusalem

Jesus meets with individuals, preaches to great crowds, trains his disciples, and debates with the religious leaders. The message that he is the Son of God receives a mixed reaction. Some worship him, some are puzzled, some shrink back, and some move to silence him. We see the same varied reactions today. Times have changed, but people's hearts remain hard. May we see ourselves in these encounters Jesus had with people, and may our response be to worship and follow him.

C. DEATH AND RESURRECTION OF JESUS, THE SON OF GOD (13:1—21:25)
1. Jesus teaches his disciples
2. Jesus completes his mission

Jesus carefully instructed the disciples how to continue to believe even after his death, yet they could not take it in. After he died and the first reports came back that Jesus was alive, the disciples could not believe it. Thomas is especially remembered as one who refused to believe even when he heard the eyewitness accounts from other disciples. May we not be like Thomas, demanding a physical face-to-face encounter, but may we accept the eyewitness testimony of the disciples that John has recorded in this Gospel.

MEGATHEMES

THEME	EXPLANATION	IMPORTANCE
Jesus Christ, Son of God	John shows us that Jesus is unique as God's special Son, yet he is fully God. Because he is fully God, Jesus is able to reveal God to us clearly and accurately.	Because Jesus is God's Son, we can perfectly trust what he says. By trusting him, we can gain an open mind to understand God's message and fulfill his purpose in our lives.
Eternal Life	Because Jesus is God, he lives forever. Before the world began, he lived with God, and he will reign forever with him. In John we see Jesus revealed in power and magnificence even before his resurrection.	Jesus offers eternal life to us. We are invited to begin living in a personal, eternal relationship with him now. Although we must grow old and die, by trusting him we can have a new life that lasts forever.
Belief	John records eight specific signs, or miracles, that show the nature of Jesus' power and love. We see his power over everything created, and we see his love of all people. These signs encourage us to believe in him.	Believing is active, living, and continuous trust in Jesus as God. When we believe in his life, his words, his death, and his resurrection, we are cleansed from sin and receive power to follow him. But we must respond to him by believing.
Holy Spirit	Jesus taught his disciples that the Holy Spirit would come after he ascended from earth. The Holy Spirit would then indwell, guide, counsel, and comfort those who follow Jesus. Through the Holy Spirit, Christ's presence and power are multiplied in all who believe.	Through God's Holy Spirit, we are drawn to him in faith. We must know the Holy Spirit to understand all Jesus taught. We can experience Jesus' love and guidance as we allow the Holy Spirit to do his work in us.
Resurrection	On the third day after he died, Jesus rose from the dead. This was verified by his disciples and many eyewitnesses. This reality changed the disciples from frightened deserters to dynamic leaders in the new church. This fact is the foundation of the Christian faith.	We can be changed as the disciples were and have confidence that our bodies will one day be raised to live with Christ forever. The same power that raised Christ to life can give us the ability to follow Christ each day.

A. BIRTH AND PREPARATION OF JESUS, THE SON OF GOD (1:1—2:12)

In this Gospel, John provides clear evidence that Jesus is the Son of God and that by believing in him we may have eternal life. John also provides unique material about Jesus' birth. He did not come into being when he was born, because he is eternal.

God Became a Human (2)

1 ¹ In the beginning the Word already existed.
The Word was with God,
and the Word was God.

1:1
Gen 1:1
Phil 2:6
1 Jn 5:20

² He existed in the beginning with God.
³ God created everything through him,
and nothing was created except through him.

1:3
1 Cor 8:6
Col 1:16-17
Heb 1:2

⁴ The Word gave life to everything that was created,*
and his life brought light to everyone.

1:4
John 3:15-16, 36;
6:35, 48; 8:12;
1 Jn 5:12, 20

⁵ The light shines in the darkness,
and the darkness can never extinguish it.*

⁶ God sent a man, John the Baptist,* ⁷ to tell about the light so that everyone might believe because of his testimony. ⁸ John himself was not the light; he was simply a witness to tell about the light. ⁹ The one who is the true light, who gives light to everyone, was coming into the world.

1:9
1 Jn 2:8

¹⁰ He came into the very world he created, but the world didn't recognize him. ¹¹ He came to his own people, and even they rejected him. ¹² But to all who believed him and accepted him, he gave the right to become children of God. ¹³ They are reborn—not with a physical birth resulting from human passion or plan, but a birth that comes from God.

1:12
Rom 8:15-16, 29
1 Jn 3:1, 23

1:3-4 Or *and nothing that was created was created except through him. The Word gave life to everything.*
1:5 Or *and the darkness has not understood it.*   **1:6** Greek *a man named John.*

• **1:1** What Jesus taught and what he did are tied inseparably to who he is. John shows Jesus as fully human and fully God. Although Jesus took upon himself full humanity and lived as a man, he never ceased to be the eternal God who has always existed, the Creator and Sustainer of all things, and the source of eternal life. This is the truth about Jesus, and the foundation of all truth. If we cannot or do not believe this basic truth, we will not have enough faith to trust our eternal destiny to him. That is why John wrote this Gospel—to build faith and confidence in Jesus Christ so that we may believe that he truly was and is the Son of God (20:30, 31).

1:1 John wrote to believers everywhere, both Jews and non-Jews (Gentiles). As one of Jesus' 12 disciples, John writes with credibility and the details of an eyewitness. His book is not a biography (like the book of Luke); it is a thematic presentation of Jesus' life. Many in John's original audience had a Greek background. Greek culture encouraged worship of many mythological gods, whose supernatural characteristics were as important to Greeks as genealogies were to Jews. John shows that Jesus is not only different from but superior to these gods of mythology.

1:1ff What does John mean by "the Word"? *The Word* was a term used by theologians and philosophers, both Jews and Greeks, in many different ways. In Hebrew Scripture, *the Word* was an agent of creation (Psalm 33:6), the source of God's message to his people through the prophets (Hosea 4:1), and God's law, his standard of holiness (Psalm 119:11). In Greek philosophy, *the Word* was the principle of reason that governed the world, or the thought still in the mind, while in Hebrew thought, *the Word* was another expression for God. John's description shows clearly that he is speaking of Jesus (see especially 1:14)—a human being he knew and loved, but at the same time the Creator of the universe, the ultimate revelation of God, the living picture of God's holiness, the one who "holds all creation together" (Colossians 1:17). To Jewish readers, to say this man Jesus "was God" was blasphemous. To Greek readers, "the Word became human" (1:14) was unthinkable. To John, this new understanding of the Word was the Good News of Jesus Christ.

1:3 When God created, he made something from nothing. Because we are created beings, we have no basis for pride.

Remember that you exist only because God made you, and you have special gifts only because God gave them to you. With God you are something valuable and unique; apart from God you are nothing, and if you try to live without him, you will be abandoning the purpose for which you were made.

• **1:3-5** Do you ever feel that your life is too complex for God to understand? Remember, God created the entire universe, and nothing is too difficult for him. God created you; he is alive today, and his love is bigger than any problem you may face.

• **1:4, 5** "The darkness can never extinguish it" means the darkness of evil never has and never will overcome God's light. Jesus Christ is the Creator of life, and his life brings light to humankind. In his light, we see ourselves as we really are (sinners in need of a Savior). When we follow Jesus, the true Light, we can avoid walking blindly and falling into sin. He lights the path ahead of us so we can see how to live. He removes the darkness of sin from our lives. In what ways have you allowed the light of Christ to shine into your life? Let Christ guide your life, and you'll never need to stumble in darkness.

1:6-8 For more information on John the Baptist, see his Profile on page 1749.

• **1:8** We, like John the Baptist, are not the source of God's light; we merely reflect that light. Jesus Christ is the true Light; he helps us see our way to God and shows us how to walk along that way. But Christ has chosen to reflect his light through his followers to an unbelieving world, perhaps because unbelievers are not able to bear the full blazing glory of his light firsthand. The word *witness* indicates our role as reflectors of Christ's light. We are never to present ourselves as the light to others, but are always to point them to Christ, the Light.

1:10, 11 Although Christ created the world, the people he created didn't recognize him (1:10). Even the people chosen by God to prepare the rest of the world for the Messiah rejected him (1:11), although the entire Old Testament pointed to his coming.

1:12, 13 All who welcome Jesus Christ as Lord of their lives are reborn spiritually, receiving new life from God. Through faith in Christ, this new birth changes us from the inside out—rearrang-

1:14
Gal 4:4
Phil 2:6-8
Col 2:9
1 Tim 3:16
1 Jn 1:1; 4:2-3

¹⁴So the Word became human* and made his home among us. He was full of unfailing love and faithfulness.* And we have seen his glory, the glory of the Father's one and only Son.

1:14a Greek *became flesh.*   **1:14b** Or *grace and truth;* also in 1:17.

JOHN THE BAPTIST

There's no getting around it—John the Baptist was unique. He wore odd clothes and ate strange food and preached an unusual message to the Judeans who went out to the wastelands to see him.

But John did not aim at uniqueness for its own sake. Instead, he aimed at obedience. He knew he had a specific role to play in the world—announcing the coming of the Savior—and he put all his energies into this task. Luke tells us that John was in the wilderness when God's word of direction came to him. John was ready and waiting. The angel who had announced John's birth to Zechariah had made it clear that this child was to be a Nazirite—one set apart for God's service. John remained faithful to that calling.

This wild-looking man had no power or position in the Jewish political system, but he spoke with almost irresistible authority. People were moved by his words because he spoke the truth, challenging them to turn from their sins and baptizing them as a symbol of their repentance. They responded by the hundreds. But even as people crowded to him, he pointed beyond himself, never forgetting that his main role was to announce the coming of the Savior.

The words of truth that moved many to repentance goaded others to resistance and resentment. John even challenged Herod to admit his sin. Herodias, the woman Herod had married illegally, decided to get rid of this wilderness preacher. Although she was able to have him killed, she was not able to stop his message. The one John had announced was already on the move. John had accomplished his mission.

God has given each of us a purpose for living, and we can trust him to guide us. John did not have the complete Bible as we know it today, but he focused his life on the truth he knew from the available Old Testament Scriptures. Likewise, we can discover in God's Word the truths he wants us to know. And as these truths work in us, others will be drawn to him. God can use you in a way he can use no one else. Let him know your willingness to follow him today.

Strengths and accomplishments	• The God-appointed messenger to announce the arrival of Jesus • A preacher whose theme was repentance • A fearless confronter • Known for his remarkable lifestyle • Uncompromising
Lessons from his life	• God does not guarantee an easy or safe life to those who serve him • Doing what God desires is the greatest possible life investment • Standing for the truth is more important than life itself
Vital statistics	• Where: Judea • Occupation: Prophet • Relatives: Father: Zechariah. Mother: Elizabeth. Distant relative: Jesus. • Contemporaries: Herod, Herodias
Key verse	"I tell you the truth, of all who have ever lived, none is greater than John the Baptist. Yet even the least person in the Kingdom of Heaven is greater than he is!" (Matthew 11:11).

John's story is told in all four Gospels. His coming was predicted in Isaiah 40:3 and Malachi 4:5; and he is mentioned in Acts 1:5, 22; 10:37; 11:16; 13:24, 25; 18:25; 19:3, 4.

ing our attitudes, desires, and motives. Being born makes you physically alive and places you in your parents' family (1:13). Being born of God makes you spiritually alive and puts you in God's family (1:12). Have you asked Christ to make you a new person? This fresh start in life is available to all who believe in Christ.

• **1:14** "The Word became human." By doing so, Christ became (1) *the perfect teacher*—in Jesus' life we see how God thinks and therefore how we should think (Philippians 2:5-11); (2) *the perfect example*—as a model of what we are to become, he shows us how to live and gives us the power to live that way (1 Peter 2:21); (3) *the perfect sacrifice*—Jesus came as a sacrifice for all sins, and his death satisfied God's requirements for the removal of sin (Colossians 1:15-23).

• **1:14** "The Father's one and only Son" means Jesus is God's only and unique Son. The emphasis is on *unique.* Jesus is one of a kind and enjoys a relationship with God. He is unlike all believers, who are called "children of God."

1:14 When Jesus was conceived, God became a man. He was not part man and part God; he was completely human and completely divine (Colossians 2:9). Before Christ came, people could know God partially. After Christ came, people could know God fully because he became visible and tangible in Christ. Christ is the perfect expression of God in human form. The two most common errors people make about Jesus are to minimize his humanity or to minimize his divinity. Jesus is both God and man.

15John testified about him when he shouted to the crowds, "This is the one I was talking about when I said, 'Someone is coming after me who is far greater than I am, for he existed long before me.'"

16From his abundance we have all received one gracious blessing after another.* 17For the law was given through Moses, but God's unfailing love and faithfulness came through Jesus Christ. 18No one has ever seen God. But the unique One, who is himself God,* is near to the Father's heart. He has revealed God to us.

John the Baptist Declares His Mission (19)

19This was John's testimony when the Jewish leaders sent priests and Temple assistants* from Jerusalem to ask John, "Who are you?" 20He came right out and said, "I am not the Messiah."

21"Well then, who are you?" they asked. "Are you Elijah?"

"No," he replied.

"Are you the Prophet we are expecting?"*

"No."

22"Then who are you? We need an answer for those who sent us. What do you have to say about yourself?"

23John replied in the words of the prophet Isaiah:

"I am a voice shouting in the wilderness,
    'Clear the way for the LORD's coming!'"*

24Then the Pharisees who had been sent 25asked him, "If you aren't the Messiah or Elijah or the Prophet, what right do you have to baptize?"

26John told them, "I baptize with* water, but right here in the crowd is someone you do not recognize. 27Though his ministry follows mine, I'm not even worthy to be his slave and untie the straps of his sandal."

28This encounter took place in Bethany, an area east of the Jordan River, where John was baptizing.

1:16 Col 2:9-10
1:17 Exod 31:18; 34:28 / John 7:19
1:18 Exod 33:20 / 2 Cor 4:4, 6 / Col 1:15
1:19-28 Matt 3:1-12 / Mark 1:2-8 / Luke 3:1-16
1:20 Luke 3:15 / John 3:28
1:21 Deut 18:15 / Mal 4:5 / Matt 11:14
1:23 †Isa 40:3
1:26 Mal 3:1 / Matt 3:11 / Mark 1:8 / Luke 3:16
1:27 Mark 1:7 / John 1:15 / Acts 13:25
1:28 John 3:26; 10:40

1:16 Or received the grace of Christ rather than the grace of the law; Greek reads received grace upon grace. **1:18** Some manuscripts read But the one and only Son. **1:19** Greek and Levites. **1:21** Greek Are you the Prophet? See Deut 18:15, 18; Mal 4:5-6. **1:23** Isa 40:3. **1:26** Or in; also in 1:31, 33.

1:17 Law and grace (the combination of God's "unfailing love and faithfulness") are both aspects of God's nature that he uses in dealing with us. Moses emphasized God's law and justice, while Jesus Christ came to highlight God's mercy, love, faithfulness, and forgiveness. Moses could only be the giver of the law, while Christ came to fulfill the law (Matthew 5:17). The nature and will of God were revealed in the law; now the nature and will of God are revealed in Jesus Christ. Rather than coming through cold stone tablets, God's revelation now comes through a person's life. As we get to know Christ better, our understanding of God will increase.

• **1:18** God communicated through various people in the Old Testament, usually prophets who were told to give specific messages. But no one ever saw God. Jesus is both God and the Father's unique Son. In Christ, God revealed his nature and essence in a way that could be seen and touched. In Christ, God became a man who lived on earth.

1:19 The priests and Temple assistants (also called Levites) were respected religious leaders in Jerusalem. Priests served in the Temple, and Temple assistants helped them. The Pharisees (1:24) were a group that both John the Baptist and Jesus often denounced. Many of them outwardly obeyed God's laws to look pious, while inwardly their hearts were filled with pride and greed. The Pharisees believed that their own oral traditions were just as important as God's inspired Word. For more information on the Pharisees, see the charts in Matthew 3, p. 1541 and Mark 2, p. 1617.

These leaders came to see John the Baptist for several reasons: (1) Their duty as guardians of the faith included investigating any new teaching or movement (Deuteronomy 13:1-5;

18:20-22). (2) They wanted to find out if John had the credentials of a prophet. (3) John had quite a following, and it was growing. They were probably jealous and wanted to see why this man was so popular.

1:21-23 In the religious leaders' minds, there were four options regarding John the Baptist's identity: He was (1) the Prophet foretold by Moses (Deuteronomy 18:15), (2) Elijah (Malachi 4:5), (3) the Messiah, or (4) a false prophet. John denied being the first three personages. Instead, he called himself, in the words of the Old Testament prophet Isaiah, "The voice of someone shouting, 'Clear the way through the wilderness for the LORD!'" (Isaiah 40:3). The leaders kept pressing John to say who he was because people were expecting the Messiah to come (Luke 3:15). But John emphasized only why he had come—to prepare the way for the Messiah. The Pharisees missed the point. They wanted to know who John was, but John wanted to prepare them to recognize who Jesus was.

1:25, 26 John was baptizing Jews. The Essenes (a strict, monastic sect of Judaism) practiced baptism for purification, but normally only non-Jews (Gentiles) were baptized when they converted to Judaism. When the Pharisees questioned John's authority to baptize, they were asking who gave John the right to treat God's chosen people like Gentiles. John said, "I baptize with water"— he was merely helping the people perform a symbolic act of repentance. But soon one would come who would truly forgive sins, something only the Son of God—the Messiah—could do.

1:27 John the Baptist said he was not even worthy to be Christ's slave. But according to Luke 7:28, Jesus said that John was the greatest of all prophets. If such a great person felt inadequate even to be Christ's slave, how much more should we lay aside our pride to serve Christ! When we truly understand who Christ is, our pride and self-importance melt away.

John the Baptist Proclaims Jesus as the Messiah (20)

1:29
Isa 53:7
1 Cor 5:7
1 Pet 1:19

1:32
Matt 3:16
Mark 1:10
Luke 3:22

1:33
Luke 3:16
Acts 1:5

1:34
John 1:49; 10:36

29 The next day John saw Jesus coming toward him and said, "Look! The Lamb of God who takes away the sin of the world! 30 He is the one I was talking about when I said, 'A man is coming after me who is far greater than I am, for he existed long before me.' 31 I did not recognize him as the Messiah, but I have been baptizing with water so that he might be revealed to Israel."

32 Then John testified, "I saw the Holy Spirit descending like a dove from heaven and resting upon him. 33 I didn't know he was the one, but when God sent me to baptize with water, he told me, 'The one on whom you see the Spirit descend and rest is the one who will baptize with the Holy Spirit.' 34 I saw this happen to Jesus, so I testify that he is the Chosen One of God.*"

The First Disciples Follow Jesus (21)

35 The following day John was again standing with two of his disciples. 36 As Jesus walked by, John looked at him and declared, "Look! There is the Lamb of God!" 37 When John's two disciples heard this, they followed Jesus.

38 Jesus looked around and saw them following. "What do you want?" he asked them.

They replied, "Rabbi" (which means "Teacher"), "where are you staying?"

39 "Come and see," he said. It was about four o'clock in the afternoon when they went with him to the place where he was staying, and they remained with him the rest of the day.

1:34 Some manuscripts read *the Son of God.*

• **1:29** Every morning and evening, a lamb was sacrificed in the Temple for the sins of the people (Exodus 29:38-42). Isaiah 53:7 prophesied that the Messiah, God's servant, would be led to the slaughter like a lamb. To pay the penalty for sin, a life had to be given—and God chose to provide the sacrifice himself. The sins of the world were removed when Jesus died as the perfect sacrifice. This is the way our sins are forgiven (1 Corinthians 5:7). The "sin of the world" means everyone's sin, the sin of each individual. Jesus paid the price of *your* sin by his death. You can receive forgiveness by confessing your sin to him and asking for his forgiveness.

1:30 Although John the Baptist was a well-known preacher who attracted large crowds, he was content for Jesus to take the higher place. This is true humility, the basis for greatness in preaching, teaching, or any other work we do for Christ. When you are content to do what God wants you to do and let Jesus Christ be honored for it, God will do great things through you.

1:31-34 At Jesus' baptism, John the Baptist had declared Jesus to be the Messiah. At that time God had given John a sign to show him that Jesus truly had been sent from God (1:33). John and Jesus were related (see Luke 1:36), so John probably knew who he was. But it wasn't until Jesus' baptism that John understood that Jesus was the Messiah. Jesus' baptism is described in Matthew 3:13-17; Mark 1:9-11; and Luke 3:21, 22.

1:33 John the Baptist's baptism with water was preparatory, because it was for repentance and symbolized the washing away of sins. Jesus, by contrast, would baptize with the Holy Spirit. He would send the Holy Spirit upon all believers, empowering them to live and to teach the message of salvation. This outpouring of the Spirit came after Jesus had risen from the dead and ascended into heaven (see 20:22; Acts 2).

1:34 John the Baptist's job was to point people to Jesus, their long-awaited Messiah. Today people are looking for someone to give them security in an insecure world. Our job is to point them to Christ and to show that he is the one whom they seek.

• **1:35ff** These new disciples used several names for Jesus: Lamb of God (1:36), Rabbi (1:38), Messiah (1:41), Son of God (1:49), and King of Israel (1:49). As they got to know Jesus, their appreciation for him grew. The more time we spend getting to know Christ, the more we will understand and appreciate who he is. We may be drawn to him for his teaching, but we will come to know him as the Son of God. Although these disciples made this

verbal shift in a few days, they would not fully understand Jesus until three years later (Acts 2). What they so easily professed had to be worked out in experience. We may find that words of faith come easily, but deep appreciation for Christ comes with living by faith.

• **1:37** One of the two disciples was Andrew (1:40). The other was probably John, the writer of this book. Why did these disciples leave John the Baptist? Because that's what John wanted them to do—he was pointing the way to Jesus, the one John had prepared them to follow. These were Jesus' first disciples, along with Simon Peter (1:42) and Nathanael (1:45).

1:38 When the two disciples began to follow Jesus, he asked them, "What do you want?" Following Christ is not enough; we must follow him for the right reasons. To follow Christ for our own purposes would be asking Christ to follow us—to align with us to support and advance our cause, not his. We must examine our motives for following him. Are we seeking his glory or ours?

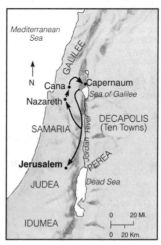

JESUS' FIRST TRAVELS
After his baptism by John in the Jordan River and the temptation by Satan in the wilderness (see the map in Mark 1, p. 1613), Jesus returned to Galilee. He visited Nazareth, Cana, and Capernaum, and then returned to Jerusalem for the Passover.

⁴⁰Andrew, Simon Peter's brother, was one of these men who heard what John said and then followed Jesus. ⁴¹Andrew went to find his brother, Simon, and told him, "We have found the Messiah" (which means "Christ"*).

⁴²Then Andrew brought Simon to meet Jesus. Looking intently at Simon, Jesus said, "Your name is Simon, son of John—but you will be called Cephas" (which means "Peter"*).

⁴³The next day Jesus decided to go to Galilee. He found Philip and said to him, "Come, follow me." ⁴⁴Philip was from Bethsaida, Andrew and Peter's hometown.

⁴⁵Philip went to look for Nathanael and told him, "We have found the very person Moses* and the prophets wrote about! His name is Jesus, the son of Joseph from Nazareth."

⁴⁶"Nazareth!" exclaimed Nathanael. "Can anything good come from Nazareth?"

"Come and see for yourself," Philip replied.

⁴⁷As they approached, Jesus said, "Now here is a genuine son of Israel—a man of complete integrity."

⁴⁸"How do you know about me?" Nathanael asked.

Jesus replied, "I could see you under the fig tree before Philip found you."

⁴⁹Then Nathanael exclaimed, "Rabbi, you are the Son of God—the King of Israel!"

⁵⁰Jesus asked him, "Do you believe this just because I told you I had seen you under the fig tree? You will see greater things than this." ⁵¹Then he said, "I tell you the truth, you will all see heaven open and the angels of God going up and down on the Son of Man, the one who is the stairway between heaven and earth.*"

Jesus Turns Water into Wine (22)

2 The next day* there was a wedding celebration in the village of Cana in Galilee. Jesus' mother was there, ²and Jesus and his disciples were also invited to the celebration. ³The wine supply ran out during the festivities, so Jesus' mother told him, "They have no more wine."

⁴"Dear woman, that's not our problem," Jesus replied. "My time has not yet come."

1:40
Matt 4:18-22
Mark 1:16
Luke 5:2-11
1:41
Ps 2:2
John 4:25
1:42
Matt 16:18
1 Cor 15:5
1 Pet 2:5
1:43
John 6:5-6;
12:20-22
1:45
Gen 3:15
Num 21:8-9; 24:17
Deut 18:15, 18
Isa 7:14; 11:1-10;
52:10, 13; 53:1-12
Jer 23:5-6; 30:9
Ezek 34:23-24;
37:24-25
Hos 11:1
Mic 5:2
Zech 3:8-9;
6:12-13; 9:9
Mal 3:1; 4:2, 5
1:49
2 Sam 7:14
Ps 2:2
John 1:34; 20:31
1:51
Gen 28:12
2:1
John 1:35, 43
2:4
John 7:30; 8:20

1:41 *Messiah* (a Hebrew term) and *Christ* (a Greek term) both mean "the anointed one."   **1:42** The names *Cephas* (from Aramaic) and *Peter* (from Greek) both mean "rock."   **1:45** Greek *Moses in the law.*   **1:51** Greek *going up and down on the Son of Man;* see Gen 28:10-17. "Son of Man" is a title Jesus used for himself.   **2:1** Greek *On the third day;* see 1:35, 43.

1:40-42 Andrew accepted John the Baptist's testimony about Jesus and immediately went to tell his brother, Simon, about him. There was no question in Andrew's mind that Jesus was the Messiah. Not only did he tell his brother, but he was also eager to introduce others to Jesus (see 6:8, 9; 12:22). How many people in your life have heard you talk about your relationship with Jesus?

1:42 Jesus saw not only who Simon was, but who he would become. That is why he gave him a new name—*Cephas* in Aramaic, *Peter* in Greek (the name means "a rock"). Peter is not presented as rock-solid throughout the Gospels, but he became a solid rock in the days of the early church, as we learn in the book of Acts. By giving Simon a new name, Jesus introduced a change in character. For more on Simon Peter, see his Profile in Matthew 27, p. 1603.

1:46 Nazareth was despised by the Jews because a Roman army garrison was located there. Some have speculated that an aloof attitude or a poor reputation in morals and religion on the part of the people of Nazareth led to Nathanael's harsh comment. Nathanael's hometown was Cana, about four miles from Nazareth.

• **1:46** When Nathanael heard that the Messiah was from Nazareth, he was surprised. Philip responded, "Come and see for yourself." Fortunately for Nathanael, he went to meet Jesus and became a disciple. If he had stuck to his prejudice without investigating further, he would have missed the Messiah! Don't let people's stereotypes about Christ cause them to miss his power and love. Invite them to come and see who Jesus really is.

1:47-49 Jesus knew about Nathanael before the two ever met. Jesus also knows what we are really like. An honest person will feel comfortable with the thought that Jesus knows him or her through and through. A dishonest person will feel uncomfortable. You can't pretend to be something you're not. God knows the real you and wants *you* to follow him.

1:51 This is a reference to Jacob's dream recorded in Genesis 28:12. As the unique God-man, Jesus would be the ladder between heaven and earth. Jesus is not saying that this would be a physical experience (that they would see the ladder with their eyes) like the Transfiguration, but that they would have spiritual insight into Jesus' true nature and purpose for coming.

2:1, 2 Jesus was on a mission to save the world, the greatest mission in the history of humankind. Yet he took time to attend a wedding and take part in its festivities. We may be tempted to think we should not take time out from our "important" work for social occasions. But maybe these social occasions are part of our mission. Jesus valued these wedding festivities because they involved people, and Jesus came to be with people. Our mission can often be accomplished in joyous times of celebration with others. Bring balance to your life by bringing Jesus into times of pleasure as well as times of work.

2:1-3 Weddings in Jesus' day were week-long festivals. Banquets would be prepared for many guests, and the week would be spent celebrating the new life of the married couple. Often the whole town was invited, and everybody would come—it was considered an insult to refuse an invitation to a wedding. To accommodate many people, careful planning was needed. To run out of wine was more than embarrassing; it broke the strong unwritten laws of hospitality. Jesus was about to respond to a heartfelt need.

2:4 Mary was probably not asking Jesus to do a miracle; she was simply hoping that her son would help solve this major problem and find some wine. Tradition says that Joseph, Mary's husband, was dead, so she probably was used to asking for her son's help in certain situations. Jesus' answer to Mary is difficult to understand, but maybe that is the point. Although Mary did not understand what Jesus was going to do, she trusted him to do what was right. Those who believe in Jesus but run into situations they

5 But his mother told the servants, "Do whatever he tells you."

2:6
Mark 7:3-4
John 3:25

6 Standing nearby were six stone water jars, used for Jewish ceremonial washing. Each could hold twenty to thirty gallons.* 7 Jesus told the servants, "Fill the jars with water." When the jars had been filled, 8 he said, "Now dip some out, and take it to the master of ceremonies." So the servants followed his instructions.

2:9
John 4:46

9 When the master of ceremonies tasted the water that was now wine, not knowing where it had come from (though, of course, the servants knew), he called the bridegroom over. 10 "A host always serves the best wine first," he said. "Then, when everyone has had a lot to drink, he brings out the less expensive wine. But you have kept the best until now!"

2:11
John 2:23; 3:2;
4:54; 6:14; 11:47;
12:37

11 This miraculous sign at Cana in Galilee was the first time Jesus revealed his glory. And his disciples believed in him.

2:6 Greek *2 or 3 measures* [75 to 113 liters].

NICODEMUS

God specializes in finding and changing people we consider out of reach. It took a while for Nicodemus to come out of the dark, but God was patient with this "undercover" believer.

Afraid of being discovered, Nicodemus made an appointment to see Jesus at night. Daylight conversations between Pharisees and Jesus tended to be antagonistic, but Nicodemus really wanted to learn. He probably got a lot more than he expected—a challenge to a new life! We know very little about Nicodemus, but we know that he left that evening's encounter a changed man. He came away with a whole new understanding of both God and himself.

Nicodemus next appears as part of the Jewish high council (7:50). As the group discussed ways to eliminate Jesus, Nicodemus raised the question of justice. Although his objection was overruled, he had spoken up. He had begun to change.

Our last picture of Nicodemus shows him joining Joseph of Arimathea in asking for Jesus' body in order to provide for its burial (19:39). Realizing what he was risking, Nicodemus was making a bold move. He was continuing to grow.

God looks for steady growth, not instant perfection. How well does your present level of spiritual growth match up with how long you have known Jesus?

Strengths and accomplishments	• One of the few religious leaders who believed in Jesus • A member of the powerful Jewish high council • A Pharisee who was attracted by Jesus' character and miracles • Joined with Joseph of Arimathea in burying Jesus
Weakness and mistake	• Limited by his fear of being publicly exposed as Jesus' follower
Lessons from his life	• Unless we are born again, we can never be part of the Kingdom of God • God is able to change those we might consider unreachable • God is patient, but persistent • If we are available, God can use us
Vital statistics	• Where: Jerusalem • Occupation: Religious leader • Contemporaries: Jesus, Annas, Caiaphas, Pilate, Joseph of Arimathea
Key verse	"'What do you mean?' exclaimed Nicodemus. 'How can an old man go back into his mother's womb and be born again?'" (John 3:4).

Nicodemus's story is told in John 3:1-21; 7:50-52; and 19:39-40.

---

cannot understand must continue to trust that he will work in the best way.

• **2:5** Mary submitted to Jesus' way of doing things. She recognized that Jesus was more than her human son—he was the Son of God. When we bring our problems to Christ, we may think we know how he should take care of them. But he may have a completely different plan. Like Mary, we should submit and allow him to deal with the problem as he sees best.

2:6 The six stone water jars were normally used for ceremonial washing. When full, the pots would hold 20 to 30 gallons. According to the Jews' ceremonial law, people became symbolically unclean by touching objects of everyday life. Before eating, the Jews would pour water over their hands to cleanse themselves of any bad influences associated with what they had touched.

2:10 People look everywhere but to God for excitement and meaning. For some reason, they expect God to be dull and life-

less. Just as the wine Jesus made was the best, so life in him is better than life on our own. Why wait until everything else runs out before trying God? Why save the best until last?

2:11 When the disciples saw Jesus' miracle, they believed. The miracle showed his power over nature and revealed the way he would go about his ministry—helping others, speaking with authority, and being in personal touch with people.

Miracles are not merely superhuman events, but events that demonstrate God's power. Almost every miracle Jesus did was a renewal of fallen creation—restoring sight, making the lame walk, even restoring life to the dead. Believe in Christ not because he is a superman but because he is the God who continues his creation, even in those of us who are poor, weak, crippled, orphaned, blind, deaf, or with some other desperate need.

¹²After the wedding he went to Capernaum for a few days with his mother, his brothers, and his disciples.

2:12
Matt 12:46-50

B. MESSAGE AND MINISTRY OF JESUS, THE SON OF GOD (2:13—12:50)

John stresses the deity of Christ. He gives us eight miracles that serve as signs that Jesus is the Messiah. In this section he records Jesus describing himself as the bread of life, the water of life, the light of the world, the gate, and the good shepherd. John provides teachings of Jesus found nowhere else. This is the most theological of the four Gospels.

1. Jesus encounters belief and unbelief from the people

Jesus Clears the Temple (**23**)

¹³It was nearly time for the Jewish Passover celebration, so Jesus went to Jerusalem. ¹⁴In the Temple area he saw merchants selling cattle, sheep, and doves for sacrifices; he also saw dealers at tables exchanging foreign money. ¹⁵Jesus made a whip from some ropes and chased them all out of the Temple. He drove out the sheep and cattle, scattered the money changers' coins over the floor, and turned over their tables. ¹⁶Then, going over to the people who sold doves, he told them, "Get these things out of here. Stop turning my Father's house into a marketplace!"

2:13-22
Matt 21:12-17
Mark 11:15-19
Luke 19:45-48

2:16
Luke 2:49

¹⁷Then his disciples remembered this prophecy from the Scriptures: "Passion for God's house will consume me."*

2:17
†Ps 69:9

¹⁸But the Jewish leaders demanded, "What are you doing? If God gave you authority to do this, show us a miraculous sign to prove it."

¹⁹"All right," Jesus replied. "Destroy this temple, and in three days I will raise it up."

2:19
Matt 26:61; 27:40
Mark 14:58
Acts 6:14

2:17 Or *"Concern for God's house will be my undoing."* Ps 69:9.

2:12 Capernaum became Jesus' home base during his ministry in Galilee. Located on a major trade route, it was an important city in the region, with a Roman garrison and a customs station. At Capernaum, Matthew was called to be a disciple (Matthew 9:9). The city was also the home of several other disciples (Matthew 4:13-19) and a high-ranking government official (4:46). It had at least one major synagogue. Although Jesus made this city his base of operations in Galilee, he condemned it for the people's unbelief (Matthew 11:23; Luke 10:15).

2:13 The Passover celebration took place yearly at the Temple in Jerusalem. Every Jewish male was expected to make a pilgrimage to Jerusalem during this time (Deuteronomy 16:16). This was a week-long festival—the Passover was one day, and the Festival of Unleavened Bread lasted the rest of the week. The entire week commemorated the freeing of the Jews from slavery in Egypt (Exodus 12:1-13).

2:13 Jerusalem was both the religious and the political seat of Palestine, and the place where the Messiah was expected to arrive. The Temple was located there, and many Jewish families from all over the world would travel to Jerusalem during the key festivals. The Temple was on an imposing site, a hill overlooking the city. Solomon had built the first Temple on this same site almost 1,000 years earlier (959 B.C.), but his Temple had been destroyed by the Babylonians (2 Kings 25). The Temple was rebuilt in 515 B.C., and Herod the Great had enlarged and remodeled it.

• **2:14** The Temple area was always crowded during Passover with thousands of out-of-town visitors. The religious leaders crowded it even further by allowing money changers and merchants to set up booths in the Court of the Gentiles. They rationalized this practice as a convenience for the worshipers and as a way to make money for Temple upkeep. But the religious leaders did not seem to care that the Court of the Gentiles was so full of merchants that foreigners found it difficult to worship. And worship was the main purpose for visiting the Temple. No wonder Jesus was angry!

• **2:14** The Temple tax had to be paid in local currency, so foreigners had to have their money changed. But the money changers often charged exorbitant exchange rates. The people also were required to make sacrifices for sins. Because of the long journey, many could not bring their own animals. Some who brought animals had them rejected for imperfections. So animal merchants conducted a flourishing business in the Temple courtyard. The price of sacrificial animals was much higher in the Temple area than elsewhere. Jesus

was angry at the dishonest, greedy practices of the money changers and merchants, and he particularly disliked their presence on the Temple grounds. They were making a mockery of God's house of worship.

2:14ff John records this first clearing, or cleansing, of the Temple. A second clearing occurred at the end of Jesus' ministry, about three years later, and that event is recorded in Matthew 21:12-17; Mark 11:12-19; Luke 19:45-48.

• **2:14-16** God's Temple was being misused by people who had turned it into a marketplace. They had forgotten, or didn't care, that God's house is a place of worship, not a place for making a profit. Our attitude toward the church is wrong if we see it as a place for personal contacts or business advantage. Make sure you attend church to worship God.

• **2:15, 16** Jesus was obviously angry at the merchants who exploited those who had come to God's house to worship. There is a difference between uncontrolled rage and righteous indignation—yet both are called anger. We must be very careful how we use the powerful emotion of anger. It is right to be angry about injustice and sin; it is wrong to be angry over trivial personal offenses.

2:15, 16 Jesus made a whip and chased out the money changers. Does his example permit us to use violence against wrongdoers? Certain authority is granted to some, but not to all. For example, the authority to use weapons and restrain people is granted to police officers, but not to the general public. The authority to imprison people is granted to judges, but not to individual citizens. Jesus had God's authority, something we cannot have. While we want to live like Christ, we should never try to claim his authority where it has not been given to us.

2:17 Jesus took the evil acts in the Temple as an insult against God, and thus, he did not deal with them halfheartedly. He was consumed with righteous anger against such flagrant disrespect for God.

2:19, 20 The Jews understood Jesus to mean the Temple out of which he had just driven the merchants and money changers. This was the Temple Zerubbabel had built over 500 years earlier, but Herod the Great had begun remodeling it, making it much larger and far more beautiful. It had been 46 years since this remodeling had started (20 B.C.), and it still wasn't completely finished. They understood Jesus' words to mean that this imposing building could be torn down and rebuilt in three days, and they were startled.

2:21
John 10:38;
14:2, 10; 17:21
1 Cor 3:16; 6:19

2:22
Luke 24:6-8
John 12:16; 14:26

2:23
John 7:31;
11:47-48

3:1-2
John 7:50; 19:39

3:2
Matt 22:16
Acts 2:22; 10:38

3:3
John 1:13

3:5
Ezek 36:26-27
Titus 3:5
2 Pet 1:11

3:6
John 1:13
Rom 8:15-16
1 Cor 15:50
Gal 4:6

20 "What!" they exclaimed. "It has taken forty-six years to build this Temple, and you can rebuild it in three days?" 21 But when Jesus said "this temple," he meant his own body. 22 After he was raised from the dead, his disciples remembered he had said this, and they believed both the Scriptures and what Jesus had said.

Nicodemus Visits Jesus at Night (24)

23 Because of the miraculous signs Jesus did in Jerusalem at the Passover celebration, many began to trust in him. 24 But Jesus didn't trust them, because he knew human nature. 25 No one needed to tell him what mankind is really like.

3 There was a man named Nicodemus, a Jewish religious leader who was a Pharisee. 2 After dark one evening, he came to speak with Jesus. "Rabbi," he said, "we all know that God has sent you to teach us. Your miraculous signs are evidence that God is with you."

3 Jesus replied, "I tell you the truth, unless you are born again,* you cannot see the Kingdom of God."

4 "What do you mean?" exclaimed Nicodemus. "How can an old man go back into his mother's womb and be born again?"

5 Jesus replied, "I assure you, no one can enter the Kingdom of God without being born of water and the Spirit.* 6 Humans can reproduce only human life, but the Holy Spirit gives

3:3 Or *born from above;* also in 3:7.   **3:5** Or *and spirit.* The Greek word for *Spirit* can also be translated *wind;* see 3:8.

2:21, 22 Jesus was not talking about the Temple made of stones, but about his body. His listeners didn't realize it, but Jesus was greater than the Temple (Matthew 12:6). His words would take on meaning for his disciples after his resurrection. That Christ so perfectly fulfilled this prediction became the strongest proof for his claims to be God.

• **2:23-25** The Son of God knows all about human nature. Jesus was well aware of the truth of Jeremiah 17:9, which states, "The human heart is the most deceitful of all things, and desperately wicked. Who really knows how bad it is?" Jesus was discerning, and he knew that the faith of some followers was superficial. Some of the same people claiming to believe in Jesus at this time would later yell "Crucify him!" It's easy to believe when it is exciting and everyone else believes the same way. But keep your faith firm even when it isn't popular to follow Christ.

• **3:1** Nicodemus was a Pharisee and a member of the ruling council (called the high council, or the Sanhedrin). The Pharisees were a group of religious leaders whom Jesus and John the Baptist often criticized for being hypocrites (see the note on Matthew 3:7 for more on the Pharisees). Most Pharisees were intensely jealous of Jesus because he undermined their authority and challenged their views. But Nicodemus was searching, and he believed that Jesus had some answers. A learned teacher himself, he came to Jesus to be taught. No matter how intelligent and well educated you are, you must come to Jesus with an open mind and heart so he can teach you the truth about God.

3:1ff Nicodemus came to Jesus personally, although he could have sent one of his assistants. He wanted to examine Jesus for himself to separate fact from rumor. Perhaps Nicodemus was afraid of what his peers, the Pharisees, would say about his visit, so he came after dark. Later, when he understood that Jesus was truly the Messiah, he spoke up boldly in his defense (7:50, 51). Like Nicodemus, we must examine Jesus for ourselves—others cannot do it for us. Then, if we believe he is who he says, we will want to speak up for him.

• **3:3** What did Nicodemus know about the Kingdom? From the Bible he knew it would be ruled by God, it would be restored on earth, and it would incorporate God's people. Jesus revealed to this devout Pharisee that the Kingdom would come to the whole world (3:16), not just the Jews, and that Nicodemus wouldn't be a part of it unless he was personally born again (3:5). This was a revolutionary concept: The Kingdom is personal, not national or ethnic, and its entrance requirements are repentance and spiritual rebirth. Jesus later taught that God's Kingdom has *already begun* in the hearts of believers (Luke 17:21). It will be fully realized when Jesus returns again to judge the world and abolish evil forever (Revelation 21–22).

3:5, 6 "Being born of water and the Spirit" could refer to (1) the contrast between physical birth (water) and spiritual birth (Spirit), or (2) being regenerated by the Spirit and signifying that rebirth by Christian baptism. The water may also represent the cleansing action of God's Holy Spirit (Titus 3:5). Nicodemus undoubtedly would have been familiar with God's promise in Ezekiel 36:25, 26. Jesus was explaining the importance of a spiritual rebirth, saying that people don't enter the Kingdom by living a better life, but by being spiritually reborn.

3:6 Who is the Holy Spirit? God is three persons in one—the Father, the Son, and the Holy Spirit. God became a man in Jesus so that Jesus could die for our sins. Jesus rose from the dead to offer salvation to all people through spiritual renewal and rebirth. When Jesus ascended into heaven, his physical presence left the earth, but he promised to send the Holy Spirit so that his spiritual presence would still be among humankind (see Luke 24:49). The Holy Spirit first became available to all believers at Pentecost (Acts 2). Whereas in Old Testament days the Holy Spirit empowered specific individuals for specific purposes, now all believers have the power of the Holy Spirit available to them. For more on the Holy Spirit, read 14:16-28; Romans 8:9; 1 Corinthians 12:13; and 2 Corinthians 1:22.

THE VISIT IN SAMARIA
Jesus went to Jerusalem for the Passover, cleared the Temple, and talked with Nicodemus, a religious leader, about eternal life. He then left Jerusalem and traveled in Judea. On his way to Galilee, he visited Sychar and other villages in Samaria. Unlike most Jews of the day, he did not try to avoid the region of Samaria.

birth to spiritual life.* 7 So don't be surprised when I say, ' You* must be born again.' 8 The
wind blows wherever it wants. Just as you can hear the wind but can't tell where it comes
from or where it is going, so you can't explain how people are born of the Spirit."

9 "How are these things possible?" Nicodemus asked.

10 Jesus replied, "You are a respected Jewish teacher, and yet you don't understand these
things? 11 I assure you, we tell you what we know and have seen, and yet you won't believe our
testimony. 12 But if you don't believe me when I tell you about earthly things, how can you
possibly believe if I tell you about heavenly things? 13 No one has ever gone to heaven and returned. But the Son of Man* has come down from heaven. 14 And as Moses lifted up the
bronze snake on a pole in the wilderness, so the Son of Man must be lifted up, 15 so that
everyone who believes in him will have eternal life.*

16 "For God loved the world so much that he gave his one and only Son, so that everyone
who believes in him will not perish but have eternal life. 17 God sent his Son into the world
not to judge the world, but to save the world through him.

18 "There is no judgment against anyone who believes in him. But anyone who does not
believe in him has already been judged for not believing in God's one and only Son. 19 And
the judgment is based on this fact: God's light came into the world, but people loved the
darkness more than the light, for their actions were evil. 20 All who do evil hate the light and
refuse to go near it for fear their sins will be exposed. 21 But those who do what is right come
to the light so others can see that they are doing what God wants.*"

John the Baptist Tells More about Jesus (25)

22 Then Jesus and his disciples left Jerusalem and went into the Judean countryside. Jesus
spent some time with them there, baptizing people.

23 At this time John the Baptist was baptizing at Aenon, near Salim, because there was
plenty of water there; and people kept coming to him for baptism. 24 (This was before John
was thrown into prison.) 25 A debate broke out between John's disciples and a certain Jew*

Cross-references (right margin):
- **3:8** Eccl 11:5
- **3:13** John 6:38, 42; Eph 4:8-10
- **3:14** Num 21:8-9; John 8:28; 12:34
- **3:15** John 20:31; 1 Jn 5:11-12
- **3:16** Rom 5:8; 8:32; 1 Jn 4:9-10; 5:13
- **3:17** John 12:47
- **3:18** John 5:24
- **3:19** John 1:5, 9; 8:12; 9:5; 12:46
- **3:20** Eph 5:11-13
- **3:21** 1 Jn 1:6
- **3:22** John 3:26; 4:1-2
- **3:24** Matt 4:12

3:6 Greek *what is born of the Spirit is spirit.*   3:7 The Greek word for *you* is plural; also in 3:12.   3:13 Some manuscripts add *who lives in heaven.* "Son of Man" is a title Jesus used for himself.   3:15 Or *everyone who believes will
have eternal life in him.*   3:21 Or *can see God at work in what he is doing.*   3:25 Some manuscripts read *some Jews.*

3:8 Jesus explained that we cannot control the work of the Holy
Spirit. He works in ways we cannot predict or understand. Just
as you did not control your physical birth, so you cannot control
your spiritual birth. It is a gift from God through the Holy Spirit
(Romans 8:16; 1 Corinthians 2:10-12; 1 Thessalonians 1:5, 6).

3:10, 11 This Jewish teacher of the Bible knew the Old Testament thoroughly, but he didn't understand what it said about the
Messiah. Knowledge is not salvation. You should know the Bible,
but even more important, you should understand the God whom
the Bible reveals and the salvation that God offers.

3:14, 15 When the Israelites were wandering in the wilderness,
God sent a plague of snakes to punish the people for their rebel-
lious attitudes. Those doomed to die from snakebite could be
healed by obeying God's command to look up at the elevated
bronze snake and by believing that God would heal them if they
did (see Numbers 21:8, 9). Similarly, our salvation happens when
we look up to Jesus, believing he will save us. God has provided
this way for us to be healed of sin's deadly bite.

• **3:16** The message of the Good News comes to a focus in this
verse. God's love is not static or self-centered; it reaches out and
draws others in. Here God sets the pattern of true love, the basis
for all love relationships—when you love someone dearly, you are
willing to give freely to the point of self-sacrifice. God paid dearly
with the life of his Son, the highest price he could pay. Jesus
accepted our punishment, paid the price for our sins, and then
offered us the new life that he had bought for us. When we share
the Good News with others, our love must be like Jesus'—willingly giving up our own comfort and security so that others
might join us in receiving God's love.

• **3:16** Some people are repulsed by the idea of eternal life because
their lives are miserable. But eternal life is not an extension of a
person's miserable, mortal life; eternal life is God's life embodied
in Christ given to all believers now as a guarantee that they will
live forever. In eternal life there is no death, sickness, enemy, evil,

or sin. When we don't know Christ, we make choices as though
this life is all we have. In reality, this life is just the introduction to
eternity. Receive this new life by faith and begin to evaluate all that
happens from an eternal perspective.

• **3:16** To "believe" is more than intellectual agreement that Jesus
is God. It means to put our trust and confidence in him that he
alone can save us. It is to put Christ in charge of our present plans
and eternal destiny. Believing is both trusting his words as reliable,
and relying on him for the power to change. If you have never
trusted Christ, let this promise of everlasting life be yours—and
believe.

3:18 People often try to protect themselves from their fears by
putting their faith in something they do or have: good deeds, skill
or intelligence, money or possessions. But only God can save us
from the one thing that we really need to fear—eternal condem-
nation. We believe in God by recognizing the insufficiency of our
own efforts to find salvation and by asking him to do his work
in us. When Jesus talks about unbelievers, he means those who
reject or ignore him completely, not those who have momentary
doubts.

• **3:19-21** Many people don't want their lives exposed to God's
light because they are afraid of what will be revealed. They don't
want to be changed. Don't be surprised when these same people
are threatened by your desire to obey God and do what is right,
because they are afraid that the light in you may expose some
of the darkness in their lives. Rather than giving in to discourage-
ment, keep praying that they will come to see how much better
it is to live in light than in darkness.

• **3:25ff** Some people look for points of disagreement so they
can sow seeds of discord, discontent, and doubt. John the Baptist ended this theological argument by focusing on his devotion
to Christ. It is divisive to try to force others to believe our way.
Instead, let's witness about what Christ has done for us. How can
anyone argue with us about that?

3:26
John 1:7, 34

3:27
1 Cor 4:7
Heb 5:4

3:28
Mal 3:1

3:29
Matt 9:15
Rev 21:9

3:31
1 Jn 4:5

3:33
1 Jn 5:10

3:34
Luke 4:18

3:35
John 5:20; 15:9

3:36
John 3:16
1 Jn 5:12-13

over ceremonial cleansing. ²⁶So John's disciples came to him and said, "Rabbi, the man you met on the other side of the Jordan River, the one you identified as the Messiah, is also baptizing people. And everybody is going to him instead of coming to us."

²⁷John replied, "No one can receive anything unless God gives it from heaven. ²⁸You yourselves know how plainly I told you, 'I am not the Messiah. I am only here to prepare the way for him.' ²⁹It is the bridegroom who marries the bride, and the best man is simply glad to stand with him and hear his vows. Therefore, I am filled with joy at his success. ³⁰He must become greater and greater, and I must become less and less.

³¹"He has come from above and is greater than anyone else. We are of the earth, and we speak of earthly things, but he has come from heaven and is greater than anyone else.* ³²He testifies about what he has seen and heard, but how few believe what he tells them! ³³Anyone who accepts his testimony can affirm that God is true. ³⁴For he is sent by God. He speaks God's words, for God gives him the Spirit without limit. ³⁵The Father loves his Son and has put everything into his hands. ³⁶And anyone who believes in God's Son has eternal life. Anyone who doesn't obey the Son will never experience eternal life but remains under God's angry judgment."

Jesus Talks to a Woman at the Well (27)

4:1
John 3:22, 26

4:4
Matt 10:5
Luke 9:52

4:5-6
Gen 33:19; 48:22
Josh 24:32

4 Jesus* knew the Pharisees had heard that he was baptizing and making more disciples than John ²(though Jesus himself didn't baptize them—his disciples did). ³So he left Judea and returned to Galilee.

⁴He had to go through Samaria on the way. ⁵Eventually he came to the Samaritan village of Sychar, near the field that Jacob gave to his son Joseph. ⁶Jacob's well was there; and Jesus,

3:31 Some manuscripts do not include *and is greater than anyone else.*   **4:1** Some manuscripts read *The Lord.*

• **3:26** John the Baptist's disciples were disturbed because people were following Jesus instead of John. It is easy to grow jealous of the popularity of another person's ministry. But we must remember that our true mission is to influence people to follow Christ, not us.

3:27 Why did John the Baptist continue to baptize after Jesus came onto the scene? Why didn't he become a disciple, too? John explained that because God had given him his work, he had to continue it until God called him to do something else. John's main purpose was to point people to Christ. Even with Jesus beginning his own ministry, John could still turn people to Jesus.

3:30 John's willingness to decrease in importance shows unusual humility. Pastors and other Christian leaders can be tempted to focus more on the success of their ministries than on Christ. Beware of those who put more emphasis on their own achievements than on God's Kingdom.

3:31-35 Jesus' testimony was trustworthy because he had come from heaven and was speaking of what he had seen there. His words were the very words of God. Your whole spiritual life depends on your answer to one question: Who is Jesus Christ? If you accept Jesus as only a prophet or teacher, you have to reject his teaching, for he claimed to be God's Son, even God himself. The heartbeat of John's Gospel is the dynamic truth that Jesus Christ is God's Son, the Messiah, the Savior, who existed from the beginning and will continue to live forever. This same Jesus has invited us to accept him and live with him eternally. When we understand who Jesus is, we are compelled to believe what he said.

3:34 God's Spirit was upon Jesus without measure or limit. Thus, Jesus was the highest revelation of God to humanity (Hebrews 1:2).

3:36 Jesus says that those who believe in him *have* (not *will* have) eternal life. To receive eternal life is to join in God's life, which by nature is eternal. Thus, eternal life begins at the moment of spiritual rebirth.

3:36 John, the author of this Gospel, has been demonstrating that Jesus is the true Son of God. Jesus sets before us the greatest choice in life. We are responsible to decide today whom we will obey (Joshua 24:15), and God wants us to choose him and

life (Deuteronomy 30:15-20). God's angry judgment refers to his final rejection of those who reject him. To put off the choice is to choose not to follow Christ. Indecision is a fatal decision.

4:1-3 Already opposition was rising against Jesus, especially from the Pharisees. They resented Jesus' popularity as well as his message, which challenged much of their teachings. Because Jesus was just beginning his ministry, it wasn't yet time to confront these leaders openly; so he left Jerusalem and traveled north toward Galilee.

• **4:4** To go from the territory of Judea to Galilee meant passing through a central territory called Samaria. Most Jews did everything they could to avoid traveling through Samaria. The reason goes way back into their history.

After the northern kingdom, with its capital at Samaria, fell to the Assyrians, many Jews were deported to Assyria, and foreigners were brought in to settle the land and help keep the peace (2 Kings 17:24). The intermarriage between those foreigners and the remaining Jews resulted in a mixed race, impure in the opinion of Jews who lived in the southern kingdom. Thus, the pure Jews hated this mixed race, called Samaritans, because they felt that their fellow Jews who had intermarried had betrayed their people and nation. The Samaritans had set up an alternate center for worship on Mount Gerizim (4:20) to parallel the Temple at Jerusalem, but it had been destroyed 150 years earlier. While there was long-standing prejudice between Jews and Samaritans, Jesus did not live by such restrictions. The route through Samaria was shorter, and that was the route he took.

• **4:5-7** Jacob's well was on the property originally owned by Jacob (Genesis 33:18, 19). It was not a spring-fed well, but a well into which water seeped from rain and dew, collecting at the bottom. Wells were almost always located outside the city along the main road. Twice each day, morning and evening, women came to draw water. This woman came at noon, however, probably to avoid meeting people who knew her reputation. Jesus gave this woman an extraordinary message about fresh and pure water that would quench her spiritual thirst forever.

tired from the long walk, sat wearily beside the well about noontime. ⁷Soon a Samaritan woman came to draw water, and Jesus said to her, "Please give me a drink." ⁸He was alone at the time because his disciples had gone into the village to buy some food.

⁹The woman was surprised, for Jews refuse to have anything to do with Samaritans.* She said to Jesus, "You are a Jew, and I am a Samaritan woman. Why are you asking me for a drink?"

¹⁰Jesus replied, "If you only knew the gift God has for you and who you are speaking to, you would ask me, and I would give you living water."

¹¹"But sir, you don't have a rope or a bucket," she said, "and this well is very deep. Where would you get this living water? ¹²And besides, do you think you're greater than our ancestor Jacob, who gave us this well? How can you offer better water than he and his sons and his animals enjoyed?"

¹³Jesus replied, "Anyone who drinks this water will soon become thirsty again. ¹⁴But those who drink the water I give will never be thirsty again. It becomes a fresh, bubbling spring within them, giving them eternal life."

¹⁵"Please, sir," the woman said, "give me this water! Then I'll never be thirsty again, and I won't have to come here to get water."

¹⁶"Go and get your husband," Jesus told her.

¹⁷"I don't have a husband," the woman replied.

Jesus said, "You're right! You don't have a husband—¹⁸for you have had five husbands, and you aren't even married to the man you're living with now. You certainly spoke the truth!"

¹⁹"Sir," the woman said, "you must be a prophet. ²⁰So tell me, why is it that you Jews insist that Jerusalem is the only place of worship, while we Samaritans claim it is here at Mount Gerizim,* where our ancestors worshiped?"

²¹Jesus replied, "Believe me, dear woman, the time is coming when it will no longer matter whether you worship the Father on this mountain or in Jerusalem. ²²You Samaritans know very little about the one you worship, while we Jews know all about him, for salvation comes through the Jews. ²³But the time is coming—indeed it's here now—when true worshipers will worship the Father in spirit and in truth. The Father is looking for those who will worship him that way. ²⁴For God is Spirit, so those who worship him must worship in spirit and in truth."

4:9 Some manuscripts do not include this sentence.　**4:20** Greek *on this mountain.*

Marginal cross-references

4:7
Gen 24:17
1 Kgs 17:10

4:9
Ezra 4:1-3; 9–10
Matt 10:5
Luke 9:52-53
John 8:48
Acts 10:48

4:10
Isa 12:3; 44:3
Jer 2:13; 17:13
John 7:37-39
1 Cor 12:13
Rev 7:17; 21:6;
22:17

4:14
John 6:35; 7:38

4:15
John 6:34

4:19
Matt 21:46
John 7:40; 9:17

4:20
Deut 11:29;
12:5-14
Josh 8:33

4:21
Mal 1:11
1 Tim 2:8

4:22
2 Kgs 17:28-41
Isa 2:3
Rom 3:1-2; 9:4-5

4:23-24
2 Cor 3:17-18
Phil 3:3

4:7-9 This woman (1) was a Samaritan, a member of the hated mixed race, (2) was known to be living in sin, and (3) was in a public place. No respectable Jewish man would talk to a woman under such circumstances. But Jesus did. The Good News is for every person, no matter what his or her race, social position, or past sins. We must be prepared to share this Good News at any time and in any place. Jesus crossed all barriers to share the Good News, and we who follow him must do no less.

4:10 What did Jesus mean by "living water"? In the Old Testament, many verses speak of thirsting after God as one thirsts for water (Psalm 42:1; Isaiah 55:1; Jeremiah 2:13; Zechariah 13:1). God is called the fountain of life (Psalm 36:9) and the fountain of living water (Jeremiah 17:13). In saying he would bring living water that could forever quench a person's thirst for God, Jesus was claiming to be the Messiah. Only the Messiah could give this gift that satisfies the soul's desire.

4:13-15 Many spiritual functions parallel physical functions. As our bodies hunger and thirst, so do our souls. But our souls need *spiritual* food and water. The woman confused the two kinds of water, perhaps because no one had ever talked with her about her spiritual hunger and thirst before. We would not think of depriving our bodies of food and water when they hunger or thirst. Why then should we deprive our souls? The living Word, Jesus Christ, and the written Word, the Bible, can satisfy our hungry and thirsty souls.

4:15 The woman mistakenly believed that if she received the water Jesus offered, she would not have to return to the well each day. She was interested in Jesus' message because she thought it could make her life easier. But if that were always the case, people would accept Christ's message for the wrong reasons. Christ did not come to take away challenges, but to change us on the inside and to empower us to deal with problems from God's perspective.

4:16-20 When this woman discovered that Jesus knew all about her private life, she quickly changed the subject. Often people become uncomfortable when the conversation is too close to home, and they try to talk about something else. As we witness, we should gently guide the conversation back to Christ. His presence exposes sin and makes people squirm, but only Christ can forgive sins and give new life.

4:20-24 The woman brought up a popular theological issue—the correct place to worship. But her question was a smoke screen to keep Jesus away from her deepest need. Jesus directed the conversation to a much more important point: The *location* of worship is not nearly as important as the *attitude* of the worshipers.

4:22 When Jesus said, "Salvation comes through the Jews," he meant that only through the Jewish Messiah would the whole world find salvation. God had promised that through the Jewish race the whole earth would be blessed (Genesis 12:3). The Old Testament prophets had called the Jews to be a light to the other nations of the world, bringing them to a knowledge of God; and they had predicted the Messiah's coming. The woman at the well may have known of these passages and was expecting the Messiah, but she didn't realize that she was talking to him!

4:24 "God is Spirit" means he is not a physical being limited to one place. He is present everywhere, and he can be worshiped anywhere, at any time. It is not where we worship that counts, but how we worship. Is your worship genuine and true? Do you have the Holy Spirit's help? How does the Holy Spirit help us worship?

4:25
Deut 18:15
4:26
Mark 14:61-62
John 9:37

²⁵The woman said, "I know the Messiah is coming—the one who is called Christ. When he comes, he will explain everything to us."*

²⁶Then Jesus told her, "I AM the Messiah!"*

Jesus Tells about the Spiritual Harvest (28)

²⁷Just then his disciples came back. They were shocked to find him talking to a woman, but none of them had the nerve to ask, "What do you want with her?" or "Why are you talking to her?" ²⁸The woman left her water jar beside the well and ran back to the village, telling everyone, ²⁹"Come and see a man who told me everything I ever did! Could he possibly be the Messiah?" ³⁰So the people came streaming from the village to see him.

4:29
Matt 9:37
John 7:26

³¹Meanwhile, the disciples were urging Jesus, "Rabbi, eat something."

³²But Jesus replied, "I have a kind of food you know nothing about."

³³"Did someone bring him food while we were gone?" the disciples asked each other.

4:34
John 5:30, 36;
6:38; 17:4
4:35
Matt 9:37
Luke 10:2
4:37
Job 31:8
Mic 6:15

³⁴Then Jesus explained: "My nourishment comes from doing the will of God, who sent me, and from finishing his work. ³⁵You know the saying, 'Four months between planting and harvest.' But I say, wake up and look around. The fields are already ripe* for harvest. ³⁶The harvesters are paid good wages, and the fruit they harvest is people brought to eternal life. What joy awaits both the planter and the harvester alike! ³⁷You know the saying, 'One plants and another harvests.' And it's true. ³⁸I sent you to harvest where you didn't plant; others had already done the work, and now you will get to gather the harvest."

Many Samaritans Believe in Jesus (29)

³⁹Many Samaritans from the village believed in Jesus because the woman had said, "He told me everything I ever did!" ⁴⁰When they came out to see him, they begged him to stay in their village. So he stayed for two days, ⁴¹long enough for many more to hear his message and be-

4:42
Luke 2:11
1 Jn 4:14

lieve. ⁴²Then they said to the woman, "Now we believe, not just because of what you told us, but because we have heard him ourselves. Now we know that he is indeed the Savior of the world."

Jesus Preaches in Galilee (30/Matthew 4:12-17; Mark 1:14-15; Luke 4:14-15)

4:44
Matt 13:57
Luke 4:24

⁴³At the end of the two days, Jesus went on to Galilee. ⁴⁴He himself had said that a prophet is not honored in his own hometown. ⁴⁵Yet the Galileans welcomed him, for they had been in Jerusalem at the Passover celebration and had seen everything he did there.

Jesus Heals a Government Official's Son (31)

4:46
John 2:1-11

⁴⁶As he traveled through Galilee, he came to Cana, where he had turned the water into wine. There was a government official in nearby Capernaum whose son was very sick. ⁴⁷When he

4:26 Or *"The 'I AM' is here";* or *"I am the LORD";* Greek reads *"I am, the one speaking to you."* See Exod 3:14.
4:35 Greek *white.*

The Holy Spirit prays for us (Romans 8:26), teaches us the words of Christ (14:26), and tells us we are loved (Romans 5:5).

4:34 The "nourishment" about which Jesus was speaking was his spiritual nourishment. It includes more than Bible study, prayer, and attending church. Spiritual nourishment also comes from doing God's will and helping to bring his work of salvation to completion. We are nourished not only by what we take in, but also by what we give out for God. In 17:4, Jesus refers to completing God's work on earth.

• **4:35** Sometimes Christians excuse themselves from witnessing by saying that their family or friends aren't ready to believe. Jesus, however, makes it clear that around us a continual harvest waits to be reaped. Don't let Jesus find you making excuses. Look around. You will find people ready to hear God's Word.

4:36-38 The wages Jesus offers are the joy of working for him and seeing the harvest of believers. These wages come to planter and harvester alike because both find joy in seeing new believers come into Christ's Kingdom. The phrase "others had already done the work" (4:38) may refer to the Old Testament prophets and to John the Baptist, who paved the way for the Good News.

• **4:39** The Samaritan woman immediately shared her experience with others. Despite her reputation, many took her invitation and came out to meet Jesus. Perhaps there are sins in our past of which we're ashamed. But Christ changes us. As people see

these changes, they become curious. Use these opportunities to introduce them to Christ.

JESUS RETURNS TO GALILEE
Jesus stayed in Sychar for two days, then went on to Galilee. He visited Nazareth and various towns in Galilee before arriving in Cana. From there he spoke the word of healing, and a government official's son in Capernaum was healed. The Gospel of Matthew tells us Jesus then settled in Capernaum (Matthew 4:12, 13).

heard that Jesus had come from Judea to Galilee, he went and begged Jesus to come to Capernaum to heal his son, who was about to die.

⁴⁸Jesus asked, "Will you never believe in me unless you see miraculous signs and wonders?"

⁴⁹The official pleaded, "Lord, please come now before my little boy dies."

⁵⁰Then Jesus told him, "Go back home. Your son will live!" And the man believed what Jesus said and started home.

⁵¹While the man was on his way, some of his servants met him with the news that his son was alive and well. ⁵²He asked them when the boy had begun to get better, and they replied, "Yesterday afternoon at one o'clock his fever suddenly disappeared!" ⁵³Then the father realized that that was the very time Jesus had told him, "Your son will live." And he and his entire household believed in Jesus. ⁵⁴This was the second miraculous sign Jesus did in Galilee after coming from Judea.

4:48
1 Cor 1:22

4:50
Matt 8:13
Mark 7:29

4:53
Acts 11:14;
16:14-15

4:54
John 2:11

Jesus Heals a Lame Man by a Pool (42)

5 Afterward Jesus returned to Jerusalem for one of the Jewish holy days. ²Inside the city, near the Sheep Gate, was the pool of Bethesda,* with five covered porches. ³Crowds of sick people—blind, lame, or paralyzed—lay on the porches.* ⁵One of the men lying there had been sick for thirty-eight years. ⁶When Jesus saw him and knew he had been ill for a long time, he asked him, "Would you like to get well?"

⁷"I can't, sir," the sick man said, "for I have no one to put me into the pool when the water bubbles up. Someone else always gets there ahead of me."

⁸Jesus told him, "Stand up, pick up your mat, and walk!"

⁹Instantly, the man was healed! He rolled up his sleeping mat and began walking! But this miracle happened on the Sabbath, ¹⁰so the Jewish leaders objected. They said to the man who was cured, "You can't work on the Sabbath! The law doesn't allow you to carry that sleeping mat!"

5:1
Lev 23:1-2
Deut 16:1
John 2:13

5:2
Neh 3:1; 12:39

5:8
Matt 9:6
Mark 2:11
Luke 5:24

5:10
Neh 13:15-20
Jer 17:21
Matt 12:2

5:2 Other manuscripts read *Beth-zatha;* still others read *Bethsaida.* **5:3** Some manuscripts add an expanded conclusion to verse 3 and all of verse 4: *waiting for a certain movement of the water,* ⁴*for an angel of the Lord came from time to time and stirred up the water. And the first person to step in after the water was stirred was healed of whatever disease he had.*

• **4:46-49** This government official was probably an officer in Herod's service. He had walked 20 miles to see Jesus and addressed him as "Lord," putting himself under Jesus even though he had legal authority over Jesus.

4:48 This miracle was more than a favor to one official; it was a sign to all the people. John's Gospel was written to all humankind to urge faith in Christ. Here a government official had faith that Jesus could do what he claimed. The official believed; *then* he saw a miraculous sign.

• **4:50** This government official not only believed Jesus could heal; he also obeyed Jesus by returning home, thus demonstrating his

JESUS TEACHES IN JERUSALEM
Between chapters 4 and 5 of John, Jesus ministered throughout Galilee, especially in Capernaum. He had been calling certain men to follow him, but it wasn't until after this trip to Jerusalem (5:1) that he chose his 12 disciples from among them.

faith. It isn't enough for us to say we believe that Jesus can take care of our problems. We need to act as if we can. When you pray about a need or problem, live as though you believe Jesus can do what he says.

• **4:51** Jesus' miracles were not mere illusions. Although the official's son was 20 miles away, he was healed when Jesus spoke the word. Distance was no problem because Christ has mastery over space. We can never put so much space between ourselves and Christ that he can no longer help us.

4:53 Notice how the official's faith grew. First, he believed enough to ask Jesus to help his son. Second, he believed Jesus' assurance that his son would live, and he acted on it. Third, he and his whole house believed in Jesus. Faith is a gift that grows as we use it.

5:1 Three festivals (or "holy days") required all Jewish males to come to Jerusalem: (1) the Festival of Passover and Unleavened Bread, (2) the Festival of Pentecost (also called the Festival of Harvest or the Festival of Weeks), and (3) the Festival of Shelters.

5:6 After 38 years, this man's problem had become a way of life. No one had ever helped him. He had no hope of ever being healed. The man's situation looked hopeless. But no matter how trapped you feel in your infirmities, God can minister to your deepest needs. Don't let a problem or hardship cause you to lose hope. God may have special work for you to do in spite of your condition, or even because of it. Many have ministered effectively to hurting people because they have triumphed over their own hurts.

• **5:10** According to the Pharisees, carrying a mat on the Sabbath was work and was therefore unlawful. It did not break an Old Testament law, but it broke the Pharisees' *interpretation* of God's command to "remember to observe the Sabbath day by keeping it holy" (Exodus 20:8). This was just one of hundreds of rules they had added to the Old Testament law.

5:10 A man who hadn't walked for 38 years had been healed, but the Pharisees were more concerned about their petty rules than the life and health of a human being. The Jewish leaders saw both a

¹¹But he replied, "The man who healed me told me, 'Pick up your mat and walk.'"

¹²"Who said such a thing as that?" they demanded.

5:14
John 8:11

¹³The man didn't know, for Jesus had disappeared into the crowd. ¹⁴But afterward Jesus found him in the Temple and told him, "Now you are well; so stop sinning, or something even worse may happen to you." ¹⁵Then the man went and told the Jewish leaders that it was Jesus who had healed him.

Jesus Claims to Be the Son of God (43)

¹⁶So the Jewish leaders began harassing* Jesus for breaking the Sabbath rules. ¹⁷But Jesus

5:18
Phil 2:6
Titus 2:13
2 Pet 1:1
1 Jn 5:21

replied, "My Father is always working, and so am I." ¹⁸So the Jewish leaders tried all the harder to find a way to kill him. For he not only broke the Sabbath, he called God his Father, thereby making himself equal with God.

5:19
John 8:28; 12:49;
14:10

¹⁹So Jesus explained, "I tell you the truth, the Son can do nothing by himself. He does only what he sees the Father doing. Whatever the Father does, the Son also does. ²⁰For the Father loves the Son and shows him everything he is doing. In fact, the Father will show him how to

5:21
John 11:25

do even greater works than healing this man. Then you will truly be astonished. ²¹For just as the Father gives life to those he raises from the dead, so the Son gives life to anyone he wants. ²²In addition, the Father judges no one. Instead, he has given the Son absolute authority to

5:16 Or *persecuting.*

THE CLAIMS OF CHRIST	Jesus claimed to be:	Matthew	Mark	Luke	John
	the fulfillment of Old Testament prophecies	5:17; 14:33; 16:16, 17; 26:31, 53-56; 27:43	14:21, 61, 62	4:16-21; 7:18-23; 18:31; 22:37; 24:44	2:22; 5:45-47; 6:45; 7:40; 10:34-36; 13:18; 15:25; 20:9
	the Son of Man	8:20; 12:8; 16:27; 19:28; 20:18, 19; 24:27, 44; 25:31; 26:2, 45, 64	8:31, 38; 9:9; 10:45; 14:41	6:22; 7:33, 34; 12:8; 17:22; 18:8, 31; 19:10; 21:36	1:51; 3:13, 14; 6:27, 53; 12:23, 34
	the Son of God	11:27; 14:33; 16:16, 17; 27:43	3:11, 12; 14:61, 62	8:28; 10:22	1:18; 3:35, 36; 5:18-26; 6:40; 10:36; 11:4; 17:1; 19:7
	the Messiah/ the Christ	23:9, 10; 26:63, 64	8:29, 30	4:41; 23:1, 2; 24:25-27	4:25, 26; 10:24, 25; 11:27
	Teacher/Master	26:18			13:13, 14
	one with authority to forgive		2:1-12	7:48, 49	
	Lord		5:19		13:13, 14; 20:28, 29
	Savior			19:10	3:17; 10:9

Those who read the life of Christ are faced with one unavoidable question—was Jesus God? Part of any reasonable conclusion has to include the fact that he did claim to be God. We have no other choice but to agree or disagree with his claim. Eternal life is at stake in the choice.

---

mighty miracle of healing and a broken rule. They threw the miracle aside as they focused their attention on the broken rule, because the rule was more important to them than the miracle. It is easy to get so caught up in our man-made structures and rules that we forget the people involved. Are your guidelines for living God-made or man-made? Are they helping people, or have they become needless stumbling blocks?

5:14 This man had been lame, or paralyzed, and suddenly he could walk. This was a great miracle. But he needed an even greater miracle—to have his sins forgiven. The man was delighted to be physically healed, but he had to turn from his sins and seek God's forgiveness to be spiritually healed. God's forgiveness is the greatest gift you will ever receive. Don't neglect his gracious offer.

5:17 If God stopped every kind of work on the Sabbath, nature would fall into chaos, and sin would overrun the world. Genesis

2:2 says that God rested on the seventh day, but this can't mean that he stopped doing good. Jesus wanted to teach that when the opportunity to do good presents itself, it should not be ignored, even on the Sabbath.

● **5:17ff** Jesus was identifying himself with God, his Father. There could be no doubt as to his claim to be God. Jesus does not leave us the option to believe in God while ignoring God's Son (5:23). The Pharisees also called God their Father, but they realized Jesus was claiming a unique relationship with him. In response to Jesus' claim, the Pharisees had two choices: to believe him, or to accuse him of blasphemy. They chose the second.

5:19-23 Because of his unity with God, Jesus lived as God wanted him to live. Because of our identification with Jesus, we must honor him and live as he wants us to live. The question "What would Jesus do?" may help us make the right choices.

judge, 23 so that everyone will honor the Son, just as they honor the Father. Anyone who does not honor the Son is certainly not honoring the Father who sent him.

24 "I tell you the truth, those who listen to my message and believe in God who sent me have eternal life. They will never be condemned for their sins, but they have already passed from death into life.

25 "And I assure you that the time is coming, indeed it's here now, when the dead will hear my voice—the voice of the Son of God. And those who listen will live. 26 The Father has life in himself, and he has granted that same life-giving power to his Son. 27 And he has given him authority to judge everyone because he is the Son of Man.* 28 Don't be so surprised! Indeed, the time is coming when all the dead in their graves will hear the voice of God's Son, 29 and they will rise again. Those who have done good will rise to experience eternal life, and those who have continued in evil will rise to experience judgment. 30 I can do nothing on my own. I judge as God tells me. Therefore, my judgment is just, because I carry out the will of the one who sent me, not my own will.

Jesus Supports His Claim (44)

31 "If I were to testify on my own behalf, my testimony would not be valid. 32 But someone else is also testifying about me, and I assure you that everything he says about me is true. 33 In fact, you sent investigators to listen to John the Baptist, and his testimony about me was true. 34 Of course, I have no need of human witnesses, but I say these things so you might be saved. 35 John was like a burning and shining lamp, and you were excited for a while about his message. 36 But I have a greater witness than John—my teachings and my miracles. The Father gave me these works to accomplish, and they prove that he sent me. 37 And the Father who sent me has testified about me himself. You have never heard his voice or seen him face to face, 38 and you do not have his message in your hearts, because you do not believe me— the one he sent to you.

39 "You search the Scriptures because you think they give you eternal life. But the Scriptures point to me! 40 Yet you refuse to come to me to receive this life.

41 "Your approval means nothing to me, 42 because I know you don't have God's love within you. 43 For I have come to you in my Father's name, and you have rejected me. Yet if others come in their own name, you gladly welcome them. 44 No wonder you can't believe! For you gladly honor each other, but you don't care about the honor that comes from the one who alone is God.*

45 "Yet it isn't I who will accuse you before the Father. Moses will accuse you! Yes, Moses, in whom you put your hopes. 46 If you really believed Moses, you would believe me, because he wrote about me. 47 But since you don't believe what he wrote, how will you believe what I say?"

5:27 "Son of Man" is a title Jesus used for himself.   **5:44** Some manuscripts read *from the only One.*

5:23
1 Jn 2:23
5:24
John 3:15;
20:30-31
1 Jn 3:14; 5:13
5:25
John 4:21; 6:63, 68
5:26
John 1:4; 6:57
1 Jn 5:11-12
5:27
John 9:39
Acts 10:42; 17:31
5:29
Dan 12:2
Matt 25:46
Acts 24:15
5:30
John 5:19; 6:38
5:31
John 8:13-14
5:32
John 8:18
5:36
John 10:25, 38;
14:11; 15:24
1 Jn 5:9
5:37
Deut 4:12
John 1:18; 8:18
1 Tim 1:17
5:38
1 Jn 2:14
5:39
Luke 24:27, 44
Acts 13:27
Rom 2:17-20
5:41
John 12:43
5:45
John 9:28
Rom 2:17
5:46
Gen 3:15
Deut 18:15, 18
Luke 24:27, 44
Acts 26:22-23
5:47
Luke 16:31

5:24 "Eternal life"—living forever with God—begins when you accept Jesus Christ as Savior. At that moment, new life begins in you (2 Corinthians 5:17). It is a completed transaction. You still will face physical death, but when Christ returns again, your body will be resurrected to live forever (1 Corinthians 15).

5:25 In saying that the dead will hear his voice, Jesus was talking about the spiritually dead who hear, understand, and accept him. Those who accept Jesus, the Word, will have eternal life. Jesus was also talking about the physically dead. He raised several dead people while he was on earth, and at his second coming, "the Christians who have died" will rise to meet him (1 Thessalonians 4:16).

5:26 God is the source and Creator of life, for there is no life apart from God, here or hereafter. The life in us is a gift from him (see Deuteronomy 30:20; Psalm 36:9). Because Jesus is eternally existent with God, the Creator, he, too, is "the life" (14:6) through whom we may live eternally (see 1 John 5:11).

5:27 The Old Testament mentioned three signs of the coming Messiah. In this chapter, John shows that Jesus has fulfilled all three signs. Authority to judge is given to him as the Son of Man (cf. 5:27 with Daniel 7:13, 14). The lame and sick are healed (cf. 5:20, 21 with Isaiah 35:6; Jeremiah 31:8, 9). The dead are raised to life (cf. 5:21, 28 with Deuteronomy 32:39; 1 Samuel 2:6; 2 Kings 5:7).

5:29 Those who have rebelled against Christ will be resurrected,

too, but they will hear God's judgment against them and will be sentenced to eternity apart from him. There are those who wish to live well on earth, ignore God, and then see death as final rest. Jesus does not allow unbelieving people to see death as the end of it all. There is a judgment to face.

• **5:31ff** Jesus claimed to be equal with God (5:18), to give eternal life (5:24), to be the source of life (5:26), and to judge sin (5:27). These statements make it clear that Jesus was claiming to be divine—an almost unbelievable claim, but one that was supported by another witness, John the Baptist.

• **5:39, 40** The religious leaders knew what the Bible said but failed to apply its words to their lives. They knew the teachings of the Scriptures but failed to see the Messiah to whom the Scriptures pointed. They knew the rules but missed the Savior. Entrenched in their own religious system, they refused to let the Son of God change their lives. Don't become so involved in "religion" that you miss Christ.

5:41 Whose praise do you seek? The religious leaders enjoyed great prestige in Israel, but their stamp of approval meant nothing to Jesus. He was concerned about God's approval. This is a good principle for us. If even the highest officials in the world approve of our actions and God does not, we should be concerned. But if God approves, even though others don't, we should be content.

• **5:45** The Pharisees prided themselves on being the true follow-

Jesus Feeds Five Thousand (**96**/Matthew 14:13-21; Mark 6:30-44; Luke 9:10-17)

6 After this, Jesus crossed over to the far side of the Sea of Galilee, also known as the Sea of Tiberias. ²A huge crowd kept following him wherever he went, because they saw his miraculous signs as he healed the sick. ³Then Jesus climbed a hill and sat down with his disciples around him. ⁴(It was nearly time for the Jewish Passover celebration.) ⁵Jesus soon saw a huge crowd of people coming to look for him. Turning to Philip, he asked, "Where can we buy bread to feed all these people?" ⁶He was testing Philip, for he already knew what he was going to do.

⁷Philip replied, "Even if we worked for months, we wouldn't have enough money* to feed them!"

⁸Then Andrew, Simon Peter's brother, spoke up. ⁹"There's a young boy here with five barley loaves and two fish. But what good is that with this huge crowd?"

¹⁰"Tell everyone to sit down," Jesus said. So they all sat down on the grassy slopes. (The men alone numbered about 5,000.) ¹¹Then Jesus took the loaves, gave thanks to God, and distributed them to the people. Afterward he did the same with the fish. And they all ate as much as they wanted. ¹²After everyone was full, Jesus told his disciples, "Now gather the leftovers, so that nothing is wasted." ¹³So they picked up the pieces and filled twelve baskets with scraps left by the people who had eaten from the five barley loaves.

¹⁴When the people saw him* do this miraculous sign, they exclaimed, "Surely, he is the Prophet we have been expecting!"* ¹⁵When Jesus saw that they were ready to force him to be their king, he slipped away into the hills by himself.

Jesus Walks on Water (**97**/Matthew 14:22-33; Mark 6:45-52)

¹⁶That evening Jesus' disciples went down to the shore to wait for him. ¹⁷But as darkness fell and Jesus still hadn't come back, they got into the boat and headed across the lake toward

6:7 Greek *Two hundred denarii would not be enough.* A denarius was equivalent to a laborer's full day's wage. **6:14a** Some manuscripts read *Jesus.* **6:14b** See Deut 18:15, 18; Mal 4:5-6.

6:4 John 11:55
6:5 John 1:43
6:8 John 1:40
6:9 2 Kgs 4:43 John 21:9, 13
6:14 Deut 18:15, 18 Acts 3:22; 7:37

---

ers of their ancestor Moses. They were trying to follow every one of his laws to the letter, and they even added some of their own. Jesus' warning that Moses would accuse them stung them to fury. Moses wrote about Jesus (Genesis 3:15; Numbers 21:9; 24:17; Deuteronomy 18:15), yet the religious leaders refused to believe Jesus when he came.

6:5 If anyone knew where to get food, it would have been Philip because he was from Bethsaida, a town about nine miles away (1:44). Jesus was testing Philip to strengthen his faith. By asking for a human solution (knowing that there was none), Jesus highlighted the powerful and miraculous act that he was about to perform.

• **6:5-7** When Jesus asked Philip where they could buy a great amount of bread, Philip started assessing the probable cost. Jesus wanted to teach him that financial resources are not the most important ones. We can limit what God does in us by assuming what is and is not possible. Is there some impossible task that you believe God wants you to do? Don't let your estimate of what can't be done keep you from taking on the task. God can do the miraculous; trust him to provide the resources.

6:8, 9 The disciples are contrasted with the youngster who brought what he had. They certainly had more resources than the boy, but they knew they didn't have enough, so they didn't give anything at all. The boy gave what little he had, and it made all the difference. If we offer nothing to God, he will have nothing to use. But he can take what little we have and turn it into something great.

6:8, 9 In performing his miracles, Jesus usually preferred to work through people. Here he took what a young child offered and used it to accomplish one of the most spectacular miracles recorded in the Gospels. Age is no barrier to Christ. Never think you are too young or old to be of service to him.

• **6:13** There is a lesson in the leftovers. God gives in abundance. He takes whatever we can offer him in time, ability, or resources and multiplies its effectiveness beyond our wildest expectations. If you take the first step in making yourself available to God, he

will show you how greatly you can be used to advance the work of his Kingdom.

6:14 "The Prophet" is the one prophesied by Moses (Deuteronomy 18:15).

JESUS WALKS ON THE WATER
Jesus fed the 5,000 on a hill near the Sea of Galilee at Bethsaida. The disciples set out across the sea toward Capernaum. But they encountered a storm—and Jesus came walking to them on the water! The boat landed at Gennesaret (Mark 6:53); from there they went back to Capernaum.

Capernaum. [18]Soon a gale swept down upon them, and the sea grew very rough. [19]They had rowed three or four miles* when suddenly they saw Jesus walking on the water toward the boat. They were terrified, [20]but he called out to them, "Don't be afraid. I am here!*" [21]Then they were eager to let him in the boat, and immediately they arrived at their destination!

6:19
Job 9:8
6:20
Matt 14:27

Jesus Is the True Bread from Heaven (99)

[22]The next day the crowd that had stayed on the far shore saw that the disciples had taken the only boat, and they realized Jesus had not gone with them. [23]Several boats from Tiberias landed near the place where the Lord had blessed the bread and the people had eaten. [24]So when the crowd saw that neither Jesus nor his disciples were there, they got into the boats and went across to Capernaum to look for him. [25]They found him on the other side of the lake and asked, "Rabbi, when did you get here?"

6:23
John 6:11

[26]Jesus replied, "I tell you the truth, you want to be with me because I fed you, not because you understood the miraculous signs. [27]But don't be so concerned about perishable things like food. Spend your energy seeking the eternal life that the Son of Man* can give you. For God the Father has given me the seal of his approval."

6:27
Matt 3:17; 17:5
Mark 1:11; 9:7
Luke 3:22
John 1:33; 4:14;
6:50-51, 54, 58
Acts 2:22
Rom 6:23

[28]They replied, "We want to perform God's works, too. What should we do?"

[29]Jesus told them, "This is the only work God wants from you: Believe in the one he has sent."

6:29
1 Jn 3:23

[30]They answered, "Show us a miraculous sign if you want us to believe in you. What can you do? [31]After all, our ancestors ate manna while they journeyed through the wilderness! The Scriptures say, 'Moses gave them bread from heaven to eat.'*"

6:31
Exod 16:15
Num 11:7-9
Neh 9:15
†Pss 78:24; 105:40

[32]Jesus said, "I tell you the truth, Moses didn't give you bread from heaven. My Father did. And now he offers you the true bread from heaven. [33]The true bread of God is the one who comes down from heaven and gives life to the world."

6:33
John 6:41, 50

[34]"Sir," they said, "give us that bread every day."

[35]Jesus replied, "I am the bread of life. Whoever comes to me will never be hungry again. Whoever believes in me will never be thirsty. [36]But you haven't believed in me even though you have seen me. [37]However, those the Father has given me will come to me, and I will never reject them. [38]For I have come down from heaven to do the will of God who sent me, not to do my own will. [39]And this is the will of God, that I should not lose even one of all those he has given me, but that I should raise them up at the last day. [40]For it is my Father's will that all who see his Son and believe in him should have eternal life. I will raise them up at the last day."

6:35
John 4:14; 6:48;
7:37-38
6:37
John 10:28-29;
17:2, 24
6:38
John 4:34; 5:30
6:39
John 10:28-29;
17:12; 18:9
6:40
John 12:45

6:19 Greek *25 or 30 stadia* [4.6 or 5.5 kilometers].   **6:20** Or *The 'I Am' is here;* Greek reads *I am.* See Exod 3:14.
6:27 "Son of Man" is a title Jesus used for himself.   **6:31** Exod 16:4; Ps 78:24.

6:18 The Sea of Galilee is 650 feet below sea level, 150 feet deep, and surrounded by hills. These physical features make it subject to sudden windstorms that would cause extremely high waves. Such storms were expected on this lake, but they were nevertheless frightening. When Jesus came to the disciples during a storm, walking on the water (three and a half miles from shore), he told them not to be afraid. We often face spiritual and emotional storms and feel tossed about like a small boat on a big lake. In spite of terrifying circumstances, if we trust our lives to Christ for his safekeeping, he will give us peace in any storm.

6:18, 19 The disciples, terrified, probably thought they were seeing a ghost (Mark 6:49). But if they had thought about all they had already seen Jesus do, they could have accepted this miracle. They were frightened—they didn't expect Jesus to come, and they weren't prepared for his help. Faith is a mind-set that *expects* God to act. When we act on this expectation, we can overcome our fears.

• **6:26** Jesus criticized the people who followed him only for the physical and temporal benefits and not for the satisfying of their spiritual hunger. Many people use religion to gain prestige, comfort, or even political votes. But those are self-centered motives. True believers follow Jesus simply because they know he has the truth and his way is the way to live.

• **6:28, 29** Many sincere seekers for God are puzzled about what he wants them to do. The religions of the world are people's attempts to answer this question. But Jesus' reply is brief and simple: We must believe on him whom God has sent. Satisfying God does not come from the work we *do*, but from whom we *believe*. The first step involves accepting that Jesus is who he claims to be. All spiritual development is built on this affirmation. Declare to Jesus, "You are the Messiah, the Son of the living God" (Matthew 16:16), and embark on a life of belief that is satisfying to your Creator.

6:35 People eat bread to satisfy physical hunger and to sustain physical life. We can satisfy spiritual hunger and sustain spiritual life only by a right relationship with Jesus Christ. No wonder he called himself the bread of life. But bread must be eaten to sustain life, and Christ must be invited into our daily walk to sustain spiritual life.

6:37, 38 Jesus did not work independently of God the Father, but in union with him. This should give us even more assurance of being welcomed into God's presence and being protected by him. Jesus' purpose was to do the will of God, not to satisfy Jesus' human desires. When we follow Jesus, we should have the same purpose.

6:39 Jesus said he would not lose even one person whom the Father had given him. Thus, anyone who makes a sincere commitment to believe in Jesus Christ as Savior is secure in God's promise of eternal life. Christ will not let his people be overcome by Satan and lose their salvation (see also 17:12; Philippians 1:6).

6:40 Those who put their faith in Christ will be resurrected from physical death to eternal life with God when Christ comes again (see 1 Corinthians 15:52; 1 Thessalonians 4:16).

The People Disagree That Jesus Is from Heaven (100)

6:41
John 6:33, 35, 51

⁴¹Then the people* began to murmur in disagreement because he had said, "I am the bread that came down from heaven." ⁴²They said, "Isn't this Jesus, the son of Joseph? We know his

6:42
Luke 4:22
John 7:27-28

father and mother. How can he say, 'I came down from heaven'?"

6:44
Jer 31:3
John 6:65; 12:32

⁴³But Jesus replied, "Stop complaining about what I said. ⁴⁴For no one can come to me unless the Father who sent me draws them to me, and at the last day I will raise them up. ⁴⁵As it is written in the Scriptures,* 'They will all be taught by God.' Everyone who listens to the

6:45
†Isa 54:13
Jer 31:33-34
1 Thes 4:9
Heb 8:10-11

Father and learns from him comes to me. ⁴⁶(Not that anyone has ever seen the Father; only I, who was sent from God, have seen him.)

6:46
John 1:18; 5:37

⁴⁷"I tell you the truth, anyone who believes has eternal life. ⁴⁸Yes, I am the bread of life!

6:47
John 3:15-16, 36

⁴⁹Your ancestors ate manna in the wilderness, but they all died. ⁵⁰Anyone who eats the bread from heaven, however, will never die. ⁵¹I am the living bread that came down from heaven. Anyone who eats this bread will live forever; and this bread, which I will offer so the

6:48
John 6:35, 41,
51, 58

world may live, is my flesh."

6:51
John 10:10-11
Heb 10:10

⁵²Then the people began arguing with each other about what he meant. "How can this man give us his flesh to eat?" they asked.

⁵³So Jesus said again, "I tell you the truth, unless you eat the flesh of the Son of Man and drink his blood, you cannot have eternal life within you. ⁵⁴But anyone who eats my flesh and

6:54
John 6:39-40, 44

drinks my blood has eternal life, and I will raise that person at the last day. ⁵⁵For my flesh is true food, and my blood is true drink. ⁵⁶Anyone who eats my flesh and drinks my blood

6:56
John 14:20; 15:4-7;
17:21-23
1 Jn 2:24; 3:24

remains in me, and I in him. ⁵⁷I live because of the living Father who sent me; in the same way, anyone who feeds on me will live because of me. ⁵⁸I am the true bread that came down from heaven. Anyone who eats this bread will not die as your ancestors did (even though

6:57
John 5:26

they ate the manna) but will live forever."

6:58
John 6:31

⁵⁹He said these things while he was teaching in the synagogue in Capernaum.

Many Disciples Desert Jesus (101)

6:62
Acts 1:9-11
Eph 4:8

⁶⁰Many of his disciples said, "This is very hard to understand. How can anyone accept it?"

⁶¹Jesus was aware that his disciples were complaining, so he said to them, "Does this offend you? ⁶²Then what will you think if you see the Son of Man ascend to heaven again?

6:63
Rom 8:2
1 Cor 15:45
1 Pet 3:18

⁶³The Spirit alone gives eternal life. Human effort accomplishes nothing. And the very words I have spoken to you are spirit and life. ⁶⁴But some of you do not believe me." (For Jesus knew from the beginning which ones didn't believe, and he knew who would betray

6:64
John 13:11

him.) ⁶⁵Then he said, "That is why I said that people can't come to me unless the Father gives

6:65
John 6:44

them to me."

6:41 Greek *Jewish people;* also in 6:52.   6:45 Greek *in the prophets.* Isa 54:13.

• **6:41** Some of the people grumbled in disagreement because they could not accept Jesus' claim of divinity. They saw him only as a carpenter from Nazareth. They refused to believe that Jesus was God's divine Son, and they could not tolerate his message. Many people reject Christ because they say they cannot believe he is the Son of God. In reality, the demands that Christ makes for their loyalty and obedience are what they can't accept. So to protect themselves from the message, they reject the messenger.

6:44 God, not people, plays the most active role in salvation. When someone chooses to believe in Jesus Christ as Savior, he or she does so only in response to the urging of God's Holy Spirit. God does the urging; then we decide whether or not to believe. Thus, no one can believe in Jesus without God's help.

6:45 Jesus was alluding to an Old Testament view of the messianic Kingdom in which all people are taught directly by God (Isaiah 54:13; Jeremiah 31:31-34). He was stressing the importance of not merely hearing, but learning. We are taught by God through the Bible, our experiences, the thoughts the Holy Spirit brings, and relationships with other Christians. Are you open to God's teaching?

6:47 As used here, *believes* means "continues to believe." We do not believe merely once; we keep on believing in and trusting Jesus.

6:47ff The religious leaders frequently asked Jesus to prove to them why he was better than the prophets they already had. Jesus here referred to the manna that Moses had given their

ancestors in the wilderness (see Exodus 16). This bread was physical and temporal. The people ate it, and it sustained them for a day. But they had to get more bread every day, and this bread could not keep them from dying. Jesus, who is much greater than Moses, offers himself as the spiritual bread from heaven that satisfies completely and leads to eternal life.

6:51 How can Jesus give us his flesh as bread to eat? To eat living bread means to accept Christ into our lives and become united with him. We are united with Christ in two ways: (1) by believing in his death (the sacrifice of his flesh) and resurrection and (2) by devoting ourselves to living as he requires, depending on his teaching for guidance and trusting in the Holy Spirit for power.

6:56 This was a shocking message—to eat flesh and drink blood sounded cannibalistic. The idea of drinking any blood, let alone human blood, was repugnant to the religious leaders because the law forbade it (Leviticus 17:10, 11). Jesus was not talking about literal blood, of course. He was saying that his life had to become their own, but they could not accept this concept. The Gospel writers as well as the apostle Paul used the body and blood imagery in talking about Communion (see 1 Corinthians 11:23-26).

6:63, 65 The Holy Spirit gives spiritual life; without the work of the Holy Spirit, we cannot even see our need for new life (14:17). All spiritual renewal begins and ends with God. He reveals truth to us, lives within us, and then enables us to respond to that truth.

66At this point many of his disciples turned away and deserted him. 67Then Jesus turned to the Twelve and asked, "Are you also going to leave?"

68Simon Peter replied, "Lord, to whom would we go? You have the words that give eternal life. 69We believe, and we know you are the Holy One of God.*"

70Then Jesus said, "I chose the twelve of you, but one is a devil." 71He was speaking of Judas, son of Simon Iscariot, one of the Twelve, who would later betray him.

6:68
John 6:63

6:69
Matt 16:16
Mark 1:24; 8:29
Luke 9:20
1 Jn 2:20

2. Jesus encounters conflict with the religious leaders

Jesus' Brothers Ridicule Him (121)

7 After this, Jesus traveled around Galilee. He wanted to stay out of Judea, where the Jewish leaders were plotting his death. 2But soon it was time for the Jewish Festival of Shelters, 3and Jesus' brothers said to him, "Leave here and go to Judea, where your followers can see your miracles! 4You can't become famous if you hide like this! If you can do such wonderful things, show yourself to the world!" 5For even his brothers didn't believe in him.

6Jesus replied, "Now is not the right time for me to go, but you can go anytime. 7The world can't hate you, but it does hate me because I accuse it of doing evil. 8You go on. I'm not going* to this festival, because my time has not yet come." 9After saying these things, Jesus remained in Galilee.

7:1
John 5:18; 7:19;
8:37, 40

7:2
Lev 23:34
Deut 16:16

7:3
Matt 12:46

7:6
John 2:4; 7:30;
8:20

7:7
John 15:18

Jesus Teaches Openly at the Temple (123)

10But after his brothers left for the festival, Jesus also went, though secretly, staying out of public view. 11The Jewish leaders tried to find him at the festival and kept asking if anyone had seen him. 12There was a lot of grumbling about him among the crowds. Some argued, "He's a good man," but others said, "He's nothing but a fraud who deceives the people." 13But no one had the courage to speak favorably about him in public, for they were afraid of getting in trouble with the Jewish leaders.

7:11
John 11:56

7:12
John 7:40-43

7:13
John 9:22-23

6:69 Other manuscripts read *you are the Christ, the Holy One of God;* still others read *you are the Christ, the Son of God;* and still others read *you are the Christ, the Son of the living God.*   **7:8** Some manuscripts read *not yet going.*

• **6:66** Why did Jesus' words cause many of his followers to desert him? (1) They may have realized that he wasn't going to be the conquering Messiah-King they expected. (2) He refused to give in to their self-centered requests. (3) He emphasized faith, not deeds. (4) His teachings were difficult to understand, and some of his words were offensive. As we grow in our faith, we may be tempted to turn away because Jesus' lessons are difficult. Will your response be to give up, ignore certain teachings, or reject Christ? Instead, ask God to show you what the teachings mean and how they apply to your life. Then have the courage to act on God's truth.

6:67 There is no middle ground with Jesus. When he asked the disciples if they would also leave, he was showing that they could either accept or reject him. Jesus was not trying to repel people with his teachings. He was simply telling the truth. The more the people heard Jesus' real message, the more they divided into two camps—the honest seekers who wanted to understand more, and those who rejected Jesus because they didn't like what they had heard.

• **6:67, 68** After many of Jesus' followers had deserted him, he asked the 12 disciples if they were also going to leave. Peter replied, "To whom would we go?" In his straightforward way, Peter answered for all of us—there is no other way. Though there are many philosophies and self-styled authorities, Jesus alone has the words of eternal life. People look everywhere for eternal life and miss Christ, the only source. Stay with him, especially when you are confused or feel alone.

• **6:70** In response to Jesus' message, some people left; others stayed and truly believed; and some, like Judas, stayed but tried to use Jesus for personal gain. Many people today turn away from Christ. Others pretend to follow, going to church for status, approval of family and friends, or business contacts. But there are only two real responses to Jesus—you either accept him or reject him. How have you responded to Christ?

6:71 For more information on Judas, see his Profile in Mark 14, p. 1655.

7:2 The Festival of Shelters is described in Leviticus 23:33ff. This event occurred in October, about six months after the Passover celebration mentioned in John 6:2-5. The festival commemorated the days when the Israelites wandered in the wilderness and lived in shelters (Leviticus 23:43).

• **7:3-5** Jesus' brothers had a difficult time believing in him. Some of these brothers would eventually become leaders in the church (James, for example), but for several years they were embarrassed by Jesus. After Jesus died and rose again, they finally believed. We today have every reason to believe because we have the full record of Jesus' miracles, death, and resurrection. We also have the evidence of what the Good News has done in people's lives through the centuries. Don't miss this opportunity to believe in God's Son.

7:7 Because the world hated Jesus, we who follow him can expect that many people will hate us as well. If circumstances are going too well, ask if you are following Christ as you should. We can be grateful when life goes well, but we must make sure it is not at the cost of following Jesus halfheartedly or not at all.

7:10 Jesus came with the greatest gift ever offered, so why did he often act secretly? The religious leaders hated him, and many would refuse his gift of salvation, no matter what he said or did. The more Jesus taught and worked publicly, the more these leaders would cause trouble for him and his followers. So it was necessary for Jesus to teach and work as quietly as possible. Many people today have the privilege of teaching, preaching, and worshiping publicly with little persecution. These believers should be grateful and make the most of their opportunities to proclaim the Good News.

• **7:13** The Jewish religious leaders had a great deal of power over the common people. Apparently these leaders couldn't do much to Jesus at this time, but they threatened anyone who might publicly support him, most likely with excommunication. Excommunication from the synagogue was one of the reprisals for believing in Jesus (9:22). To a Jew, this was a severe punishment.

7:15
Matt 13:54
Luke 2:47
Acts 4:13

7:16
John 8:28; 12:49;
14:10

7:18
John 5:41, 44;
8:50, 54

7:19
John 1:17; 7:1, 25;
8:37-40

7:20
John 8:48, 52;
10:20

7:21-22
Gen 17:10-13
Lev 12:3

7:23
John 5:8-10, 16
Acts 7:8

7:24
Isa 11:3-4
John 8:15

7:27
John 9:29

7:28-29
John 8:26, 55;
17:25

7:30
John 8:20

7:31
John 2:23; 8:30;
10:42; 11:45;
12:11, 42

7:33
John 13:33; 16:5

7:34
John 8:21; 13:33

¹⁴Then, midway through the festival, Jesus went up to the Temple and began to teach. ¹⁵The people* were surprised when they heard him. "How does he know so much when he hasn't been trained?" they asked.

¹⁶So Jesus told them, "My message is not my own; it comes from God who sent me. ¹⁷Anyone who wants to do the will of God will know whether my teaching is from God or is merely my own. ¹⁸Those who speak for themselves want glory only for themselves, but a person who seeks to honor the one who sent him speaks truth, not lies. ¹⁹Moses gave you the law, but none of you obeys it! In fact, you are trying to kill me."

²⁰The crowd replied, "You're demon possessed! Who's trying to kill you?"

²¹Jesus replied, "I did one miracle on the Sabbath, and you were amazed. ²²But you work on the Sabbath, too, when you obey Moses' law of circumcision. (Actually, this tradition of circumcision began with the patriarchs, long before the law of Moses.) ²³For if the correct time for circumcising your son falls on the Sabbath, you go ahead and do it so as not to break the law of Moses. So why should you be angry with me for healing a man on the Sabbath? ²⁴Look beneath the surface so you can judge correctly."

²⁵Some of the people who lived in Jerusalem started to ask each other, "Isn't this the man they are trying to kill? ²⁶But here he is, speaking in public, and they say nothing to him. Could our leaders possibly believe that he is the Messiah? ²⁷But how could he be? For we know where this man comes from. When the Messiah comes, he will simply appear; no one will know where he comes from."

²⁸While Jesus was teaching in the Temple, he called out, "Yes, you know me, and you know where I come from. But I'm not here on my own. The one who sent me is true, and you don't know him. ²⁹But I know him because I come from him, and he sent me to you." ³⁰Then the leaders tried to arrest him; but no one laid a hand on him, because his time* had not yet come.

³¹Many among the crowds at the Temple believed in him. "After all," they said, "would you expect the Messiah to do more miraculous signs than this man has done?"

Religious Leaders Attempt to Arrest Jesus (124)

³²When the Pharisees heard that the crowds were whispering such things, they and the leading priests sent Temple guards to arrest Jesus. ³³But Jesus told them, "I will be with you only a little longer. Then I will return to the one who sent me. ³⁴You will search for me but not find me. And you cannot go where I am going."

³⁵The Jewish leaders were puzzled by this statement. "Where is he planning to go?" they asked. "Is he thinking of leaving the country and going to the Jews in other lands?* Maybe he will even teach the Greeks! ³⁶What does he mean when he says, 'You will search for me but not find me,' and 'You cannot go where I am going'?"

7:15 Greek *Jewish people.*   **7:30** Greek *his hour.*   **7:35** Or *the Jews who live among the Greeks?*

7:13 Everyone was talking about Jesus! But when it came time to speak up for him in public, no one said a word. All were afraid. Fear can stifle our witness. Although many people talk about Christ in church, when it comes to making a public statement about their faith, they are often embarrassed. Jesus says that he will acknowledge us before God if we acknowledge him before others (Matthew 10:32). Be courageous! Speak up for Christ!

7:16-18 Those who attempt to know God's will and do it will know intuitively that Jesus was telling the truth about himself. Have you ever listened to religious speakers and wondered if they were telling the truth? Test them: (1) Their words should agree with, not contradict, the Bible; (2) their words should point to God and his will, not to themselves.

• **7:19** The Pharisees spent their days trying to achieve holiness by keeping the meticulous rules that they had added to God's laws. Jesus' accusation that they didn't keep Moses' laws stung them deeply. In spite of their pompous pride in themselves and their rules, they did not even fulfill a legalistic religion, for they were living far below what the law of Moses required. Murder was certainly against the law. Jesus' followers should do *more* than the moral law requires, not by adding to its requirements, but by going beyond and beneath the mere dos and don'ts of the law to the spirit of the law.

7:20 Most of the people were probably not aware of the plot to kill Jesus (5:18). There was a small group looking for the right opportunity to kill him, but most were still trying to decide what they believed about him.

7:21-23 According to Moses' law, circumcision was to be performed eight days after a baby's birth (Genesis 17:9-14; Leviticus 12:3). This rite was carried out on all Jewish males to demonstrate their identity as part of God's covenant people. If the eighth day after birth was a Sabbath, the circumcision would still be performed (even though it was considered work). While the religious leaders allowed certain exceptions to Sabbath laws, they allowed none to Jesus, who was simply showing mercy to those who needed healing.

• **7:26** This chapter shows the many reactions people had toward Jesus. They called him a good man (7:12), a fraud (7:12), demon possessed (7:20), the Messiah (7:26), and the Prophet, whose coming had been predicted by Moses (7:40). We must make up our own minds about who Jesus is, knowing that whatever we decide will have eternal consequences.

7:27 There was a popular tradition that the Messiah would simply appear. But those who believed this tradition were ignoring the Scriptures that clearly predicted the Messiah's birthplace (Micah 5:2).

37On the last day, the climax of the festival, Jesus stood and shouted to the crowds, "Anyone who is thirsty may come to me! 38 Anyone who believes in me may come and drink! For the Scriptures declare, 'Rivers of living water will flow from his heart.'"* 39(When he said "living water," he was speaking of the Spirit, who would be given to everyone believing in him. But the Spirit had not yet been given,* because Jesus had not yet entered into his glory.)

40When the crowds heard him say this, some of them declared, "Surely this man is the Prophet we've been expecting."* 41Others said, "He is the Messiah." Still others said, "But he can't be! Will the Messiah come from Galilee? 42For the Scriptures clearly state that the Messiah will be born of the royal line of David, in Bethlehem, the village where King David was born."* 43So the crowd was divided about him. 44Some even wanted him arrested, but no one laid a hand on him.

45When the Temple guards returned without having arrested Jesus, the leading priests and Pharisees demanded, "Why didn't you bring him in?"

46"We have never heard anyone speak like this!" the guards responded.

47"Have you been led astray, too?" the Pharisees mocked. 48"Is there a single one of us rulers or Pharisees who believes in him? 49This foolish crowd follows him, but they are ignorant of the law. God's curse is on them!"

50Then Nicodemus, the leader who had met with Jesus earlier, spoke up. 51"Is it legal to convict a man before he is given a hearing?" he asked.

52They replied, "Are you from Galilee, too? Search the Scriptures and see for yourself—no prophet ever comes* from Galilee!"

[*The most ancient Greek manuscripts do not include John 7:53–8:11.*]

53Then the meeting broke up, and everybody went home.

Jesus Forgives an Adulterous Woman (125)

8 Jesus returned to the Mount of Olives, 2but early the next morning he was back again at the Temple. A crowd soon gathered, and he sat down and taught them. 3As he was speaking, the teachers of religious law and the Pharisees brought a woman who had been caught in the act of adultery. They put her in front of the crowd.

7:37-38 Or *"Let anyone who is thirsty come to me and drink.* 38*For the Scriptures declare, 'Rivers of living water will flow from the heart of anyone who believes in me.'"* **7:39** Some manuscripts read *But as yet there was no Spirit.* Still others read *But as yet there was no Holy Spirit.* **7:40** See Deut 18:15, 18; Mal 4:5-6. **7:42** See Mic 5:2. **7:52** Some manuscripts read *the prophet does not come.*

7:37
Isa 55:1
John 4:10, 14; 6:35
Rev 22:17

7:38
Prov 18:4
Isa 58:11
Ezek 47:1-10
Joel 3:18

7:39
John 14:17-18;
16:7; 20:22
Rom 8:9
1 Cor 15:45
2 Cor 3:17

7:40
Deut 18:15
John 6:14

7:41
John 1:46

7:42
2 Sam 7:12
Mic 5:2
Matt 1:1; 2:5-10
Luke 2:4

7:44
John 7:30

7:46
Matt 7:28

7:48
John 12:42

7:50
John 3:1-2; 19:39

7:51
Deut 1:16

7:52
Isa 9:1-2
Matt 4:14-16
John 1:46

8:2
Matt 26:55

7:38 Jesus' words, "come and drink," alluded to the theme of many Bible passages that talk about the Messiah's life-giving blessings (Isaiah 12:2, 3; 44:3, 4; 58:11). In promising to give the Holy Spirit to all who believed, Jesus was claiming to be the Messiah, for that was something only the Messiah could do.

7:38 Jesus used the term *living water* in 4:10 to indicate eternal life. Here he uses the term to refer to the Holy Spirit. The two go together: Wherever the Holy Spirit is accepted, he brings eternal life. Jesus teaches more about the Holy Spirit in chapters 14–16. The Holy Spirit empowered Jesus' followers at Pentecost (Acts 2) and has since been available to all who believe in Jesus as Savior.

7:40-44 The crowd was asking questions about Jesus. Some believed, others were hostile, and others disqualified Jesus as the Messiah because he was from Nazareth, not Bethlehem (Micah 5:2). But he *was* born in Bethlehem (Luke 2:1-7), although he grew up in Nazareth. He may have had a pronounced Galilean accent. If they had looked more carefully, they would not have jumped to the wrong conclusions. When you search for God's truth, make sure you look carefully and thoughtfully at the Bible with an open heart and mind. Don't jump to conclusions before knowing more of what the Bible says.

7:44-46 Although the Romans ruled Palestine, they gave the Jewish religious leaders authority over minor civil and religious affairs. The religious leaders supervised their own Temple guards and gave the officers power to arrest anyone causing a disturbance or breaking any of their ceremonial laws. Because these leaders had developed hundreds of trivial laws, it was almost impossible for anyone, even the leaders themselves, not to break, neglect, or ignore at least a few of them some of the time. But

these Temple guards couldn't find one reason to arrest Jesus. And as they listened to Jesus to try to find evidence, they couldn't help hearing the wonderful words he said.

• **7:46-49** The Jewish leaders saw themselves as an elite group that alone had the truth, and they resisted the truth about Christ because it wasn't *theirs* to begin with. It is easy to think that we have the truth and that those who disagree with us do not have any truth at all. But God's truth is available to everyone. Don't copy the Pharisees' self-centered and narrow attitude.

• **7:50-52** This passage offers additional insight into Nicodemus, the Pharisee who visited Jesus at night (chapter 3). Apparently Nicodemus had become a secret believer. Since most of the Pharisees hated Jesus and wanted to kill him, Nicodemus risked his reputation and high position even though he only spoke up indirectly for Jesus. His statement was bold, and the Pharisees immediately became suspicious. After Jesus' death, Nicodemus brought spices for his body (19:39). That is the last time he is mentioned in Scripture.

• **7:51** Nicodemus confronted the Pharisees with their failure to keep their own laws. The Pharisees were losing ground—the Temple guards came back impressed by Jesus (7:46), and one of the Pharisees' own, Nicodemus, was defending him. With their hypocritical motives being exposed and their prestige slowly eroding, they began to move to protect themselves. Pride would interfere with their ability to reason, and soon they would become obsessed with getting rid of Jesus just to save face. What was good and right no longer mattered.

8:3-6 The Jewish leaders had already disregarded the law by arresting the woman without the man. The law required that both

8:5
Lev 20:10
Deut 22:22-24
Job 31:11

8:6
Matt 22:15

8:7
Deut 17:7

4"Teacher," they said to Jesus, "this woman was caught in the act of adultery. 5 The law of Moses says to stone her. What do you say?"

6 They were trying to trap him into saying something they could use against him, but Jesus stooped down and wrote in the dust with his finger. 7 They kept demanding an answer, so he stood up again and said, "All right, but let the one who has never sinned throw the first stone!" 8 Then he stooped down again and wrote in the dust.

9 When the accusers heard this, they slipped away one by one, beginning with the oldest, until only Jesus was left in the middle of the crowd with the woman. 10 Then Jesus stood up again and said to the woman, "Where are your accusers? Didn't even one of them condemn you?"

8:11
John 5:14

11 "No, Lord," she said.

And Jesus said, "Neither do I. Go and sin no more."

Jesus Is the Light of the World (126)

8:12
Isa 9:1-2
John 1:4-5, 9; 3:19;
9:5; 12:35-36, 46
2 Cor 4:6

8:14
John 7:28; 9:29

8:16
John 5:30

8:17-18
Deut 17:6; 19:15
John 5:37
1 Jn 5:7-9

8:19
John 14:7, 9

8:20
Mark 12:41
John 7:30

12 Jesus spoke to the people once more and said, "I am the light of the world. If you follow me, you won't have to walk in darkness, because you will have the light that leads to life."

13 The Pharisees replied, "You are making those claims about yourself! Such testimony is not valid."

14 Jesus told them, "These claims are valid even though I make them about myself. For I know where I came from and where I am going, but you don't know this about me. 15 You judge me by human standards, but I do not judge anyone. 16 And if I did, my judgment would be correct in every respect because I am not alone. The Father* who sent me is with me. 17 Your own law says that if two people agree about something, their witness is accepted as fact.* 18 I am one witness, and my Father who sent me is the other."

19 "Where is your father?" they asked.

Jesus answered, "Since you don't know who I am, you don't know who my Father is. If you knew me, you would also know my Father." 20 Jesus made these statements while he was teaching in the section of the Temple known as the Treasury. But he was not arrested, because his time* had not yet come.

8:16 Some manuscripts read *The One.*   **8:17** See Deut 19:15.   **8:20** Greek *his hour.*

---

parties to adultery be stoned (Leviticus 20:10; Deuteronomy 22:22). The leaders were using the woman as a trap so they could trick Jesus. If Jesus said the woman should not be stoned, they would accuse him of violating Moses' law. If he urged them to execute her, they would report him to the Romans, who did not permit the Jews to carry out their own executions (18:31).

8:7 This is a significant statement about judging others. Because Jesus upheld the legal penalty for adultery, stoning, he could not be accused of being against the law. But by saying that only a sinless person could throw the first stone, he highlighted the importance of compassion and forgiveness. When others are caught in sin, are you quick to pass judgment? To do so is to act as though you have never sinned. It is God's role to judge, not ours. Our role is to show forgiveness and compassion.

8:9 When Jesus said that only someone who had not sinned should throw the first stone, the leaders slipped quietly away, from oldest to youngest. Evidently the older men were more aware of their sins than the younger. Age and experience often temper youthful self-righteousness. But whatever your age, take an honest look at your life. Recognize your sinful nature, and look for ways to help others rather than hurt them.

8:11 Jesus didn't condemn the woman accused of adultery, but neither did he ignore or condone her sin. He told her to leave her life of sin. Jesus stands ready to forgive any sin in your life, but confession and repentance mean a change of heart. With God's help we can accept Christ's forgiveness and stop our wrongdoing.

8:12 To understand what Jesus meant by "the light of the world," see the note on 1:4, 5.

8:12 Jesus was speaking in the Treasury—the part of the Temple where the offerings were put (8:20) and where candles burned to

symbolize the pillar of fire that led the people of Israel through the wilderness (Exodus 13:21, 22). In this context, Jesus called himself the light of the world. The pillar of fire represented God's presence, protection, and guidance. Likewise, Jesus brings God's presence, protection, and guidance. Is he the light of *your* world?

8:12 What does it mean to follow Christ? As a soldier follows his captain, so we should follow Christ, our commander. As a slave follows his master, so we should follow Christ, our Lord. As we follow the advice of a trusted counselor, so we should follow Jesus' commands to us in Scripture. As we follow the laws of our nation, so we should follow the laws of the Kingdom of Heaven.

8:13, 14 The Pharisees thought Jesus was either a lunatic or a liar. Jesus provided them with a third alternative: He was telling the truth. Because most of the Pharisees refused to consider the third alternative, they never recognized him as Messiah and Lord. If you are seeking to know who Jesus is, do not close any door before looking through it honestly. Only with an open mind will you know the truth that he is Messiah and Lord.

8:13-18 The Pharisees argued that Jesus' claim was legally invalid because he had no other witnesses. Jesus responded that his confirming witness was God himself. Jesus and the Father made two witnesses, the number required by the law (Deuteronomy 19:15).

8:20 The Temple Treasury was located in the Court of Women. In this area, 13 collection boxes were set up to receive money offerings. Seven of the boxes were for the Temple tax; the other 6 were for freewill offerings. On another occasion, a widow placed her money in one of these boxes, and Jesus taught a profound lesson from her action (Luke 21:1-4).

Jesus Warns of Coming Judgment (127)

²¹Later Jesus said to them again, "I am going away. You will search for me but will die in your sin. You cannot come where I am going."

²²The people* asked, "Is he planning to commit suicide? What does he mean, 'You cannot come where I am going'?"

²³Jesus continued, "You are from below; I am from above. You belong to this world; I do not. ²⁴That is why I said that you will die in your sins; for unless you believe that I AM who I claim to be,* you will die in your sins."

²⁵"Who are you?" they demanded.

Jesus replied, "The one I have always claimed to be.* ²⁶I have much to say about you and much to condemn, but I won't. For I say only what I have heard from the one who sent me, and he is completely truthful." ²⁷But they still didn't understand that he was talking about his Father.

²⁸So Jesus said, "When you have lifted up the Son of Man on the cross, then you will understand that I AM he.* I do nothing on my own but say only what the Father taught me. ²⁹And the one who sent me is with me—he has not deserted me. For I always do what pleases him." ³⁰Then many who heard him say these things believed in him.

Jesus Speaks about God's True Children (128)

³¹Jesus said to the people who believed in him, "You are truly my disciples if you remain faithful to my teachings. ³²And you will know the truth, and the truth will set you free."

³³"But we are descendants of Abraham," they said. "We have never been slaves to anyone. What do you mean, 'You will be set free'?"

³⁴Jesus replied, "I tell you the truth, everyone who sins is a slave of sin. ³⁵A slave is not a permanent member of the family, but a son is part of the family forever. ³⁶So if the Son sets you free, you are truly free. ³⁷Yes, I realize that you are descendants of Abraham. And yet some of you are trying to kill me because there's no room in your hearts for my message. ³⁸I am telling you what I saw when I was with my Father. But you are following the advice of your father."

³⁹"Our father is Abraham!" they declared.

"No," Jesus replied, "for if you were really the children of Abraham, you would follow his example.* ⁴⁰Instead, you are trying to kill me because I told you the truth, which I heard from God. Abraham never did such a thing. ⁴¹No, you are imitating your real father."

They replied, "We aren't illegitimate children! God himself is our true Father."

⁴²Jesus told them, "If God were your Father, you would love me, because I have come to you from God. I am not here on my own, but he sent me. ⁴³Why can't you understand what I am saying? It's because you can't even hear me! ⁴⁴For you are the children of your father the devil, and you love to do the evil things he does. He was a murderer from the beginning. He has always hated the truth, because there is no truth in him. When he lies, it is consistent with his character; for he is a liar and the father of lies. ⁴⁵So when I tell the truth, you just

8:21
John 7:34, 36;
13:33

8:22
John 7:35

8:23
John 3:31; 17:14

8:24
Exod 3:14-15
John 4:26;
8:28, 58; 13:19

8:26
John 3:32-34;
12:49

8:28
John 3:14; 5:19;
8:24; 12:32

8:29
John 4:34; 6:38;
8:16; 14:10; 16:32

8:30
John 7:31

8:31
John 15:7
2 Jn 1:9

8:32
Rom 8:2
2 Cor 3:17
Gal 5:1, 13

8:33
Matt 3:9
Luke 3:8

8:34
Rom 6:16, 20
2 Pet 2:19

8:35
Gen 21:10
Gal 4:30

8:39
Matt 3:9
John 8:33
Gal 3:7, 14, 29

8:41
Deut 32:6
Isa 63:16; 64:8
Mal 1:6

8:42
1 Jn 5:1

8:44
Gen 3:4; 4:9
1 Jn 3:8

8:45
John 18:37

8:22 Greek *Jewish people;* also in 8:31, 48, 52, 57.   **8:24** Greek *unless you believe that I am.* See Exod 3:14.   **8:25** Or *Why do I speak to you at all?*   **8:28** Greek *When you have lifted up the Son of Man, then you will know that I am.* "Son of Man" is a title Jesus used for himself.   **8:39** Some manuscripts read *if you are really the children of Abraham, follow his example.*

8:24 People will die in their sins if they reject Christ, because they are rejecting the only way to be rescued from sin. Sadly, many are so taken up with the values of this world that they are blind to the priceless gift Christ offers. Where are you looking? Don't focus on this world's values and miss what is most valuable—eternal life with God.

• **8:32** Jesus himself is the truth that sets us free (8:36). He is the source of truth, the perfect standard of what is right. He frees us from continued slavery to sin, from self-deception, and from deception by Satan. He shows us clearly the way to eternal life with God. Thus, Jesus does not give us freedom to do what we want, but freedom to follow God. As we seek to serve God, Jesus' perfect truth frees us to be all that God meant us to be.

• **8:34, 35** Sin has a way of enslaving us, controlling us, dominating us, and dictating our actions. Jesus can free you from this slavery that keeps you from becoming the person God created you to be. If sin is restraining, mastering, or enslaving you, Jesus can break its power over your life.

8:41 Jesus made a distinction between illegitimate children and true children. The religious leaders were descendants of Abraham (founder of the Jewish nation) and therefore claimed to be children of God. But their actions showed them to be true children of Satan, for they lived under Satan's guidance. True children of Abraham (faithful followers of God) would not act as they did. Your church membership and family connections will not make you a true child of God. Your true father is the one you imitate and obey.

8:43 The religious leaders were unable to understand because they refused to listen. Satan used their stubbornness, pride, and prejudices to keep them from believing in Jesus.

8:44, 45 The attitudes and actions of these leaders clearly identified them as followers of Satan. They may not have been conscious of this, but their hatred of truth, their lies, and their murderous intentions indicated how much control the devil had over them. They were his tools in carrying out his plans; they spoke the very same language of lies. Satan still uses people to obstruct God's work (Genesis 4:8; Romans 5:12; 1 John 3:12).

8:47
1 Jn 4:6

naturally don't believe me! 46 Which of you can truthfully accuse me of sin? And since I am telling you the truth, why don't you believe me? 47 Anyone who belongs to God listens gladly to the words of God. But you don't listen because you don't belong to God."

Jesus States He Is Eternal (129)

48 The people retorted, "You Samaritan devil! Didn't we say all along that you were possessed by a demon?"

8:50
John 5:41

8:51
John 5:24;
11:25-26

49 "No," Jesus said, "I have no demon in me. For I honor my Father—and you dishonor me. 50 And though I have no wish to glorify myself, God is going to glorify me. He is the true judge. 51 I tell you the truth, anyone who obeys my teaching will never die!"

8:53
John 4:12

8:54
John 16:14; 17:5

8:55
John 7:28-29;
15:10

52 The people said, "Now we know you are possessed by a demon. Even Abraham and the prophets died, but you say, 'Anyone who obeys my teaching will never die!' 53 Are you greater than our father Abraham? He died, and so did the prophets. Who do you think you are?"

54 Jesus answered, "If I want glory for myself, it doesn't count. But it is my Father who will glorify me. You say, 'He is our God,*' 55 but you don't even know him. I know him. If I said otherwise, I would be as great a liar as you! But I do know him and obey him. 56 Your father Abraham rejoiced as he looked forward to my coming. He saw it and was glad."

8:56
Gen 18:18;
22:17-18
Matt 13:17
Heb 11:13

57 The people said, "You aren't even fifty years old. How can you say you have seen Abraham?*"

8:58
Exod 3:14
Isa 43:10, 13
John 1:1; 8:24, 28

58 Jesus answered, "I tell you the truth, before Abraham was even born, I AM!*" 59 At that point they picked up stones to throw at him. But Jesus was hidden from them and left the Temple.

9:2
Exod 20:5
Ezek 18:20
Luke 13:2
John 9:34

Jesus Heals the Man Who Was Born Blind (148)

9 As Jesus was walking along, he saw a man who had been blind from birth. 2 "Rabbi," his disciples asked him, "why was this man born blind? Was it because of his own sins or his parents' sins?"

9:3
John 11:4

3 "It was not because of his sins or his parents' sins," Jesus answered. "This happened so the power of God could be seen in him. 4 We must quickly carry out the tasks assigned us by the one who sent us.* The night is coming, and then no one can work. 5 But while I am here in the world, I am the light of the world."

9:4
John 5:17; 11:9;
12:35

9:5
Isa 49:6
John 1:4-5, 9; 8:12;
12:46

6 Then he spit on the ground, made mud with the saliva, and spread the mud over the

9:6
Mark 8:23

8:54 Some manuscripts read *your God.* **8:57** Some manuscripts read *How can you say Abraham has seen you?* **8:58** Or *before Abraham was even born, I have always been alive;* Greek reads *before Abraham was, I am.* See Exod 3:14. **9:4** Other manuscripts read *I must quickly carry out the tasks assigned me by the one who sent me;* still others read *We must quickly carry out the tasks assigned us by the one who sent me.*

8:46, 47 In a number of places Jesus intentionally challenged his listeners to test him. He welcomed those who wanted to question his claims and character as long as they were willing to follow through on what they discovered. Jesus' challenge clarifies the two most frequent reasons that people miss when encountering him: (1) They never accept his challenge to test him, or (2) they test him but are not willing to believe what they discover. Have you made either of those mistakes?

8:51 When Jesus says those who obey won't die, he is talking about spiritual death, not physical death. Even physical death, however, will eventually be overcome. Those who follow Christ will be raised to live eternally with him.

8:56 God told Abraham, the father of the Jewish nation, that through him all nations would be blessed (Genesis 12:1-7; 15:1-21). Abraham had been able to see this through the eyes of faith. Jesus, a descendant of Abraham, blessed all people through his death, resurrection, and offer of salvation.

8:58 This is one of the most powerful statements uttered by Jesus. When he said that he existed before Abraham was born, he undeniably proclaimed his divinity. Not only did Jesus say that he existed before Abraham; he also applied God's holy name (*I AM*—Exodus 3:14) to himself. This claim demands a response. It cannot be ignored. The Jewish leaders tried to stone Jesus for blasphemy because he claimed equality with God. But Jesus *is* God. How have you responded to Jesus, the Son of God?

8:59 In accordance with the law given in Leviticus 24:16, the religious leaders were ready to stone Jesus for claiming to be God. They well understood what Jesus was claiming, and because they

didn't believe he was God, they charged him with blasphemy. It is ironic that *they* were really the blasphemers, cursing and attacking the very God they claimed to serve!

9:1ff In chapter 9, we see four different reactions to Jesus. The neighbors revealed surprise and skepticism; the Pharisees showed disbelief and prejudice; the parents believed but kept quiet for fear of excommunication; and the healed man showed consistent, growing faith. Each reaction to Jesus allowed the man to reach a clearer understanding of the one who had healed him.

• **9:2, 3** A common belief in Jewish culture was that calamity or suffering was the result of some great sin. But Christ used this man's suffering to teach about faith and to glorify God. We live in a fallen world where good behavior is not always rewarded and bad behavior not always punished. Therefore, innocent people sometimes suffer. If God took suffering away whenever we asked, we would follow him for comfort and convenience, not out of love and devotion. Regardless of the reasons for our suffering, Jesus has the power to help us deal with it. When you suffer from a disease, tragedy, or disability, try not to ask, Why did this happen to me? or What did I do wrong? Instead, ask God to give you strength for the trial and a clearer perspective on what is happening.

9:6 When Jesus spit on the ground and made mud in order to repair the man's eyes, he was working with original materials. Genesis 2:7 states that God formed Adam's body from the dust of the ground. Jesus was demonstrating a creator's awareness of the materials he first used to shape the human body.

blind man's eyes. ⁷He told him, "Go wash yourself in the pool of Siloam" (Siloam means "sent"). So the man went and washed and came back seeing!

⁸His neighbors and others who knew him as a blind beggar asked each other, "Isn't this the man who used to sit and beg?" ⁹Some said he was, and others said, "No, he just looks like him!"

But the beggar kept saying, "Yes, I am the same one!"

¹⁰They asked, "Who healed you? What happened?"

¹¹He told them, "The man they call Jesus made mud and spread it over my eyes and told me, 'Go to the pool of Siloam and wash yourself.' So I went and washed, and now I can see!"

¹²"Where is he now?" they asked.

"I don't know," he replied.

Religious Leaders Question the Blind Man (149)

¹³Then they took the man who had been blind to the Pharisees, ¹⁴because it was on the Sabbath that Jesus had made the mud and healed him. ¹⁵The Pharisees asked the man all about it. So he told them, "He put the mud over my eyes, and when I washed it away, I could see!"

¹⁶Some of the Pharisees said, "This man Jesus is not from God, for he is working on the Sabbath." Others said, "But how could an ordinary sinner do such miraculous signs?" So there was a deep division of opinion among them.

¹⁷Then the Pharisees again questioned the man who had been blind and demanded, "What's your opinion about this man who healed you?"

The man replied, "I think he must be a prophet."

¹⁸The Jewish leaders still refused to believe the man had been blind and could now see, so they called in his parents. ¹⁹They asked them, "Is this your son? Was he born blind? If so, how can he now see?"

²⁰His parents replied, "We know this is our son and that he was born blind, ²¹but we don't know how he can see or who healed him. Ask him. He is old enough to speak for himself."

²²His parents said this because they were afraid of the Jewish leaders, who had announced that anyone saying Jesus was the Messiah would be expelled from the synagogue. ²³That's why they said, "He is old enough. Ask him."

²⁴So for the second time they called in the man who had been blind and told him, "God should get the glory for this,* because we know this man Jesus is a sinner."

²⁵"I don't know whether he is a sinner," the man replied. "But I know this: I was blind, and now I can see!"

²⁶"But what did he do?" they asked. "How did he heal you?"

²⁷"Look!" the man exclaimed. "I told you once. Didn't you listen? Why do you want to hear it again? Do you want to become his disciples, too?"

²⁸Then they cursed him and said, "You are his disciple, but we are disciples of Moses! ²⁹We know God spoke to Moses, but we don't even know where this man comes from."

³⁰"Why, that's very strange!" the man replied. "He healed my eyes, and yet you don't know where he comes from? ³¹We know that God doesn't listen to sinners, but he is ready to hear those who worship him and do his will. ³²Ever since the world began, no one has been able to open the eyes of someone born blind. ³³If this man were not from God, he couldn't have done it."

9:24 Or *Give glory to God, not to Jesus;* Greek reads *Give glory to God.*

9:7
2 Kgs 5:10
Isa 35:5

9:8
Acts 3:10

9:14
Luke 13:14
John 5:9

9:16
John 3:2; 7:43

9:17
Matt 21:11

9:22
Luke 6:22
John 7:13; 12:42;
16:2; 19:38
Acts 5:13

9:24
Josh 7:19

9:28
John 5:45

9:29
John 8:14

9:31
Job 27:8-9
Pss 34:15; 66:18;
145:19
Prov 15:29
Isa 1:15
Jer 11:11; 14:12
Mic 3:4
Zech 7:13

9:33
John 3:2

9:7 The pool of Siloam was built by Hezekiah. His workers constructed an underground tunnel from a spring outside the city walls to carry water into the city. Thus, the people could always get water without fear of being attacked. This was especially important during times of siege (see 2 Kings 20:20; 2 Chronicles 32:30).

• **9:13-17** While the Pharisees conducted investigations and debated about Jesus, people were being healed and lives were being changed. The Pharisees' skepticism was based not on insufficient evidence, but on jealousy of Jesus' popularity and his influence on the people.

9:14-16 The Jewish Sabbath, Saturday, was the weekly holy day of rest. The Pharisees had made a long list of specific dos and don'ts regarding the Sabbath. Kneading the mud and healing the man were considered work and therefore were forbidden. Jesus may have purposely made the clay in order to emphasize his teaching about the Sabbath—that it is right to care for others' needs even if it involves working on a day of rest.

• **9:25** By now the man who had been blind had heard the same questions over and over. He did not know how or why he was healed, but he knew that his life had been miraculously changed and he was not afraid to tell the truth. You don't need to know all the answers in order to share Christ with others. It is important to tell them how he has changed your life. Then trust that God will use your words to help others believe in him, too.

• **9:28, 34** The man's new faith was severely tested by some of the authorities. He was cursed and evicted from the synagogue. Persecution may come when you follow Jesus. You may lose friends; you may even lose your life. But no one can ever take away the eternal life that Jesus gives you.

9:34
John 9:2

34"You were born a total sinner!" they answered. "Are you trying to teach us?" And they threw him out of the synagogue.

Jesus Teaches about Spiritual Blindness (**150**)

35When Jesus heard what had happened, he found the man and asked, "Do you believe in the Son of Man?*"

36The man answered, "Who is he, sir? I want to believe in him."

9:37
John 4:26

37"You have seen him," Jesus said, "and he is speaking to you!"

38"Yes, Lord, I believe!" the man said. And he worshiped Jesus.

9:39
Luke 4:18

39Then Jesus told him,* "I entered this world to render judgment—to give sight to the blind and to show those who think they see* that they are blind."

9:40
Rom 2:19

40Some Pharisees who were standing nearby heard him and asked, "Are you saying we're blind?"

9:41
John 15:22

41"If you were blind, you wouldn't be guilty," Jesus replied. "But you remain guilty because you claim you can see.

10:2
Acts 20:28

10:4
Ps 80:2
John 10:27

Jesus Is the Good Shepherd (**151**)

10 "I tell you the truth, anyone who sneaks over the wall of a sheepfold, rather than going through the gate, must surely be a thief and a robber! 2But the one who enters through the gate is the shepherd of the sheep. 3The gatekeeper opens the gate for him, and the sheep recognize his voice and come to him. He calls his own sheep by name and leads them out. 4After he has gathered his own flock, he walks ahead of them, and they follow him because they know his voice. 5They won't follow a stranger; they will run from him because they don't know his voice."

10:6
John 16:25

10:7
John 14:6

10:8
Jer 23:1-2
Ezek 34:2-3

10:9
Ps 118:20
John 14:6

6Those who heard Jesus use this illustration didn't understand what he meant, 7so he explained it to them: "I tell you the truth, I am the gate for the sheep. 8All who came before me* were thieves and robbers. But the true sheep did not listen to them. 9Yes, I am the gate. Those who come in through me will be saved.* They will come and go freely and will find good pastures. 10The thief's purpose is to steal and kill and destroy. My purpose is to give them a rich and satisfying life.

10:10
John 5:40
Acts 20:29
2 Pet 2:1

10:11
Isa 40:11
Ezek 34:11-16, 23
Heb 13:20
1 Pet 2:25
1 Jn 3:16
Rev 7:17

11"I am the good shepherd. The good shepherd sacrifices his life for the sheep. 12A hired hand will run when he sees a wolf coming. He will abandon the sheep because they don't belong to him and he isn't their shepherd. And so the wolf attacks them and scatters the flock. 13The hired hand runs away because he's working only for the money and doesn't really care about the sheep.

10:14
2 Tim 2:19

10:15
Matt 11:27

14"I am the good shepherd; I know my own sheep, and they know me, 15 just as my Father knows me and I know the Father. So I sacrifice my life for the sheep. 16I have other sheep,

10:16
Isa 56:8
Ezek 37:24
John 11:52
Eph 2:14-18

9:35 Some manuscripts read *the Son of God?* "Son of Man" is a title Jesus used for himself.   **9:38-39a** Some manuscripts do not include *"Yes, Lord, I believe!" the man said. And he worshiped Jesus. Then Jesus told him.*   **9:39b** Greek *those who see.*   **10:8** Some manuscripts do not include *before me.*   **10:9** Or *will find safety.*

9:38 This man gained not only physical sight but also spiritual sight as he recognized Jesus first as a prophet (9:17), then as his Lord. When you turn to Christ, you begin to see him differently. The longer you walk with him, the better you will understand who he is. Peter tells us to "grow in the grace and knowledge of our Lord and Savior Jesus Christ" (2 Peter 3:18). If you want to know more about Jesus, keep trusting him in every area of life.

9:40, 41 The Pharisees were shocked that Jesus thought they were spiritually blind. Jesus countered by saying that it was only blindness (stubbornness and stupidity) that could excuse their behavior. To those who remained open and recognized how sin had truly blinded them from knowing the truth, he gave spiritual understanding and insight. But he rejected those who had become complacent, self-satisfied, and blind.

• **10:1** At night, sheep were often gathered into a sheepfold to protect them from thieves, weather, or wild animals. The sheepfolds were caves, sheds, or open areas surrounded by walls made of stones or branches. The shepherd often slept across the doorway of the fold to protect the sheep. Just as a shepherd cares for his sheep, Jesus, the good shepherd, cares for his flock (those who follow him). The prophet Ezekiel, in predicting the coming of the Messiah, called him a shepherd (Ezekiel 34:23).

10:7 In the sheepfold, the shepherd functioned as a gate, letting the sheep in and protecting them. Jesus is the gate to God's salvation for us. He offers access to safety and security. Christ is our protector. Some people resent that Jesus is the gate, the only way of access to God. But Jesus is God's Son—why should we seek any other way or want to customize a different approach to God? (See also the notes on 14:6.)

10:10 In contrast to the thief who takes life, Jesus gives life. The life he gives right now is abundantly rich and full. It is eternal, yet it begins immediately. Life in Christ is lived on a higher plane because of his overflowing forgiveness, love, and guidance. Have you taken Christ's offer of life?

• **10:11, 12** A hired hand tends the sheep for money, while the shepherd does it out of love. The shepherd owns the sheep and is committed to them. Jesus is not merely doing a job; he is committed to love us and even lay down his life for us. False teachers and false prophets do not have this commitment.

• **10:16** The "other sheep" were non-Jews. Jesus came to save Gentiles as well as Jews. This is an insight into his worldwide mission—to die for the sins of the world. People tend to want to restrict God's blessings to their own group, but Jesus refuses to be limited by the fences we build.

too, that are not in this sheepfold. I must bring them also. They will listen to my voice, and there will be one flock with one shepherd.

17"The Father loves me because I sacrifice my life so I may take it back again. 18No one can take my life from me. I sacrifice it voluntarily. For I have the authority to lay it down when I want to and also to take it up again. For this is what my Father has commanded."

19When he said these things, the people* were again divided in their opinions about him. 20Some said, "He's demon possessed and out of his mind. Why listen to a man like that?" 21Others said, "This doesn't sound like a man possessed by a demon! Can a demon open the eyes of the blind?"

Religious Leaders Surround Jesus at the Temple (152)

22It was now winter, and Jesus was in Jerusalem at the time of Hanukkah, the Festival of Dedication. 23He was in the Temple, walking through the section known as Solomon's Colonnade. 24The people surrounded him and asked, "How long are you going to keep us in suspense? If you are the Messiah, tell us plainly."

25Jesus replied, "I have already told you, and you don't believe me. The proof is the work I do in my Father's name. 26But you don't believe me because you are not my sheep. 27My sheep listen to my voice; I know them, and they follow me. 28I give them eternal life, and they will never perish. No one can snatch them away from me, 29for my Father has given them to me, and he is more powerful than anyone else.* No one can snatch them from the Father's hand. 30The Father and I are one."

31Once again the people picked up stones to kill him. 32Jesus said, "At my Father's direction I have done many good works. For which one are you going to stone me?"

33They replied, "We're stoning you not for any good work, but for blasphemy! You, a mere man, claim to be God."

34Jesus replied, "It is written in your own Scriptures* that God said to certain leaders of the people, 'I say, you are gods!'* 35And you know that the Scriptures cannot be altered. So if

10:19 Greek *Jewish people;* also in 10:24, 31.   **10:29** Other manuscripts read *for what my Father has given me is more powerful than anything;* still others read *for regarding that which my Father has given me, he is greater than all.*   **10:34a** Greek *your own law.*   **10:34b** Ps 82:6.

10:17-18
Phil 2:8-9
Heb 5:8; 7:16

10:23
Acts 3:11; 5:12

10:24
Luke 22:67

10:25
John 5:36; 10:38;
14:11

10:26
John 8:47

10:28
John 6:37, 39;
17:12

10:29
John 14:28
17:2, 6, 24

10:30
John 1:1; 10:38;
14:8-11; 17:21-24

10:33
Lev 24:16
Matt 26:63-66
John 1:1, 18;
5:18; 20:28
Rom 9:5
Phil 2:6
Titus 2:13
2 Pet 1:1
1 Jn 5:20

10:34
†Ps 82:6

10:17, 18 Jesus' death and resurrection, as part of God's plan for the salvation of the world, were under God's full control. No one could kill Jesus without his consent.

10:19, 20 If Jesus had been merely a man, his claims to be God would have proven him insane. But his miracles proved his words true—he really was God. The Jewish leaders could not see beyond their own prejudices, and they looked at Jesus only from a human perspective—Jesus confined in a human box. But Jesus was not limited by their restricted vision.

10:22, 23 Hanukkah commemorated the cleansing of the Temple under Judas Maccabeus in 164 B.C. after Antiochus

MINISTRY EAST OF THE JORDAN
Jesus had been in Jerusalem for the Festival of Shelters (7:2); then he preached in various towns, probably in Judea, before returning to Jerusalem for Hanukkah. He again angered the religious leaders, who tried to arrest him, but he left the city and went to the region east of the Jordan to preach.

Epiphanes had defiled it by sacrificing a pig on the altar of burnt offering. The festival was celebrated toward the end of December.

10:23 Solomon's Colonnade was a roofed walkway supported by large stone columns, just inside the walls of the Temple courtyard.

• **10:24** Many people asking for proof do so for the wrong reasons. Most of these questioners didn't want to follow Jesus in the way that required them to submit to his leadership. They hoped that Jesus would declare himself Messiah for perverted reasons. They, along with the disciples and everyone else in the Jewish nation, would have been delighted to have him drive out the Romans. Many of them didn't think he was going to do that, however. These doubters hoped he would identify himself so they could accuse him of telling lies (as the Pharisees did in 8:13).

10:28, 29 Just as a shepherd protects his sheep, Jesus protects his people from eternal harm. While believers can expect to suffer on earth, Satan cannot harm their souls or take away their eternal life with God. There are many reasons to be afraid here on earth because this is the devil's domain (1 Peter 5:8). But if you choose to follow Jesus, he will give you everlasting safety.

10:30 This is the clearest statement of Jesus' divinity he ever made. Jesus and his Father are not the same person, but they are one in essence and nature. Thus, Jesus is not merely a good teacher—he is God. His claim to be God was unmistakable. The religious leaders wanted to kill him because their laws said that anyone claiming to be God should die. Nothing could persuade them that Jesus' claim was true.

10:31 The Jewish leaders attempted to carry out the directive found in Leviticus 24:16 regarding those who blaspheme (claim to be God). They intended to stone Jesus.

10:34-36 Jesus referred to Psalm 82:6, where the Israelite rulers and judges are called "gods" (see also Exodus 4:16; 7:1). If God called the Israelite leaders gods because they were agents of

10:36
John 5:17-20

those people who received God's message were called 'gods,' [36] why do you call it blasphemy when I say, 'I am the Son of God'? After all, the Father set me apart and sent me into the world. [37] Don't believe me unless I carry out my Father's work. [38] But if I do his work, believe in the evidence of the miraculous works I have done, even if you don't believe me. Then you will know and understand that the Father is in me, and I am in the Father."

[39] Once again they tried to arrest him, but he got away and left them. [40] He went beyond the Jordan River near the place where John was first baptizing and stayed there awhile.

10:42
John 2:23; 7:31;
8:30; 11:45;
12:11, 42

[41] And many followed him. "John didn't perform miraculous signs," they remarked to one another, "but everything he said about this man has come true." [42] And many who were there believed in Jesus.

3. Jesus encounters crucial events in Jerusalem
Lazarus Becomes Sick and Dies (**165**)

11:1
Matt 21:17
Luke 10:38
11:2
John 12:3
11:4
John 9:3

11 A man named Lazarus was sick. He lived in Bethany with his sisters, Mary and Martha. [2] This is the Mary who later poured the expensive perfume on the Lord's feet and wiped them with her hair.* Her brother, Lazarus, was sick. [3] So the two sisters sent a message to Jesus telling him, "Lord, your dear friend is very sick."

[4] But when Jesus heard about it he said, "Lazarus's sickness will not end in death. No, it happened for the glory of God so that the Son of God will receive glory from this." [5] So although Jesus loved Martha, Mary, and Lazarus, [6] he stayed where he was for the next two days. [7] Finally, he said to his disciples, "Let's go back to Judea."

11:2 This incident is recorded in chapter 12.

THE NAMES OF JESUS	Reference	Name	Significance
In different settings, Jesus gave himself names that pointed to special roles he was ready to fulfill for people. Some of these refer back to the Old Testament promises of the Messiah. Others were ways to help people understand him.	6:27	Son of Man	Jesus' favorite reference to himself. It emphasized his humanity—but the way he used it, it was a claim to divinity.
	6:35	Bread of life	Refers to his life-giving role—that he is the only source of eternal life.
	8:12	Light of the world	Light is a symbol of spiritual truth. Jesus is the universal answer for people's need of spiritual truth.
	10:7	Gate for the sheep	Jesus is the only way into God's Kingdom.
	10:11	Good shepherd	Jesus appropriated the prophetic images of the Messiah pictured in the Old Testament. This is a claim to divinity, focusing on Jesus' love and guidance.
	11:25	The resurrection and the life	Not only is Jesus the source of life; he is the power over death.
	14:6	The way, the truth, and the life	Jesus is the method, the message, and the meaning for all people. With this title, he summarized his purpose in coming to earth.
	15:1	The true vine	This title has an important second part, "you are the branches." As in so many of his other names, Jesus reminds us that just as branches gain life from the vine and cannot live apart from it, so we are completely dependent on Christ for spiritual life.

God's revelation and will, how could it be blasphemy for Jesus to call himself the Son of God? Jesus was rebuking the religious leaders, because he is the Son of God in a unique, unparalleled relationship of oneness with the Father.

10:35 "The Scriptures cannot be altered" is a clear statement of the truth of the Bible. If we accept Christ as Lord, we also must accept his testimony to the Bible as God's Word.

11:1 The village of Bethany was located about two miles east of Jerusalem on the road to Jericho. It was near enough to Jerusalem for Jesus and the disciples to be in danger, but far enough away so as not to attract attention prematurely.

11:3 As their brother grew very sick, Mary and Martha turned to Jesus for help. They believed in his ability to help because they had seen his miracles. We, too, know of Jesus' miracles, both from Scripture and through changed lives we have seen. When we need extraordinary help, Jesus offers extraordinary resources. We should not hesitate to ask him for assistance.

11:4 Any trial a believer faces can ultimately bring glory to God because God can bring good out of any bad situation (Genesis 50:20; Romans 8:28). When trouble comes, do you grumble, complain, and blame God, or do you see your problems as opportunities to honor him?

• **11:5-7** Jesus loved this family and often stayed with them. He knew their pain but did not respond immediately. His delay had a specific purpose. God's timing, especially his delays, may make us think he is not answering or is not answering the way we want. But he will meet all our needs according to his perfect schedule and purpose (Philippians 4:19). Patiently await his timing.

8But his disciples objected. "Rabbi," they said, "only a few days ago the people* in Judea were trying to stone you. Are you going there again?"

9Jesus replied, "There are twelve hours of daylight every day. During the day people can walk safely. They can see because they have the light of this world. 10But at night there is danger of stumbling because they have no light." 11Then he said, "Our friend Lazarus has fallen asleep, but now I will go and wake him up."

12The disciples said, "Lord, if he is sleeping, he will soon get better!" 13They thought Jesus meant Lazarus was simply sleeping, but Jesus meant Lazarus had died.

14So he told them plainly, "Lazarus is dead. 15And for your sakes, I'm glad I wasn't there, for now you will really believe. Come, let's go see him."

16Thomas, nicknamed the Twin,* said to his fellow disciples, "Let's go, too—and die with Jesus."

Jesus Comforts Mary and Martha (166)

17When Jesus arrived at Bethany, he was told that Lazarus had already been in his grave for four days. 18Bethany was only a few miles* down the road from Jerusalem, 19and many of the people had come to console Martha and Mary in their loss. 20When Martha got word that Jesus was coming, she went to meet him. But Mary stayed in the house. 21Martha said to Jesus, "Lord, if only you had been here, my brother would not have died. 22But even now I know that God will give you whatever you ask."

23Jesus told her, "Your brother will rise again."

24"Yes," Martha said, "he will rise when everyone else rises, at the last day."

25Jesus told her, "I am the resurrection and the life.* Anyone who believes in me will live, even after dying. 26Everyone who lives in me and believes in me will never ever die. Do you believe this, Martha?"

27"Yes, Lord," she told him. "I have always believed you are the Messiah, the Son of God, the one who has come into the world from God." 28Then she returned to Mary. She called Mary aside from the mourners and told her, "The Teacher is here and wants to see you." 29So Mary immediately went to him.

30Jesus had stayed outside the village, at the place where Martha met him. 31When the people who were at the house consoling Mary saw her leave so hastily, they assumed she was going to Lazarus's grave to weep. So they followed her there. 32When Mary arrived and saw Jesus, she fell at his feet and said, "Lord, if only you had been here, my brother would not have died."

11:8 John 8:59; 10:31
11:9 John 9:4
11:10 John 12:35
11:11 Dan 12:2; Matt 9:24; 27:52; Mark 5:39; Luke 8:52; Acts 7:60; 1 Cor 11:30
11:16 Matt 10:3; John 14:5; 20:24-28; 21:2; Acts 1:3
11:20 Luke 10:38-42
11:22 John 16:30
11:23-24 Dan 12:2; John 5:28-29; Acts 24:15; Phil 3:21; 1 Thes 4:14
11:25 John 1:4; 3:36; 5:21; 6:39-40; 14:6; Col 1:18; 3:4; 1 Jn 1:1-2; 5:10-11; Rev 1:17-18
11:26 John 8:51
11:27 Matt 16:16; John 6:14

11:8 Greek *Jewish people;* also in 11:19, 31, 33, 36, 45, 54.   **11:16** Greek *Thomas, who was called Didymus.*
11:18 Greek *was about 15 stadia* [about 2.8 kilometers].   **11:25** Some manuscripts do not include *and the life.*

11:9, 10 "Daylight" symbolizes the knowledge of God's will and reliance on his guidance, and "night," the absence of this knowledge combined with self-reliance. When we move ahead in darkness, we will be likely to stumble.

JESUS RAISES LAZARUS
Jesus had been preaching in the villages beyond the Jordan, probably in Perea, when he received the news of Lazarus's sickness. Jesus did not leave immediately, but waited two days before returning to Judea. He knew Lazarus would be dead when he arrived in Bethany, but he was going to do a great miracle.

• **11:14, 15** If Jesus had been with Lazarus during the final moments of Lazarus's sickness, he might have healed him rather than let him die. But Lazarus died so that Jesus' power over death could be shown to his disciples and others. The raising of Lazarus was an essential display of his power, and the resurrection from the dead is a crucial belief of the Christian faith. Jesus not only raised himself from the dead (10:18), but he has the power to raise others.

11:16 We often remember Thomas as "the doubter," because he doubted Jesus' resurrection (John 20:25). But here he demonstrated love and courage. The disciples knew the dangers of going with Jesus to Jerusalem, and they tried to talk him out of it. Thomas merely expressed what all of them felt. When their objections failed, they were willing to go, even though it appeared they might have to die with Jesus. They may not have understood why Jesus would be killed, but they were loyal. There are unknown dangers in doing God's work. It is wise to consider the high cost of being Jesus' disciple.

11:25, 26 Jesus has power over life and death as well as power to forgive sins. This is because he is the Creator of life (see 14:6). He who *is* life can surely restore life. Whoever believes in Christ has a spiritual life that death cannot conquer or diminish in any way. When we realize his power and how wonderful his offer to us really is, how can we not commit our lives to him? To those of us who believe, what wonderful assurance and certainty we have: "Since I live, you too will live" (14:19).

11:27 Martha is best known for being too busy to sit down and

33 When Jesus saw her weeping and saw the other people wailing with her, a deep anger welled up within him,* and he was deeply troubled. 34 "Where have you put him?" he asked them.

11:35
Luke 19:41
11:37
John 9:6-7

They told him, "Lord, come and see." 35 Then Jesus wept. 36 The people who were standing nearby said, "See how much he loved him!" 37 But some said, "This man healed a blind man. Couldn't he have kept Lazarus from dying?"

Jesus Raises Lazarus from the Dead (167)

11:39
John 11:17

38 Jesus was still angry as he arrived at the tomb, a cave with a stone rolled across its entrance. 39 "Roll the stone aside," Jesus told them.

But Martha, the dead man's sister, protested, "Lord, he has been dead for four days. The smell will be terrible."

11:41
Matt 11:25

40 Jesus responded, "Didn't I tell you that you would see God's glory if you believe?" 41 So they rolled the stone aside. Then Jesus looked up to heaven and said, "Father, thank you for

11:33 Or *he was angry in his spirit.*

LAZARUS

The details surrounding death may vary, but the reality is universal. Scenes like Lazarus's funeral in Bethany are repeated many times around the world each day. A grieving family gathers at a graveside. Friends agonize over what to say. Their helpless silence, downcast eyes, and shuffling feet provide more distraction than comfort. When death is unexpected, the whys hang in the air like choking smog.

Drawn by grief and duty, people came from Jerusalem and the surrounding area to pay their last respects to a citizen of Bethany. Jesus' friend Lazarus was dead. His brief sickness proved stronger than any available medicine. Jesus had been sent for, but had failed to arrive in time. Death didn't wait. Following the wisdom of hot countries, the body was soon wrapped and buried. Four days later, Jesus arrived.

Lazarus's sisters Mary and Martha reacted in shock. Grief-stricken, they struggled to understand why Jesus had delayed in coming. We have no idea how Lazarus reacted to his own death. In fact, we don't have a record of a single word he said. We do know that he listened to Jesus. Even when the curtain of death was between them, Lazarus responded to Jesus' voice. He came hobbling out of his cave-tomb, still wrapped in the grave clothes. Jesus raised him from the dead!

When all is said and done, only what God accomplished through us will really matter. We will take little credit. Jesus worked in and around Lazarus just as he does with us. We have Christ's invitation to participate in his work, but we must not forget that he will do much more than we will know. Meanwhile, we delight in what Christ does with the little we have to offer him.

Lazarus's resurrection poses an important question: When you die, do you fully expect that your next conscious experience will be hearing the voice of Jesus call you by name?

Strengths and accomplishments	• Regularly hosted Jesus in his home • Raised from the dead by Jesus after four days in the grave
Lessons from his life	• Once we have given God ownership of our lives, we can't predict what he will do with them • Jesus' circle of relationships went beyond the 12 disciples • Jesus declared that the events surrounding Lazarus's sickness and death would glorify God
Vital statistics	• Where: Bethany • Relatives: Sisters: Mary and Martha
Key verse	"But when Jesus heard about it he said, 'Lazarus's sickness will not end in death. No, it happened for the glory of God so that the Son of God will receive glory from this'" (John 11:4).

Lazarus's role as an "active spectator" is recorded in John 11:1–12:11.

---

talk with Jesus (Luke 10:38-42). But here we see her as a woman of deep faith. Her statement of faith is exactly the response that Jesus wants from us.

• **11:33-37** John stresses that we have a God who cares. When Jesus saw the weeping and wailing, he too wept openly. Perhaps he empathized with their grief, or perhaps he was troubled at their unbelief. In either case, Jesus showed that he cares enough for us to weep with us in our sorrow. This portrait contrasts with the Greek concept of God that was popular in that day—a God with no emotions and no messy involvement with humans. Here we

see many of Jesus' emotions—compassion, indignation, sorrow, even frustration. He often expressed deep emotion, and we must never be afraid to reveal our true feelings to him. He understands them, for he experienced them. Be honest, and don't try to hide anything from your Savior. He cares.

11:38 Tombs at this time were usually caves carved in the limestone rock of a hillside. A tomb was often large enough for people to walk inside. Several bodies would be placed in one tomb. After burial, a large stone was rolled across the entrance to the tomb.

hearing me. ⁴²You always hear me, but I said it out loud for the sake of all these people standing here, so that they will believe you sent me." ⁴³Then Jesus shouted, "Lazarus, come out!" ⁴⁴And the dead man came out, his hands and feet bound in graveclothes, his face wrapped in a headcloth. Jesus told them, "Unwrap him and let him go!"

11:42 John 12:30
11:43 Luke 7:14

Religious Leaders Plot to Kill Jesus (168)

⁴⁵Many of the people who were with Mary believed in Jesus when they saw this happen. ⁴⁶But some went to the Pharisees and told them what Jesus had done. ⁴⁷Then the leading priests and Pharisees called the high council* together. "What are we going to do?" they asked each other. "This man certainly performs many miraculous signs. ⁴⁸If we allow him to go on like this, soon everyone will believe in him. Then the Roman army will come and destroy both our Temple* and our nation."

11:47 Matt 26:3-5

⁴⁹Caiaphas, who was high priest at that time,* said, "You don't know what you're talking about! ⁵⁰You don't realize that it's better for you that one man should die for the people than for the whole nation to be destroyed."

11:49 Matt 26:3
11:50 John 18:13-14

⁵¹He did not say this on his own; as high priest at that time he was led to prophesy that Jesus would die for the entire nation. ⁵²And not only for that nation, but to bring together and unite all the children of God scattered around the world.

11:51 Exod 28:30 Num 27:21
11:52 Isa 49:6 John 10:16 1 Jn 2:2

⁵³So from that time on, the Jewish leaders began to plot Jesus' death. ⁵⁴As a result, Jesus stopped his public ministry among the people and left Jerusalem. He went to a place near the wilderness, to the village of Ephraim, and stayed there with his disciples.

11:53 Matt 26:4

⁵⁵It was now almost time for the Jewish Passover celebration, and many people from all over the country arrived in Jerusalem several days early so they could go through the purification ceremony before Passover began. ⁵⁶They kept looking for Jesus, but as they stood around in the Temple, they said to each other, "What do you think? He won't come for Passover, will he?" ⁵⁷Meanwhile, the leading priests and Pharisees had publicly ordered that anyone seeing Jesus must report it immediately so they could arrest him.

11:55 Exod 12:13 2 Chr 30:17-19 Matt 26:1-2 Mark 14:1

A Woman Anoints Jesus with Perfume (182/Matthew 26:6-13; Mark 14:3-9)

12 Six days before the Passover celebration began, Jesus arrived in Bethany, the home of Lazarus—the man he had raised from the dead. ²A dinner was prepared in Jesus' honor. Martha served, and Lazarus was among those who ate* with him. ³Then Mary took a twelve-ounce jar* of expensive perfume made from essence of nard, and she anointed Jesus' feet with it, wiping his feet with her hair. The house was filled with the fragrance.

12:1 John 11:1
12:2 Luke 10:38-42
12:3 Luke 7:37-38

11:47 Greek *the Sanhedrin.*   **11:48** Or *our position;* Greek reads *our place.*   **11:49** Greek *that year;* also in 11:51.
12:2 Or *who reclined.*   **12:3** Greek *took 1 litra* [327 grams].

TIME WITH THE DISCIPLES
Lazarus's return to life became the last straw for the religious leaders, who were bent on killing Jesus. So Jesus stopped his public ministry and took his disciples away from Jerusalem to Ephraim. From there they returned to Galilee for a while (see the map in Luke 17, p. 1723).

11:44 Jesus raised others from the dead, including Jairus's daughter (Matthew 9:18-26; Mark 5:42, 43; Luke 8:40-56) and a widow's son (Luke 7:11-15).

11:45-53 Even when confronted point-blank with the power of Jesus' deity, some refused to believe. These eyewitnesses not only rejected Jesus; they plotted his murder. They were so hardened that they preferred to reject God's Son rather than admit that they were wrong. They preferred "closure" instead of being open to God's marvelous power. Beware of pride. If we allow it to grow, it can lead us into enormous sin.

11:48 The Jewish leaders knew that if they didn't stop Jesus, the Romans would lash out against all of them. Rome gave partial freedom to the Jews as long as they were quiet and obedient. Jesus' miracles often caused a disturbance. The leaders feared that Rome's displeasure would bring additional hardship to their nation.

11:51 John regarded Caiaphas's statement as a prophecy. As high priest, Caiaphas was used by God to explain Jesus' death even though Caiaphas didn't realize what he was doing.

12:3 Essence of nard was a fragrant ointment imported from the mountains of India. Thus, it was very expensive. The amount Mary used was worth a year's wages.

12:4
John 6:71
12:6
John 13:29
12:7
John 19:40
12:8
Deut 15:11

⁴But Judas Iscariot, the disciple who would soon betray him, said, ⁵"That perfume was worth a year's wages.* It should have been sold and the money given to the poor." ⁶Not that he cared for the poor—he was a thief, and since he was in charge of the disciples' money, he often stole some for himself.

⁷Jesus replied, "Leave her alone. She did this in preparation for my burial. ⁸You will always have the poor among you, but you will not always have me."

12:5 Greek *worth 300 denarii*. A denarius was equivalent to a laborer's full day's wage.

CAIAPHAS

Caiaphas was the leader of the religious group called the Sadducees. Educated and wealthy, they were politically influential in the nation. As the elite group, they were on fairly good terms with Rome. They hated Jesus because he endangered their secure lifestyles and taught a message they could not accept. A kingdom in which leaders *served* had no appeal to them.

Caiaphas's usual policy was to remove any threats to his power by whatever means necessary. For Caiaphas, whether Jesus should die was not in question; the only point to be settled was *when* his death should take place. Not only did Jesus have to be captured and tried; the Jewish high council also needed Roman approval before they could carry out the death sentence. Caiaphas's plans were unexpectedly helped by Judas's offer to betray Christ.

Caiaphas did not realize that his schemes were actually part of a wonderful plan God was carrying out. Caiaphas's willingness to sacrifice another man to preserve his own security was decidedly selfish. By contrast, Jesus' willingness to die for us was a clear example of loving self-sacrifice. Caiaphas thought he had won the battle as Jesus hung on the cross, but he did not count on the Resurrection!

Caiaphas's mind was closed. He couldn't accept the Resurrection even when the evidence was overwhelming, and he attempted to silence those whose lives had been forever changed by the risen Christ (Matthew 28:12, 13). Caiaphas represents those people who will not believe because they think it will cost them too much to accept Jesus as Lord. They choose the fleeting power, prestige, and pleasures of this life instead of the eternal life God offers those who receive his Son. What is your choice?

Strength and accomplishment	• High priest for 18 years
Weaknesses and mistakes	• One of the most directly responsible persons for Jesus' death • Used his office as a means to power and personal security • Planned Jesus' capture, carried out his illegal trial, pressured Pilate to approve the Crucifixion, attempted to prevent the Resurrection, and later tried to cover up the fact of the Resurrection • Kept up religious appearances while compromising with Rome • Involved in the later persecution of Christians
Lessons from his life	• God uses even the twisted motives and actions of his enemies to bring about his will • When we cover selfish motives with spiritual objectives and words, God still sees our intentions
Vital statistics	• Where: Jerusalem • Occupation: High priest • Relative: Father-in-law: Annas • Contemporaries: Jesus, Pilate, Herod Antipas
Key verses	"Caiaphas, who was high priest at that time, said, 'You don't know what you're talking about! You don't realize that it's better for you that one man should die for the people than for the whole nation to be destroyed'" (John 11:49-50).

Caiaphas is mentioned in Matthew 26:57; Luke 3:2; John 11; 18; and in Acts 4:6.

12:4-6 Judas often dipped into the disciples' money bag for his own use. Quite likely, Jesus knew what Judas was doing (2:24, 25; 6:64), but never did or said anything about it. Similarly, when we choose the way of sin, God may not immediately do anything to stop us, but this does not mean he approves of our actions. What we deserve will come.

12:5, 6 Judas used a pious phrase to hide his true motives. But Jesus knew what was in his heart. Judas's life had become a lie, and the devil was gaining more and more control over him (13:27). Satan is the father of lies, and a lying character opens the door to his influence. Jesus' knowledge of us should

make us want to keep our actions consistent with our words. Because we have nothing to fear with him, we should have nothing to hide.

12:7, 8 This act and Jesus' response to it do not teach us to ignore the poor so we can spend money extravagantly for Christ. This was a unique act for a specific occasion—an anointing that anticipated Jesus' burial and a public declaration of faith in him as Messiah. Jesus' words should have taught Judas a valuable lesson about the worth of money. Unfortunately, Judas did not take heed; soon he would sell his Master's life for 30 pieces of silver.

⁹When all the people* heard of Jesus' arrival, they flocked to see him and also to see Lazarus, the man Jesus had raised from the dead. ¹⁰Then the leading priests decided to kill Lazarus, too, ¹¹for it was because of him that many of the people had deserted them* and believed in Jesus.

12:10
Luke 16:31

Jesus Rides into Jerusalem on a Young Donkey
(**183**/Matthew 21:1-11; Mark 11:1-11; Luke 19:28-44)

¹²The next day, the news that Jesus was on the way to Jerusalem swept through the city. A large crowd of Passover visitors ¹³took palm branches and went down the road to meet him. They shouted,

12:13
Lev 23:40
†Ps 118:25-26
Zeph 3:15

"Praise God!*
Blessings on the one who comes in the name of the LORD!
Hail to the King of Israel!"*

¹⁴Jesus found a young donkey and rode on it, fulfilling the prophecy that said:

¹⁵ "Don't be afraid, people of Jerusalem.*
Look, your King is coming,
riding on a donkey's colt."*

12:15
Isa 35:4
†Zech 9:9

¹⁶His disciples didn't understand at the time that this was a fulfillment of prophecy. But after Jesus entered into his glory, they remembered what had happened and realized that these things had been written about him.

12:16
John 2:22; 7:39

¹⁷Many in the crowd had seen Jesus call Lazarus from the tomb, raising him from the dead, and they were telling others* about it. ¹⁸That was the reason so many went out to meet him—because they had heard about this miraculous sign. ¹⁹Then the Pharisees said to each other, "There's nothing we can do. Look, everyone* has gone after him!"

12:17
John 11:43-44

12:18
John 12:11; 19:37

Jesus Explains Why He Must Die (**185**)

²⁰Some Greeks who had come to Jerusalem for the Passover celebration ²¹paid a visit to Philip, who was from Bethsaida in Galilee. They said, "Sir, we want to meet Jesus." ²²Philip told Andrew about it, and they went together to ask Jesus.

12:21
John 1:43-44

12:23
John 13:32; 17:1

²³Jesus replied, "Now the time has come for the Son of Man* to enter into his glory. ²⁴I tell you the truth, unless a kernel of wheat is planted in the soil and dies, it remains alone. But its death will produce many new kernels—a plentiful harvest of new lives. ²⁵Those who

12:24
1 Cor 15:36

12:25
Matt 10:39
Luke 9:24; 17:33

12:9 Greek *Jewish people;* also in 12:11.   **12:11** Or *had deserted their traditions;* Greek reads *had deserted.*
12:13a Greek *Hosanna,* an exclamation of praise adapted from a Hebrew expression that means "save now."
12:13b Ps 118:25-26; Zeph 3:15.   **12:15a** Greek *daughter of Zion.*   **12:15b** Zech 9:9.   **12:17** Greek *were testifying.*   **12:19** Greek *the world.*   **12:23** "Son of Man" is a title Jesus used for himself.

12:10, 11 The leading priests' blindness and hardness of heart caused them to sink ever deeper into sin. They rejected the Messiah and planned to kill him, and then plotted to murder Lazarus as well. One sin leads to another. From the Jewish leaders' point of view, they could accuse Jesus of blasphemy because he claimed equality with God. But Lazarus had done nothing of the kind. They wanted Lazarus dead simply because he was a living witness to Jesus' power. This is a warning to us to avoid sin. Sin leads to more sin, a downward spiral that can be stopped only by repentance and the power of the Holy Spirit to change our behavior.

• **12:13** Jesus began his last week on earth by riding into Jerusalem on a donkey under a canopy of palm branches, with crowds hailing him as their king. To announce that he was indeed the Messiah, Jesus chose a *time* when all Israel would be gathered at Jerusalem, a *place* where huge crowds could see him, and a *way* of proclaiming his mission that was unmistakable. On Palm Sunday we celebrate Jesus' Triumphal Entry into Jerusalem as Lord of lords and King of Peace.

12:13 The people who were praising God for giving them a king had the wrong idea about Jesus. They were sure he would be a national leader who would restore their nation to its former glory, and thus, they were deaf to the words of their prophets and blind to Jesus' real mission. When it became apparent that Jesus was not going to fulfill their hopes, many people turned against him.

• **12:16** After Jesus' resurrection, the disciples understood for the first time many of the prophecies that they had missed along the

way. Jesus' words and actions took on new meaning and made more sense. In retrospect, the disciples saw how Jesus had led them into a deeper and better understanding of his truth. Stop now and think about the events in your life leading up to where you are now. How has God led you to this point? As you grow older, you will look back and see God's involvement more clearly than you do now.

12:18 The people flocked to Jesus because they had heard about his great miracle in raising Lazarus from the dead. Their adoration was short-lived and their commitment shallow, for in a few days they would do nothing to stop his crucifixion. Devotion based only on curiosity or popularity fades quickly.

12:20, 21 These Greeks probably were converts to the Jewish faith. They may have gone to Philip because, though he was a Jew, he had a Greek name.

• **12:23-25** This is a beautiful picture of the necessary sacrifice of Jesus. Unless a kernel of wheat is planted in the soil, it will not become a blade of wheat producing many more seeds. Jesus had to die to pay the penalty for our sin, but also to show his power over death. His resurrection proves he has eternal life. Because Jesus is God, Jesus can give this same eternal life to all who believe in him.

12:25 We must be so committed to living for Christ that we should "care nothing" for our lives by comparison. This does not mean that we long to die or that we are careless or destructive with the life God has given, but that we are willing to die if doing

12:26
John 14:3; 17:24

12:27
Ps 6:3
Matt 26:38
Mark 14:34

12:28
Matt 3:17; 17:5
Mark 1:11; 9:7
Luke 3:22; 9:35
2 Pet 1:17-18

12:31
John 14:30; 16:11
Eph 2:2

12:32
John 3:14; 6:44

12:34
Pss 89:4, 36; 110:4
Isa 9:7
Ezek 37:25
Dan 7:14

love their life in this world will lose it. Those who care nothing for their life in this world will keep it for eternity. 26 Anyone who wants to be my disciple must follow me, because my servants must be where I am. And the Father will honor anyone who serves me.

27 "Now my soul is deeply troubled. Should I pray, 'Father, save me from this hour'? But this is the very reason I came! 28 Father, bring glory to your name."

Then a voice spoke from heaven, saying, "I have already brought glory to my name, and I will do so again." 29 When the crowd heard the voice, some thought it was thunder, while others declared an angel had spoken to him.

30 Then Jesus told them, "The voice was for your benefit, not mine. 31 The time for judging this world has come, when Satan, the ruler of this world, will be cast out. 32 And when I am lifted up from the earth, I will draw everyone to myself." 33 He said this to indicate how he was going to die.

34 The crowd responded, "We understood from Scripture* that the Messiah would live forever. How can you say the Son of Man will die? Just who is this Son of Man, anyway?"

12:34 Greek *from the law.*

GREAT EXPECTATIONS
Jesus Does the Unexpected
Wherever he went, Jesus exceeded people's expectations.

What was expected	What Jesus did	Reference
A man looked for healing.	Jesus also forgave his sins.	Mark 2:1-12
The disciples were expecting an ordinary day of fishing.	They found the Savior.	Luke 5:1-11
A widow was resigned to bury her dead son.	Jesus restored her son to life.	Luke 7:11-17
The religious leaders wanted a miracle.	Jesus offered them the Creator of miracles.	Matthew 12:38-45
A woman who wanted to be healed touched Jesus.	Jesus helped her see it was her faith that had healed her.	Mark 5:25-34
The disciples thought the crowd should be sent home because there was no food.	Jesus used a small meal to feed thousands, and there were left-overs!	John 6:1-15
The crowds looked for a political leader to set up a new kingdom to overthrow Rome's control.	Jesus offered them an eternal, spiritual kingdom to overthrow sin's control.	A theme throughout the Gospels
The disciples wanted to eat the Passover meal with Jesus, their Master.	Jesus washed their feet, showing that he was also their servant.	John 13:1-20
The religious leaders wanted Jesus killed and got their wish.	But Jesus rose from the dead!	John 11:53; 19:30; 20:1-29

---

so will glorify Christ. We must disown the tyrannical rule of our own self-centeredness. By laying aside our striving for advantage, security, and pleasure, we can serve God lovingly and freely. Releasing control of our lives and transferring control to Christ bring eternal life and genuine joy.

12:26 Many believed that Jesus came for the Jews only. But when Jesus said, "Anyone who wants to be my disciple must follow me," he was talking to these Greeks as well. No matter who the sincere seekers are, Jesus welcomes them. His message is for everyone. Don't allow social or racial differences to become barriers to the Good News. Take the Good News to all people.

• **12:27** Jesus knew his crucifixion lay ahead, and because he was human, he dreaded it. He knew he would have to take the sins of the world on himself, and he knew this would separate him from his Father. He wanted to be delivered from this horrible death, but he knew that God sent him into the world to die for our sins, in our place. Jesus said no to his human desires in order to obey his Father and glorify him. Although we will never have to face such a difficult and awesome task, we are still called to obedience. Whatever the Father asks, we should do his will and bring glory to his name.

• **12:31** The ruler of this world is Satan, an angel who rebelled against God. Satan is real, not symbolic, and is constantly work-

ing against God and those who obey him. Satan tempted Eve in the garden and persuaded her to sin; he tempted Jesus in the wilderness and did not persuade him to fall (Matthew 4:1-11). Satan has great power, but people can be delivered from his reign of spiritual darkness because of Christ's victory on the cross. Satan is powerful, but Jesus is much more powerful. Jesus' resurrection shattered Satan's deathly power (Colossians 1:13, 14). To overcome Satan we need faithful allegiance to God's Word, determination to stay away from sin, and the support of other believers.

12:32-34 The crowd could not believe what Jesus was saying about the Messiah. They were waving palm branches for a victorious Messiah who would set up a political, earthly kingdom that would never end. From their reading of certain Scriptures, they thought the Messiah would never die (Psalms 89:35, 36; 110:4; Isaiah 9:7). Other passages, however, showed that he would die (Isaiah 53:5-9). Jesus' words did not mesh with their concept of the Messiah. First he had to suffer and die—then he would one day set up his eternal Kingdom. What kind of Messiah, or Savior, are you seeking? Beware of trying to force Jesus into your own mold—he won't fit.

35 Jesus replied, "My light will shine for you just a little longer. Walk in the light while you can, so the darkness will not overtake you. Those who walk in the darkness cannot see where they are going. 36 Put your trust in the light while there is still time; then you will become children of the light."

After saying these things, Jesus went away and was hidden from them.

Most of the People Do Not Believe in Jesus (186)

37 But despite all the miraculous signs Jesus had done, most of the people still did not believe in him. 38 This is exactly what Isaiah the prophet had predicted:

"LORD, who has believed our message?
To whom has the LORD revealed his powerful arm?"*

39 But the people couldn't believe, for as Isaiah also said,

40 "The Lord has blinded their eyes
    and hardened their hearts—
so that their eyes cannot see,
    and their hearts cannot understand,
and they cannot turn to me
    and have me heal them."*

41 Isaiah was referring to Jesus when he said this, because he saw the future and spoke of the Messiah's glory. 42 Many people did believe in him, however, including some of the Jewish leaders. But they wouldn't admit it for fear that the Pharisees would expel them from the synagogue. 43 For they loved human praise more than the praise of God.

Jesus Summarizes His Message (187)

44 Jesus shouted to the crowds, "If you trust me, you are trusting not only me, but also God who sent me. 45 For when you see me, you are seeing the one who sent me. 46 I have come as a light to shine in this dark world, so that all who put their trust in me will no longer remain in the dark. 47 I will not judge those who hear me but don't obey me, for I have come to save the world and not to judge it. 48 But all who reject me and my message will be judged on the day of judgment by the truth I have spoken. 49 I don't speak on my own authority. The Father who sent me has commanded me what to say and how to say it. 50 And I know his commands lead to eternal life; so I say whatever the Father tells me to say."

12:38 Isa 53:1.   **12:40** Isa 6:10.

12:35
John 8:12; 9:4;
12:46

12:36
John 8:59
Eph 5:8
1 Thes 5:5

12:38
†Isa 53:1
Rom 10:16

12:40
†Isa 6:10
Matt 13:14

12:41
Isa 6:1

12:42
John 7:13, 48;
9:22-23; 12:11

12:43
John 5:44

12:46
John 1:4; 3:19;
8:12; 9:5

12:47
John 3:17; 8:15

12:35, 36 Jesus said he would be with them in person for only a short time, and they should take advantage of his presence while they had it. Like a light shining in a dark place, he would point out the way they should walk. If they walked in his light, they would become "children of the light," revealing the truth and pointing people to God. As Christians, we are to be Christ's light bearers, letting his light shine through us. How brightly is your light shining? Can others see Christ in your actions?

12:37, 38 Jesus had performed many miracles, but most people still didn't believe in him. Likewise, many today won't believe despite all God does. Don't be discouraged if your witness for Christ doesn't turn as many to him as you'd like. Your job is to continue as a faithful witness. You are responsible to reach out to others, but they are responsible for their own decisions.

12:39-41 People in Jesus' time, like those in the time of Isaiah, would not believe despite the evidence (12:37). As a result, God hardened their hearts. Does that mean God intentionally prevented these people from believing in him? No, he simply confirmed their own choices. After a lifetime of resisting God, they had become so set in their ways that they wouldn't even try to understand Jesus' message. For such people, it is virtually impossible to come to God—their hearts have been permanently hardened. Other instances of hardened hearts because of constant stubbornness are recorded in Exodus 9:12, Romans 1:24-28, and 2 Thessalonians 2:8-12.

12:42, 43 Along with those who refused to believe, many believed but refused to admit it. This is just as bad, and Jesus had strong words for such people (see Matthew 10:32, 33). People who will not take a stand for Jesus are afraid of rejection or ridicule. Many Jewish leaders wouldn't admit to faith in Jesus because they feared excommunication from the synagogue (which was their livelihood) and loss of their prestigious place in the community. But the praise of others is fickle and short-lived. We should be much more concerned about God's eternal acceptance than about the temporary approval of other people.

12:45 We often wonder what God is like. How can we know the Creator when he doesn't make himself visible? Jesus said plainly that those who see him see God, because he is God. If you want to know what God is like, study the person and words of Jesus Christ.

12:48 The purpose of Jesus' first mission on earth was not to judge people, but to show them the way to find salvation and eternal life. When he comes again, one of his main purposes will be to judge people for how they lived on earth. Christ's words that we would not accept and obey will condemn us. On the day of judgment, those who accepted Jesus and lived his way will be raised to eternal life (1 Corinthians 15:51-57; 1 Thessalonians 4:15-18; Revelation 21:1-7), and those who rejected Jesus and lived any way they pleased will face eternal punishment (Revelation 20:11-15). Decide now which side you'll be on, for the consequences of your decision last forever.

C. DEATH AND RESURRECTION OF JESUS, THE SON OF GOD (13:1—21:25)

John begins his Gospel with eternity and ends with Jesus coming to earth again. He features Jesus teaching his disciples privately just before his arrest and death. We see, clearly, the deep love Jesus has for the believer and the peace that comes from faith. Knowing the love Jesus has for believers, we, too, should believe and allow Jesus to forgive our sins. Only then will we experience peace in a world filled with turmoil.

1. Jesus teaches his disciples

Jesus Washes the Disciples' Feet **(210)**

13:1
John 16:28; 17:1

13 Before the Passover celebration, Jesus knew that his hour had come to leave this world and return to his Father. He had loved his disciples during his ministry on earth, and now he loved them to the very end.* ²It was time for supper, and the devil had already prompted Judas,* son of Simon Iscariot, to betray Jesus. ³Jesus knew that the Father

13:2
Luke 22:3
John 6:70-71

13:1 Or *he showed them the full extent of his love.*   **13:2** Or *the devil had already intended for Judas.*

Being loved is the most powerful motivation in the world! Our ability to love is often shaped by our experience of love. We usually love others as we have been loved.

Some of the greatest statements about God's loving nature were written by a man who experienced God's love in a unique way. John, Jesus' disciple, expressed his relationship to the Son of God by calling himself "the disciple Jesus loved" (John 21:20). Although Jesus' love is clearly communicated in all the Gospels, in John's Gospel it is a central theme. Because his own experience of Jesus' love was so strong and personal, John was sensitive to those words and actions of Jesus that illustrated how the one who *is* love loved others.

Jesus knew John fully and loved him fully. He gave John and his brother James the nickname "Sons of Thunder" (Mark 3:17), perhaps from an occasion when the brothers asked Jesus for permission to "call down fire from heaven" on a village that had refused to welcome Jesus and the disciples (Luke 9:54). In John's Gospel and letters, we see the great God of love, while the thunder of God's justice bursts from the pages of Revelation.

Jesus confronts each of us as he confronted John. We cannot know the depth of Jesus' love unless we are willing to face the fact that he knows us completely. Otherwise we are fooled into believing he must love the people we pretend to be, not the sinners we actually are. John and all the disciples convince us that God is able and willing to accept us as we are. Being aware of God's love is a great motivator for change. His love is not given in exchange for our efforts; his love frees us to really live. Have you accepted that love?

Strengths and accomplishments	• One of John the Baptist's disciples before following Jesus • One of the 12 disciples and, with Peter and James, one of the inner three that were closest to Jesus • Wrote five New Testament books: the Gospel of John; 1, 2, and 3 John; and Revelation
Weaknesses and mistakes	• Along with James, shared a tendency to outbursts of selfishness and anger • Asked for a special position in Jesus' Kingdom
Lessons from his life	• Those who realize how much they are loved are able to love much • When God changes a life, he does not take away personality characteristics, but puts them to effective use in his service
Vital statistics	• Occupations: Fisherman, disciple • Relatives: Father: Zebedee. Mother: Salome. Brother: James. • Contemporaries: Jesus, Pilate, Herod
Key verses	"Dear friends, I am not writing a new commandment for you; rather it is an old one you have had from the very beginning. This old commandment—to love one another—is the same message you heard before. Yet it is also new. Jesus lived the truth of this commandment, and you also are living it. For the darkness is disappearing, and the true light is already shining" (1 John 2:7-8).

John's story is told throughout the Gospels, Acts, and Revelation.

13:1 Jesus knew he would be betrayed by one of his disciples, denied by another, and deserted by all of them for a time. Still he "loved them to the very end." God knows us completely, as Jesus knew his disciples (2:24, 25; 6:64). He knows the sins we have committed and the ones we will yet commit. Still, he loves us. How do you respond to that kind of love?

• **13:1ff** Chapters 13–17 tell us what Jesus said to his disciples on the night before his death. These words were all spoken in one

evening when, with only the disciples as his audience, he gave final instructions to prepare them for his death and resurrection, events that would change their lives forever.

13:1-3 For more information on Judas Iscariot, see his Profile in Mark 14, p. 1655.

• **13:1-17** Jesus was the model servant, and he showed his servant attitude to his disciples. Washing guests' feet was a job for a household servant to carry out when guests arrived. But

had given him authority over everything and that he had come from God and would return
to God. ⁴So he got up from the table, took off his robe, wrapped a towel around his waist,
⁵and poured water into a basin. Then he began to wash the disciples' feet, drying them with
the towel he had around him.

⁶When Jesus came to Simon Peter, Peter said to him, "Lord, are you going to wash my
feet?"

⁷Jesus replied, "You don't understand now what I am doing, but someday you will."

⁸"No," Peter protested, "you will never ever wash my feet!"

Jesus replied, "Unless I wash you, you won't belong to me."

⁹Simon Peter exclaimed, "Then wash my hands and head as well, Lord, not just my feet!"

¹⁰Jesus replied, "A person who has bathed all over does not need to wash, except for the
feet,* to be entirely clean. And you disciples are clean, but not all of you." ¹¹For Jesus knew
who would betray him. That is what he meant when he said, "Not all of you are clean."

¹²After washing their feet, he put on his robe again and sat down and asked, "Do you
understand what I was doing? ¹³You call me ' Teacher' and 'Lord,' and you are right, because
that's what I am. ¹⁴And since I, your Lord and Teacher, have washed your feet, you ought
to wash each other's feet. ¹⁵I have given you an example to follow. Do as I have done to you.
¹⁶I tell you the truth, slaves are not greater than their master. Nor is the messenger more important than the one who sends the message. ¹⁷Now that you know these things, God will
bless you for doing them.

¹⁸"I am not saying these things to all of you; I know the ones I have chosen. But this fulfills
the Scripture that says, ' The one who eats my food has turned against me.'* ¹⁹I tell you this
beforehand, so that when it happens you will believe that I Am the Messiah.* ²⁰I tell you the
truth, anyone who welcomes my messenger is welcoming me, and anyone who welcomes
me is welcoming the Father who sent me."

Jesus and the Disciples Share the Last Supper
(211/Matthew 26:20-30; Mark 14:17-26; Luke 22:14-30)

²¹Now Jesus was deeply troubled,* and he exclaimed, "I tell you the truth, one of you will
betray me!"

²²The disciples looked at each other, wondering whom he could mean. ²³The disciple
Jesus loved was sitting next to Jesus at the table.* ²⁴Simon Peter motioned to him to ask,
"Who's he talking about?" ²⁵So that disciple leaned over to Jesus and asked, "Lord, who is it?"

²⁶Jesus responded, "It is the one to whom I give the bread I dip in the bowl." And when he
had dipped it, he gave it to Judas, son of Simon Iscariot. ²⁷When Judas had eaten the bread,
Satan entered into him. Then Jesus told him, "Hurry and do what you're going to do."

13:4
Luke 12:37; 22:27
13:5
Luke 7:44
John 12:3

13:8
Ezek 36:25
1 Cor 6:11
Eph 5:26
Titus 3:5
13:10
John 15:3
13:11
John 6:64, 70-71;
13:2

13:13
1 Cor 12:3
13:14
Luke 22:27
1 Tim 5:10
1 Pet 5:5
13:15
Phil 2:5-7
1 Pet 5:3-5
1 Jn 2:6; 3:16
13:17
Jas 1:25
13:18
†Ps 41:9
13:20
Matt 10:40
Luke 10:16

13:23
John 19:26
13:25
John 21:20

13:27
Luke 22:3
John 13:2

13:10 Some manuscripts do not include *except for the feet.*   13:18 Ps 41:9.   13:19 Or *that the 'I Am' has come;* or
that I am the Lord; Greek reads *that I am.* See Exod 3:14.   13:21 Greek *was troubled in his spirit.*   13:23 Greek
was reclining on Jesus' bosom. The "disciple Jesus loved" was probably John.

Jesus wrapped a towel around his waist, as the lowliest slave
would do, and washed and dried his disciples' feet. If even he,
God in the flesh, is willing to serve, we his followers must also
be servants, willing to serve in any way that glorifies God. Are
you willing to follow Christ's example of serving? Whom can
you serve today? There is a special blessing for those who not
only agree that humble service is Christ's way, but who also
follow through and do it (13:17).

• **13:6, 7** Imagine being Peter and watching Jesus wash the
others' feet, all the while moving closer to you. Seeing his Master
behave like a slave must have confused Peter. He still did not
understand Jesus' teaching that to be a leader, a person must be a
servant. This is not a comfortable passage for leaders who find it
hard to serve those beneath them. How do you treat those who
work under you (whether children, employees, or volunteers)?

13:8, 9 When Jesus responded: "Unless I wash you, you won't
belong to me," he may have meant (1) that unless he washed away
Peter's sins by his death on the cross, then Peter could have no
relationship with him, or (2) that unless Peter submitted to him and
allowed Jesus to minister in this way, Peter would never learn the
lesson of humility. Either way, Peter seemed to grasp the significance of Jesus' words, for he then wanted to be bathed completely:
"Then wash my hands and head as well, Lord, not just my feet!"

• **13:12ff** Jesus did not wash his disciples' feet just to get them
to be nice to each other. His far greater goal was to extend his
mission on earth after he was gone. These men were to move into
the world serving God, serving each other, and serving all people
to whom they took the message of salvation.

13:22 Judas was not the obvious betrayer. After all, he was the
one the disciples trusted to keep the money (12:6; 13:29).

13:26 The honored guest at a meal was often singled out like this.

13:27 Satan's part in the betrayal of Jesus does not remove any
of the responsibility from Judas. Disillusioned because Jesus was
talking about dying rather than setting up his Kingdom, Judas may
have been trying to force Jesus' hand and make him use his power
to prove he was the Messiah. Or perhaps Judas, not understanding
Jesus' mission, no longer believed Jesus was God's chosen one.
Whatever Judas thought, Satan assumed that Jesus' death would
end his mission and thwart God's plan. Like Judas, Satan did not
know that Jesus' death was the most important part of God's plan
all along.

13:27-38 John describes these few moments in clear detail.
We can see that Jesus knew exactly what was going to happen.
He knew about Judas and about Peter, but he did not change the
situation, nor did he stop loving them. In the same way, Jesus
knows exactly what you will do to hurt him. Yet he still loves you

13:29
John 12:6
13:30
Luke 22:53

28None of the others at the table knew what Jesus meant. 29Since Judas was their treasurer, some thought Jesus was telling him to go and pay for the food or to give some money to the poor. 30So Judas left at once, going out into the night.

Jesus Predicts Peter's Denial (**212**/Luke 22:31-38)

31As soon as Judas left the room, Jesus said, "The time has come for the Son of Man* to enter

13:34
Lev 19:18
Eph 5:2
1 Thes 4:9
1 Pet 1:22
1 Jn 2:8; 3:23;
4:10-11
13:35
1 Jn 3:14; 4:20

into his glory, and God will be glorified because of him. 32And since God receives glory because of the Son,* he will soon give glory to the Son. 33Dear children, I will be with you only a little longer. And as I told the Jewish leaders, you will search for me, but you can't come where I am going. 34So now I am giving you a new commandment: Love each other. Just as I have loved you, you should love each other. 35Your love for one another will prove to the world that you are my disciples."

13:36-38
Matt 26:33-35
Mark 14:29-31
Luke 22:33-34
13:36
John 21:18
2 Pet 1:14

36Simon Peter asked, "Lord, where are you going?"

And Jesus replied, "You can't go with me now, but you will follow me later."

37"But why can't I come now, Lord?" he asked. "I'm ready to die for you."

38Jesus answered, "Die for me? I tell you the truth, Peter—before the rooster crows tomorrow morning, you will deny three times that you even know me.

Jesus Is the Way to the Father (**213**)

14:2
Ps 90:1
John 2:16, 19-21

14 "Don't let your hearts be troubled. Trust in God, and trust also in me. 2There is more than enough room in my Father's home.* If this were not so, would I have told you that I am going to prepare a place for you?* 3When everything is ready, I will come and get you, so that you will always be with me where I am. 4And you know the way to where I am going."

14:6
John 1:4, 14, 16;
8:32; 10:10; 11:25
Rom 5:2
Eph 2:18
Heb 10:20
1 Jn 5:20

5"No, we don't know, Lord," Thomas said. "We have no idea where you are going, so how can we know the way?"

6Jesus told him, "I am the way, the truth, and the life. No one can come to the Father except through me. 7If you had really known me, you would know who my Father is.* From now on, you do know him and have seen him!"

14:7
John 6:46; 8:19
1 Jn 2:13

13:31 "Son of Man" is a title Jesus used for himself. **13:32** Some manuscripts do not include *And since God receives glory because of the Son*. **14:2a** Or *There are many rooms in my Father's house*. **14:2b** Or *If this were not so, I would have told you that I am going to prepare a place for you*. Some manuscripts read *If this were not so, I would have told you. I am going to prepare a place for you*. **14:7** Some manuscripts read *If you have really known me, you will know who my Father is*.

---

unconditionally and will forgive you whenever you ask him. Judas couldn't understand this, and his life ended tragically. Peter understood, and despite his shortcomings, his life ended triumphantly because he never let go of his faith in the one who loved him.

- **13:34** To love others was not a new commandment (see Leviticus 19:18), but to love others as much as Christ loved others was revolutionary. Now we are to love others based on Jesus' sacrificial love for us. Such love will not only bring unbelievers to Christ; it will also keep believers strong and united in a world hostile to God. Jesus was a living example of God's love, as we are to be living examples of Jesus' love.

- **13:34, 35** Jesus says that our Christlike love will show we are his disciples. Do people see petty bickering, jealousy, and division in your church? Or do they know you are Jesus' followers by your love for one another?

   Love is more than simply warm feelings; it is an attitude that reveals itself in action. How can we love others as Jesus loves us? By helping when it's not convenient, by giving when it hurts, by devoting energy to others' welfare rather than our own, by absorbing hurts from others without complaining or fighting back. This kind of loving is hard to do. That is why people notice when you do it and know you are empowered by a supernatural source. The Bible has another beautiful description of love in 1 Corinthians 13.

13:37, 38 Peter proudly told Jesus that he was ready to die for him. But Jesus corrected him. He knew Peter would deny that he knew Jesus that very night to protect himself (18:15-18, 25-27). In our enthusiasm, it is easy to make promises, but God knows the extent of our commitment. Paul tells us not to think of ourselves more highly than we ought (Romans 12:3). Instead of

bragging, demonstrate your commitment step by step as you grow in your knowledge of God's Word and in your faith.

14:1-3 Jesus' words show that the way to eternal life, though unseen, is secure—as secure as your trust in Jesus. He has already prepared the way to eternal life. The only issue that may still be unsettled is your willingness to believe.

14:2, 3 There are few verses in Scripture that describe eternal life, but these few verses are rich with promises. Here Jesus says, "I am going to prepare a place for you," and "I will come and get you." We can look forward to eternal life because Jesus has promised it to all who believe in him. Although the details of eternity are unknown, we need not fear because Jesus is preparing for us and will spend eternity with us.

14:5, 6 This is one of the most basic and important passages in Scripture. How can we know the way to God? Only through Jesus. Jesus is the way because he is both God and man. By uniting our lives with his, we are united with God. Trust Jesus to take you to the Father, and all the benefits of being God's child will be yours.

14:6 Jesus says he is the *only* way to God the Father. Some people may argue that this way is too narrow. In reality, it is wide enough for the whole world, if the world chooses to accept it. Instead of worrying about how limited it sounds to have only one way, we should be saying, "Thank you, God, for providing a sure way to get to you!"

14:6 As the *way*, Jesus is our path to the Father. As the *truth*, he is the reality of all God's promises. As the *life*, he joins his divine life to ours, both now and eternally. Jesus is, in truth, the only living way to the Father.

8Philip said, "Lord, show us the Father, and we will be satisfied."

9Jesus replied, "Have I been with you all this time, Philip, and yet you still don't know who I am? Anyone who has seen me has seen the Father! So why are you asking me to show him to you? 10Don't you believe that I am in the Father and the Father is in me? The words I speak are not my own, but my Father who lives in me does his work through me. 11Just believe that I am in the Father and the Father is in me. Or at least believe because of the work you have seen me do.

12"I tell you the truth, anyone who believes in me will do the same works I have done, and even greater works, because I am going to be with the Father. 13You can ask for anything in my name, and I will do it, so that the Son can bring glory to the Father. 14 Yes, ask me for anything in my name, and I will do it!

Jesus Promises the Holy Spirit (214)

15 "If you love me, obey* my commandments. 16 And I will ask the Father, and he will give you another Advocate,* who will never leave you. 17He is the Holy Spirit, who leads into all truth. The world cannot receive him, because it isn't looking for him and doesn't recognize him. But you know him, because he lives with you now and later will be in you.* 18No, I will not abandon you as orphans—I will come to you. 19 Soon the world will no longer see me, but you will see me. Since I live, you also will live. 20When I am raised to life again, you will know that I am in my Father, and you are in me, and I am in you. 21Those who accept my commandments and obey them are the ones who love me. And because they love me, my Father will love them. And I will love them and reveal myself to each of them."

22Judas (not Judas Iscariot, but the other disciple with that name) said to him, "Lord, why are you going to reveal yourself only to us and not to the world at large?"

23Jesus replied, "All who love me will do what I say. My Father will love them, and we will come and make our home with each of them. 24 Anyone who doesn't love me will not obey me. And remember, my words are not my own. What I am telling you is from the Father who

14:9
John 1:14, 18; 12:45
2 Cor 4:4
Col 1:15
Heb 1:3

14:10
John 5:19; 10:38; 17:11, 21-24

14:16
John 14:26; 15:26

14:17
Rom 8:15-16
1 Jn 3:24

14:18
Rom 8:9-11
2 Cor 3:17-18

14:20
John 10:38; 15:4-5; 16:16, 23; 17:21-24

14:21
John 15:10; 16:27
1 Jn 2:5
2 Jn 1:6

14:22
Luke 6:16
Acts 10:41

14:23
Ps 91:1
John 15:10
Eph 3:17
1 Jn 4:16; 5:3
Rev 3:20; 21:3

14:24
John 7:16; 14:10

14:15 Other manuscripts read *you will obey;* still others read *you should obey.*   **14:16** Or *Comforter,* or *Encourager,* or *Counselor.* Greek reads *Paraclete;* also in 14:26.   **14:17** Some manuscripts read *and is in you.*

14:9 Jesus is the visible, tangible image of the invisible God. He is the complete revelation of what God is like. Jesus explained to Philip, who wanted to see the Father, that to know Jesus is to know God. The search for God, for truth and reality, ends in Christ. (See also Colossians 1:15; Hebrews 1:1-4.)

14:12, 13 Jesus is not saying that his disciples would do greater works—after all, raising the dead is about as amazing as you can get. Rather, the disciples, working in the power of the Holy Spirit, would carry the Good News of God's Kingdom out of Palestine and into the whole world.

14:14 When Jesus says we can ask for anything, we must remember that our asking must be in his name—that is, according to God's character and will. God will not grant requests contrary to his nature or his will, and we cannot use his name as a magic formula to fulfill our selfish desires. If we are sincerely following God and seeking to do his will, then our requests will be in line with what he wants, and he will grant them. (See also 15:16; 16:23.)

14:15, 16 Jesus was soon going to leave the disciples, but he would remain with them. How could this be? The Advocate—the Spirit of God himself—would come after Jesus was gone to care for and guide the disciples. The regenerating power of the Spirit came on the disciples just before Jesus' ascension (20:22), and the Spirit was poured out on all the believers at Pentecost (Acts 2), shortly after Jesus ascended to heaven. The Holy Spirit is the very presence of God within us and all believers, helping us live as God wants and building Christ's church on earth. By faith we can appropriate the Spirit's power each day.

• **14:16** The word translated "Advocate" combines the ideas of comfort and counsel. The word could also be translated Comforter, Encourager, or Counselor. The Holy Spirit is a powerful person on our side, working for and with us.

• **14:17ff** The following chapters teach these truths about the Holy Spirit: He will never leave us (14:16); the world at large

cannot receive him (14:17); he lives with us and in us (14:17); he teaches us (14:26); he reminds us of Jesus' words (14:26; 15:26); he convinces us of sin, shows us God's righteousness, and announces God's judgment on evil (16:8); he guides us into truth and gives insight into future events (16:13); he brings glory to Christ (16:14). The Holy Spirit has been active among people from the beginning of time, but after Pentecost (Acts 2) he came to live in all believers. Many people are unaware of the Holy Spirit's activities, but to those who hear Christ's words and understand the Spirit's power, the Spirit gives a whole new way to look at life.

14:18 When Jesus said, "I will come to you," he meant it. Although Jesus ascended to heaven, he sent the Holy Spirit to live in believers, and to have the Holy Spirit is to have Jesus himself.

14:19-21 Sometimes people wish they knew the future so they could prepare for it. God has chosen not to give us this knowledge. He alone knows what will happen, but he tells us all we need to know to *prepare* for the future. When we live by his standards, he will not leave us; he will come to us, he will be in us, and he will show himself to us. God knows what will happen, and because he will be with us through it all, we need not fear. We don't have to know the future to have faith in God; we have to have faith in God to be secure about the future.

14:21 Jesus said that his followers show their love for him by obeying him. Love is more than lovely words; it is commitment and conduct. If you love Christ, then prove it by obeying what he says in his Word.

14:22, 23 Because the disciples were still expecting Jesus to establish an earthly kingdom and overthrow Rome, they found it hard to understand why he did not tell the world at large that he was the Messiah. Not everyone, however, could understand Jesus' message. Ever since Pentecost, the Good News of the Kingdom has been proclaimed in the whole world, and yet not everyone is receptive to it. Jesus saves the deepest revelations of himself for those who love and obey him.

14:26
John 1:33; 15:26;
16:7; 20:22
1 Jn 2:20, 27

14:27
John 16:33; 20:19
Phil 4:7
Col 3:15

14:29
John 13:19

14:30
John 12:31

14:31
John 10:18; 12:49

sent me. ²⁵I am telling you these things now while I am still with you. ²⁶But when the Father sends the Advocate as my representative—that is, the Holy Spirit—he will teach you everything and will remind you of everything I have told you.

²⁷"I am leaving you with a gift—peace of mind and heart. And the peace I give is a gift the world cannot give. So don't be troubled or afraid. ²⁸Remember what I told you: I am going away, but I will come back to you again. If you really loved me, you would be happy that I am going to the Father, who is greater than I am. ²⁹I have told you these things before they happen so that when they do happen, you will believe.

³⁰"I don't have much more time to talk to you, because the ruler of this world approaches. He has no power over me, ³¹but I will do what the Father requires of me, so that the world will know that I love the Father. Come, let's be going.

Jesus Teaches about the Vine and the Branches (215)

15:3
John 17:17
Eph 5:26

15:4
John 6:56

15:6
Matt 3:10; 7:19;
13:42

15:8
Matt 5:16

15 "I am the true grapevine, and my Father is the gardener. ²He cuts off every branch of mine that doesn't produce fruit, and he prunes the branches that do bear fruit so they will produce even more. ³You have already been pruned and purified by the message I have given you. ⁴Remain in me, and I will remain in you. For a branch cannot produce fruit if it is severed from the vine, and you cannot be fruitful unless you remain in me.

⁵"Yes, I am the vine; you are the branches. Those who remain in me, and I in them, will produce much fruit. For apart from me you can do nothing. ⁶Anyone who does not remain in me is thrown away like a useless branch and withers. Such branches are gathered into a pile to be burned. ⁷But if you remain in me and my words remain in you, you may ask for anything you want, and it will be granted! ⁸When you produce much fruit, you are my true disciples. This brings great glory to my Father.

14:26 Jesus promised the disciples that the Holy Spirit would help them remember what he had been teaching them. This promise ensures the validity of the New Testament. The disciples were eyewitnesses of Jesus' life and teachings, and the Holy Spirit helped them remember without taking away their individual perspectives. We can be confident that the Gospels are accurate records of what Jesus taught and did (see 1 Corinthians 2:10-14). The Holy Spirit can help us in the same way. As we study the Bible, we can trust him to plant truth in our mind, convince us of God's will, and remind us when we stray from it.

14:27 The end result of the Holy Spirit's work in our lives is deep and lasting peace. Unlike worldly peace, which is usually defined as the absence of conflict, this peace is confident assurance in any circumstance; with Christ's peace, we have no need to fear the present or the future. Sin, fear, uncertainty, doubt, and numerous other forces are at war within us. The peace of God moves into our hearts and lives to restrain these hostile forces and offer comfort in place of conflict. Jesus says he will give us that peace if we are willing to accept it from him. If your life is full of stress, allow the Holy Spirit to fill you with Christ's peace (see Philippians 4:6, 7 for more on experiencing God's peace).

14:28 As God the Son, Jesus willingly submits to God the Father. On earth, Jesus also submitted to many of the physical limitations of his humanity (Philippians 2:6).

14:30, 31 Although Satan, the ruler of this world, was unable to overpower Jesus (Matthew 4), he still had the arrogance to try. Satan's power exists only because God allows him to act. But because Jesus is sinless, Satan has no power over him. If we obey Jesus and align ourselves closely with God's purposes, Satan can have no power over us.

14:31 "Come, let's be going" suggests that chapters 15–17 may have been spoken en route to the Garden of Gethsemane. Another view is that Jesus was asking the disciples to get ready to leave the upper room, but they did not actually do so until 18:1.

15:1 The grapevine is a prolific plant; a single vine supports numerous branches and bears many grapes. In the Old Testament, grapes symbolized Israel's fruitfulness in doing God's work on the earth (Psalm 80:8; Isaiah 5:1-7; Ezekiel 19:10-14). In the Passover meal, the fruit of the vine symbolized God's goodness to his people.

• **15:1ff** Christ is the vine, and God is the gardener who cares for the branches to make them fruitful. The branches are all those who claim to be followers of Christ. The fruitful branches are true believers who by their living union with Christ produce much fruit. But those who become unproductive—those who turn back from following Christ after making a superficial commitment—will be separated from the vine. Unproductive followers are as good as dead and will be cut off and tossed aside.

• **15:2, 3** Jesus makes a distinction between two kinds of pruning: (1) cutting off and (2) cutting back branches. Fruitful branches are cut back to promote growth. In other words, God must sometimes discipline us to strengthen our character and faith. But branches that don't bear fruit are cut off at the trunk not only because they are worthless but also because they often infect the rest of the tree. People who don't bear fruit for God or who try to block the efforts of God's followers will be cut off from his life-giving power.

15:5 "Fruit" is not limited to soul winning. In this chapter, answered prayer, joy, and love are mentioned as fruit (15:7, 11, 12). Galatians 5:22-24 and 2 Peter 1:5-8 describe additional fruit: qualities of Christian character.

• **15:5, 6** Remaining in Christ means (1) believing that he is God's Son (1 John 4:15), (2) receiving him as Savior and Lord (John 1:12), (3) doing what God says (1 John 3:24), (4) continuing to believe the Good News (1 John 2:24), and (5) relating in love to the community of believers, Christ's body (John 15:12).

• **15:5-8** Many people try to be good, honest people who do what is right. But Jesus says that the only way to live a truly good life is to stay close to him, like a branch attached to the vine. Apart from Christ our efforts are unfruitful. Are you receiving the nourishment and life offered by Christ, the vine? If not, you are missing a special gift he has for you.

15:8 When a vine produces "much fruit," God is glorified, for daily he sent the sunshine and rain to make the crops grow, and constantly he nurtured each tiny plant and prepared it to blossom. What a moment of glory for the Lord of the harvest when the harvest is brought into the barns, mature and ready for use! He made it all happen! This farming analogy shows how God is glorified when people come into a right relationship with him and begin to "produce much fruit" in their lives.

9"I have loved you even as the Father has loved me. Remain in my love. 10When you obey my commandments, you remain in my love, just as I obey my Father's commandments and remain in his love. 11I have told you these things so that you will be filled with my joy. Yes, your joy will overflow! 12This is my commandment: Love each other in the same way I have loved you. 13There is no greater love than to lay down one's life for one's friends. 14You are my friends if you do what I command. 15I no longer call you slaves, because a master doesn't confide in his slaves. Now you are my friends, since I have told you everything the Father told me. 16You didn't choose me. I chose you. I appointed you to go and produce lasting fruit, so that the Father will give you whatever you ask for, using my name. 17This is my command: Love each other.

15:9 John 3:35
15:10 John 14:15
15:11 John 17:13 1 Jn 1:4
15:12 John 13:34
15:13 John 10:11 Rom 5:6-8
15:16 Rom 1:13 Phil 1:22

Jesus Warns about the World's Hatred (216)

18"If the world hates you, remember that it hated me first. 19The world would love you as one of its own if you belonged to it, but you are no longer part of the world. I chose you to come out of the world, so it hates you. 20Do you remember what I told you? 'A slave is not greater than the master.' Since they persecuted me, naturally they will persecute you. And if they had listened to me, they would listen to you. 21They will do all this to you because of me, for they have rejected the one who sent me. 22They would not be guilty if I had not come and spoken to them. But now they have no excuse for their sin. 23Anyone who hates me also hates my Father. 24If I hadn't done such miraculous signs among them that no one else could do, they would not be guilty. But as it is, they have seen everything I did, yet they still hate me and my Father. 25This fulfills what is written in their Scriptures*: ' They hated me without cause.'

26"But I will send you the Advocate*—the Spirit of truth. He will come to you from the Father and will testify all about me. 27And you must also testify about me because you have been with me from the beginning of my ministry.

15:18 John 7:7 1 Jn 3:13
15:19 John 17:14 1 Jn 4:5
15:21 Matt 5:11 1 Pet 4:14
15:22 John 9:41
15:24 John 5:36; 9:41
15:25 †Pss 35:19; 69:4
15:26 John 14:17 1 Jn 5:7

16 "I have told you these things so that you won't abandon your faith. 2For you will be expelled from the synagogues, and the time is coming when those who kill you will think they are doing a holy service for God. 3This is because they have never known the Father or me. 4Yes, I'm telling you these things now, so that when they happen, you will remember my warning. I didn't tell you earlier because I was going to be with you for a while longer.

16:2 John 9:22
16:3 John 15:21
16:4 John 13:19

15:25 Greek *in their law.* Pss 35:19; 69:4.   **15:26** Or *Comforter,* or *Encourager,* or *Counselor.* Greek reads *Paraclete.*

15:11 When things are going well, we feel elated. When hardships come, we sink into depression. But true joy transcends the rolling waves of circumstance. Joy comes from a consistent relationship with Jesus Christ. When our lives are intertwined with his, he will help us walk through adversity without sinking into debilitating lows and manage prosperity without moving into deceptive highs. The joy of living with Jesus Christ daily will keep us levelheaded, no matter how high or low our circumstances.

15:12, 13 We are to love each other as Jesus loved us, and he loved us enough to give his life for us. We may not have to die for someone, but there are other ways to practice sacrificial love: listening, helping, encouraging, giving. Think of someone in particular who needs this kind of love today. Give all the love you can, and then try to give a little more.

15:15 Because Jesus Christ is Lord and Master, he should call us servants; instead, he calls us friends. How comforting and reassuring to be chosen as Christ's friends! Because he is Lord and Master, we owe him our unqualified obedience, but most of all, Jesus asks us to obey him because we love him.

• **15:16** Jesus made the first choice—to love and to die for us, to invite us to live with him forever. We make the next choice—

to accept or reject his offer. Without *his* choice, we would have no choice to make.

15:17 Christians will get plenty of hatred from the world; from each other we need love and support. Do you allow small problems to get in the way of loving other believers? Jesus commands that you love them, and he will give you the strength to do it.

15:26 Once again Jesus offers hope. The Holy Spirit gives strength to endure the unreasonable hatred and evil in our world and the hostility many have toward Christ. This is especially comforting for those facing persecution.

• **15:26** Jesus uses two names for the Holy Spirit—"Advocate" and "Spirit of truth." The word *Advocate* conveys the helping, encouraging, and strengthening work of the Spirit. *Spirit of truth* points to the teaching, illuminating, and reminding work of the Spirit. The Holy Spirit ministers to both the head and the heart, and both dimensions are important.

• **16:1-16** In his last moments with his disciples, Jesus (1) warned them about further persecution, (2) told them where, when, and why he was going, and (3) assured them that they would not be left alone, but that the Spirit would come. Jesus knew what lay ahead, and he did not want the disciples' faith shaken or destroyed. God wants you to know you are not alone. You have the Holy Spirit to comfort you, teach you truth, and help you.

16:2 Saul (who later became Paul), under the authority of the high priest, went through the land hunting down and persecuting Christians, convinced that he was doing the right thing (Acts 9:1, 2; 26:9-11).

Jesus Teaches about the Holy Spirit (**217**)

16:5
John 7:33; 13:36

16:7
John 14:26; 15:26

16:9
John 15:22

16:10
Acts 3:14; 7:52
Rom 1:17
1 Pet 3:18

16:11
John 12:31

16:13
John 14:17, 26

16:15
John 17:10

5 "But now I am going away to the one who sent me, and not one of you is asking where I am going. 6 Instead, you grieve because of what I've told you. 7 But in fact, it is best for you that I go away, because if I don't, the Advocate* won't come. If I do go away, then I will send him to you. 8 And when he comes, he will convict the world of its sin, and of God's righteousness, and of the coming judgment. 9 The world's sin is that it refuses to believe in me. 10 Righteousness is available because I go to the Father, and you will see me no more. 11 Judgment will come because the ruler of this world has already been judged.

12 "There is so much more I want to tell you, but you can't bear it now. 13 When the Spirit of truth comes, he will guide you into all truth. He will not speak on his own but will tell you what he has heard. He will tell you about the future. 14 He will bring me glory by telling you whatever he receives from me. 15 All that belongs to the Father is mine; this is why I said, 'The Spirit will tell you whatever he receives from me.'

Jesus Teaches about Using His Name in Prayer (**218**)

16:16
John 14:18-24

16 "In a little while you won't see me anymore. But a little while after that, you will see me again."

17 Some of the disciples asked each other, "What does he mean when he says, 'In a little while you won't see me, but then you will see me,' and 'I am going to the Father'? 18 And what does he mean by 'a little while'? We don't understand."

16:20
Mark 16:10
Luke 23:27
John 20:20

16:21
Isa 13:8; 21:3;
26:17
Acts 13:33
Col 1:18

16:22
Isa 66:14
John 20:20

16:23
John 14:20; 16:26

16:24
John 15:11

16:25
Ps 78:2
John 10:6

16:27
John 8:42; 14:21;
17:8

16:28
John 13:3

19 Jesus realized they wanted to ask him about it, so he said, "Are you asking yourselves what I meant? I said in a little while you won't see me, but a little while after that you will see me again. 20 I tell you the truth, you will weep and mourn over what is going to happen to me, but the world will rejoice. You will grieve, but your grief will suddenly turn to wonderful joy. 21 It will be like a woman suffering the pains of labor. When her child is born, her anguish gives way to joy because she has brought a new baby into the world. 22 So you have sorrow now, but I will see you again; then you will rejoice, and no one can rob you of that joy. 23 At that time you won't need to ask me for anything. I tell you the truth, you will ask the Father directly, and he will grant your request because you use my name. 24 You haven't done this before. Ask, using my name, and you will receive, and you will have abundant joy.

25 "I have spoken of these matters in figures of speech, but soon I will stop speaking figuratively and will tell you plainly all about the Father. 26 Then you will ask in my name. I'm not saying I will ask the Father on your behalf, 27 for the Father himself loves you dearly because you love me and believe that I came from God.* 28 Yes, I came from the Father into the world, and now I will leave the world and return to the Father."

16:7 Or *Comforter,* or *Encourager,* or *Counselor.* Greek reads *Paraclete.*   **16:27** Some manuscripts read *from the Father.*

16:5 Although the disciples had asked Jesus about his death (13:36; 14:5), they had never wondered about its meaning. They were mostly concerned about themselves. If Jesus went away, what would become of them?

16:7 Unless Jesus did what he came to do, there would be no Good News. If he did not die, he could not remove our sins; he could not rise again and defeat death. If he did not go back to the Father, the Holy Spirit would not come. Christ's presence on earth was limited to one place at a time. His leaving meant he could be present to the whole world through the Holy Spirit.

16:8-11 Three important tasks of the Holy Spirit are (1) convicting the world of its sin and calling it to repentance, (2) revealing the standard of God's righteousness to anyone who believes, because Christ would no longer be physically present on earth, and (3) demonstrating Christ's judgment over Satan.

16:9 According to Jesus, not believing in him is *sin.*

16:10, 11 Christ's death on the cross made a personal relationship with God available to us. When we confess our sin, God declares us righteous and delivers us from judgment for our sins.

16:13 The truth into which the Holy Spirit guides us is the truth about Christ. The Spirit also helps us through patient practice to discern right from wrong.

16:13 Jesus said the Holy Spirit would tell them "about the future"—the nature of their mission, the opposition they would face, and the final outcome of their efforts. They didn't fully understand these promises until the Holy Spirit came after Jesus' death and resurrection. Then the Holy Spirit revealed truths to the disciples that they wrote down in the books that now form the New Testament.

16:16 Jesus was referring to his death, now only a few hours away, and his resurrection three days later.

16:20 What a contrast between the disciples and the world! The world rejoiced as the disciples wept, but the disciples would see Jesus again (in three days) and rejoice. The world's values are often the opposite of God's values. This can cause Christians to feel like misfits. But even if life is difficult now, one day we will rejoice. Keep your eye on the future and on God's promises!

16:23-27 Jesus is talking about a new relationship between the believer and God. Previously, people approached God through priests. After Jesus' resurrection, any believer could approach God directly. A new day has dawned and now all believers are priests, talking with God personally and directly (see Hebrews 10:19-23). We approach God, not because of our own merit, but because Jesus, our great High Priest, has made us acceptable to God.

²⁹Then his disciples said, "At last you are speaking plainly and not figuratively. ³⁰Now we understand that you know everything, and there's no need to question you. From this we believe that you came from God."

³¹Jesus asked, "Do you finally believe? ³²But the time is coming—indeed it's here now— when you will be scattered, each one going his own way, leaving me alone. Yet I am not alone because the Father is with me. ³³I have told you all this so that you may have peace in me. Here on earth you will have many trials and sorrows. But take heart, because I have overcome the world."

Jesus Prays for Himself (**219**)

17 After saying all these things, Jesus looked up to heaven and said, "Father, the hour has come. Glorify your Son so he can give glory back to you. ²For you have given him authority over everyone. He gives eternal life to each one you have given him. ³And this is the way to have eternal life—to know you, the only true God, and Jesus Christ, the one you sent to earth. ⁴I brought glory to you here on earth by completing the work you gave me to do. ⁵Now, Father, bring me into the glory we shared before the world began.

Jesus Prays for His Disciples (**220**)

⁶"I have revealed you* to the ones you gave me from this world. They were always yours. You gave them to me, and they have kept your word. ⁷Now they know that everything I have is a gift from you, ⁸for I have passed on to them the message you gave me. They accepted it and know that I came from you, and they believe you sent me.

⁹"My prayer is not for the world, but for those you have given me, because they belong to you. ¹⁰All who are mine belong to you, and you have given them to me, so they bring me glory. ¹¹Now I am departing from the world; they are staying in this world, but I am coming to you. Holy Father, you have given me your name;* now protect them by the power of your name so that they will be united just as we are. ¹²During my time here, I protected them by the power of the name you gave me.* I guarded them so that not one was lost, except the one headed for destruction, as the Scriptures foretold.

¹³"Now I am coming to you. I told them many things while I was with them in this world so they would be filled with my joy. ¹⁴I have given them your word. And the world hates

17:6 Greek *have revealed your name;* also in 17:26. **17:11** Some manuscripts read *you have given me these [disciples].* **17:12** Some manuscripts read *I protected those you gave me, by the power of your name.*

16:32	Zech 13:7 / Matt 26:31 / John 8:29
16:33	John 14:27 / Rom 5:1; 8:37 / 1 Jn 5:4
17:1	John 13:31
17:2	Matt 28:18 / John 6:37, 39
17:3	Phil 3:8 / 1 Jn 5:20
17:5	John 1:1-2; 17:24 / Phil 2:6
17:6	John 17:26
17:8	John 13:3; 16:30
17:9	1 Jn 5:19
17:10	John 16:15
17:11	John 10:30; 17:21 / Gal 3:28
17:12	John 6:39
17:13	John 7:33; 15:11
17:14	John 15:18-19

16:30 The disciples believed Jesus' words because they were convinced that he knew everything. But their belief was only a first step toward the great faith they would receive when the Holy Spirit came to live in them.

16:31-33 As Christians, we should expect continuing tension with an unbelieving world that is "out of sync" with Christ, his Good News, and his people. At the same time, we can expect our relationship with Christ to produce peace and comfort because we are "in sync" with him.

16:32 The disciples scattered after Jesus was arrested (see Mark 14:50). Jesus accepted their statement of faith even though he knew their weakness. He knew they would have to grow into people whose words and lives matched even to the point of death. He takes us through the same process. How well are you living out what you say you believe about Jesus?

16:33 Jesus summed up all he had told them this night, tying together themes from 14:27-29; 16:1-4; and 16:9-11. With these words he told his disciples to take courage. In spite of the inevitable struggles they would face, they would not be alone. Jesus does not abandon us to our struggles either. If we remember that the ultimate victory has already been won, we can claim the peace of Christ in the most troublesome times.

• **17:1ff** This entire chapter is Jesus' prayer. From it, we learn that the world is a tremendous battleground where the forces under Satan's power and those under God's authority are at war. Satan and his forces are motivated by bitter hatred for Christ and his forces. Jesus prayed for his disciples, including those of us who follow him today. He prayed that God would keep his chosen believers safe from Satan's power, setting them apart and making them pure and holy, uniting them through his truth.

17:3 How do we get eternal life? Jesus tells us clearly here— by knowing God the Father himself through his Son, Jesus Christ. Eternal life requires entering into a personal relationship with God in Jesus Christ. When we admit our sin and turn away from it, Christ's love lives in us by the Holy Spirit.

17:5 Before Jesus came to earth, he was one with God. At this point, when his mission on earth was almost finished, Jesus was asking his Father to restore him to his original place of honor and authority. Jesus' resurrection and ascension—and Stephen's dying exclamation (Acts 7:56)—attest that Jesus did return to his exalted position at the right hand of God.

17:10 What did Jesus mean when he said "they bring me glory"? God's glory is the revelation of his character and presence. The lives of Jesus' disciples reveal his character, and he is present to the world through them. Does your life reveal Jesus' character and presence?

• **17:11** Jesus was asking that the disciples be united in harmony and love as the Father, Son, and Holy Spirit are united—the strongest of all unions. (See the notes on 17:21-23.)

17:12 Judas was "the one headed for destruction," who was lost because he betrayed Jesus and never sought forgiveness (see Psalm 41:9).

17:13 Joy is a common theme in Christ's teachings—he wants us to be joyful (see 15:11; 16:24). The key to immeasurable joy is living in intimate contact with Christ, the source of all joy. When we do, we will experience God's special care and protection and see the victory God brings even when defeat seems certain.

17:14 The world hates Christians because Christians' values differ from the world's. Because Christ's followers don't cooperate with the world by joining in their sin, they are living accusations

17:15
1 Jn 5:18

17:17
John 15:3

17:18
John 20:21

17:19
Heb 2:11

them because they do not belong to the world, just as I do not belong to the world. ¹⁵ I'm not asking you to take them out of the world, but to keep them safe from the evil one. ¹⁶ They do not belong to this world any more than I do. ¹⁷ Make them holy by your truth; teach them your word, which is truth. ¹⁸ Just as you sent me into the world, I am sending them into the world. ¹⁹ And I give myself as a holy sacrifice for them so they can be made holy by your truth.

Jesus Prays for Future Believers (221)

17:20
John 17:9

17:21
John 10:38
Gal 3:28

17:22
John 17:11

17:23
John 16:27; 17:5

17:24
John 1:14; 12:26

17:25
Matt 11:27

17:26
John 15:9

²⁰ "I am praying not only for these disciples but also for all who will ever believe in me through their message. ²¹ I pray that they will all be one, just as you and I are one—as you are in me, Father, and I am in you. And may they be in us so that the world will believe you sent me.

²² "I have given them the glory you gave me, so they may be one as we are one. ²³ I am in them and you are in me. May they experience such perfect unity that the world will know that you sent me and that you love them as much as you love me. ²⁴ Father, I want these whom you have given me to be with me where I am. Then they can see all the glory you gave me because you loved me even before the world began!

²⁵ "O righteous Father, the world doesn't know you, but I do; and these disciples know you sent me. ²⁶ I have revealed you to them, and I will continue to do so. Then your love for me will be in them, and I will be in them."

2. Jesus completes his mission
Jesus Is Betrayed and Arrested
(224/Matthew 26:47-56; Mark 14:43-52; Luke 22:47-53)

18:1
2 Sam 15:23
Matt 26:36
Mark 14:32

18:3
John 7:32, 45

18 After saying these things, Jesus crossed the Kidron Valley with his disciples and entered a grove of olive trees. ² Judas, the betrayer, knew this place, because Jesus had often gone there with his disciples. ³ The leading priests and Pharisees had given Judas a contingent of Roman soldiers and Temple guards to accompany him. Now with blazing torches, lanterns, and weapons, they arrived at the olive grove.

---

against the world's immorality. The world follows Satan's agenda, and Satan is the avowed enemy of Jesus and his people.

17:17 A follower of Christ becomes pure and holy through believing and obeying the Word of God (Hebrews 4:12). He or she has already accepted forgiveness through Christ's sacrificial death (Hebrews 7:26, 27). But daily application of God's Word has a purifying effect on our minds and hearts. Scripture points out sin, motivates us to confess, renews our relationship with Christ, and guides us back to the right path.

17:18 Jesus didn't ask God to take believers *out* of the world but instead to use them *in* the world. Because Jesus sends us into the world, we should not try to escape from the world, nor should we avoid all relationships with non-Christians. We are called to be salt and light (Matthew 5:13-16), and we are to do the work that God sent us to do.

• **17:20** Jesus prayed for all who would follow him, including you and others you know. He prayed for unity (17:11), protection from the evil one (17:15), and holiness (17:17). Knowing that Jesus prayed for us should give us confidence as we work for his Kingdom.

17:21-23 Jesus' great desire for his disciples was that they would become one. He wanted them unified as a powerful witness to the reality of God's love. Are you helping to unify the body of Christ, the church? You can pray for other Christians, avoid gossip, build others up, work together in humility, give your time and money, exalt Christ, and refuse to get sidetracked arguing over divisive matters.

17:21-23 Jesus prayed for unity among believers based on the believers' unity with him and the Father. Christians can know unity among themselves if they are living in union with God. For example, each branch living in union with the vine is united with all other branches doing the same.

18:3 The Jewish religious leaders were given authority by the Romans to make arrests for minor infractions. The Roman

soldiers may not have participated in the arrest but accompanied the Temple guards to make sure matters didn't get out of control.

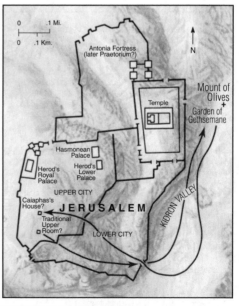

BETRAYAL IN THE GARDEN After eating the Passover meal in the upper room, Jesus and his disciples went to Gethsemane, where Judas led the Temple guard to arrest Jesus. Jesus was then taken to Caiaphas's house for his first of many trials.

⁴Jesus fully realized all that was going to happen to him, so he stepped forward to meet them. " Who are you looking for?" he asked.

⁵"Jesus the Nazarene,"* they replied.

"I Aᴍ he,"* Jesus said. (Judas, who betrayed him, was standing with them.) ⁶As Jesus said "I Aᴍ he," they all drew back and fell to the ground! ⁷Once more he asked them, "Who are you looking for?"

And again they replied, "Jesus the Nazarene."

⁸"I told you that I Aᴍ he," Jesus said. "And since I am the one you want, let these others go." ⁹He did this to fulfill his own statement: "I did not lose a single one of those you have given me."*

¹⁰Then Simon Peter drew a sword and slashed off the right ear of Malchus, the high priest's slave. ¹¹But Jesus said to Peter, "Put your sword back into its sheath. Shall I not drink from the cup of suffering the Father has given me?"

Annas Questions Jesus (225)

¹²So the soldiers, their commanding officer, and the Temple guards arrested Jesus and tied him up. ¹³First they took him to Annas, the father-in-law of Caiaphas, the high priest at that time.* ¹⁴ Caiaphas was the one who had told the other Jewish leaders, "It's better that one man should die for the people."

¹⁵Simon Peter followed Jesus, as did another of the disciples. That other disciple was acquainted with the high priest, so he was allowed to enter the high priest's courtyard with Jesus. ¹⁶Peter had to stay outside the gate. Then the disciple who knew the high priest spoke to the woman watching at the gate, and she let Peter in. ¹⁷The woman asked Peter, "You're not one of that man's disciples, are you?"

"No," he said, "I am not."

¹⁸Because it was cold, the household servants and the guards had made a charcoal fire. They stood around it, warming themselves, and Peter stood with them, warming himself.

¹⁹Inside, the high priest began asking Jesus about his followers and what he had been teaching them. ²⁰Jesus replied, "Everyone knows what I teach. I have preached regularly in the synagogues and the Temple, where the people* gather. I have not spoken in secret. ²¹Why are you asking me this question? Ask those who heard me. They know what I said."

18:4
John 6:64

18:9
John 6:39; 17:12

18:10
Luke 22:36, 38

18:11
Matt 20:22; 26:39
Mark 10:38; 14:36
Luke 22:42

18:12-14
Matt 26:57-58
Mark 14:53-54
Luke 22:54

18:13
Luke 3:2
John 18:24

18:16-18
Matt 26:69-70
Mark 14:66-68
Luke 22:55-57

18:18
Mark 14:54, 67

18:19-24
Matt 26:59-68
Mark 14:55-65
Luke 22:63-71

18:20
Matt 26:55
John 7:26

18:5a Or *Jesus of Nazareth;* also in 18:7.   **18:5b** Or *"The 'I Aᴍ' is here";* or *"I am the Lᴏʀᴅ";* Greek reads *I am;* also in 18:6, 8. See Exod 3:14.   **18:9** See John 6:39 and 17:12.   **18:13** Greek *that year.*   **18:20** Greek *Jewish people;* also in 18:38.

18:4, 5 John does not record Judas's kiss of greeting (Matthew 26:49; Mark 14:45; Luke 22:47, 48), but Judas's kiss marked a turning point for the disciples. With Jesus' arrest, each one's life would be radically different. For the first time, Judas openly betrayed Jesus before the other disciples. For the first time, Jesus' loyal disciples ran away from him (Matthew 26:56). The band of disciples would undergo severe testing before they were transformed from hesitant followers to dynamic leaders.

18:5, 6 The men may have been startled by the boldness of Jesus' question or by the words "I Aᴍ he," a declaration of his divinity (Exodus 3:14). Or perhaps they were overcome by his obvious power and authority.

• **18:10, 11** Trying to protect Jesus, Peter pulled a sword and wounded the high priest's slave. But Jesus told Peter to put away his sword and allow God's plan to unfold. At times it is tempting to take matters into our own hands, to force the issue. Most often such moves lead to sin. Instead, we must trust God to work out his plan. Think of it—if Peter had had his way, Jesus would not have gone to the cross, and God's plan of redemption would have been thwarted. Luke records that Jesus touched the man's ear and healed him (Luke 22:51).

• **18:11** "The cup" refers to the suffering, isolation, and death that Jesus would have to endure in order to atone for the sins of the world.

18:12, 13 Jesus was immediately taken to the high priest's residence, even though this was the middle of the night. The religious leaders were in a hurry—they wanted to complete the execution before the Sabbath and get on with the Passover celebration. This residence was a palace whose outer walls enclosed a court-

yard, where servants and soldiers could warm themselves around a fire.

• **18:13** Both Annas and Caiaphas had been high priests. Annas was Israel's high priest from A.D. 6 to 15, when he was deposed by Roman rulers. Caiaphas, Annas's son-in-law, was appointed high priest from A.D. 18 to 36/37. According to Jewish law, the office of high priest was held for life. Many Jews, therefore, still considered Annas the high priest and still called him by that title. But although Annas retained much authority among the Jews, Caiaphas made the final decisions.

Both Caiaphas and Annas cared more about their political ambitions than about their responsibility to lead the people to God. Though religious leaders, they had become evil. As the nation's spiritual leaders, they should have been sensitive to God's revelation. They should have known that Jesus was the Messiah about whom the Scriptures spoke, and they should have pointed the people to him. But when deceitful men and women pursue evil, they want to eliminate all opposition. Instead of honestly evaluating Jesus' claims based on their knowledge of Scripture, these religious leaders sought to further their own selfish ambitions and were even willing to kill God's Son, if that's what it took, to do it.

18:15, 16 The other disciple is probably John, the author of this Gospel. He knew the high priest and identified himself to the woman at the door. Because of his connections, John got himself and Peter into the courtyard. But Peter refused to identify himself as Jesus' follower. Peter's experiences in the next few hours would change his life. For more information about Peter, see his Profile in Matthew 27, p. 1603.

18:19ff During the night, Jesus had a pretrial hearing before Annas prior to being taken to Caiaphas and the entire high council

18:22
John 19:3

18:23
Matt 5:39
Acts 23:2-5

18:24
Matt 26:3

22 Then one of the Temple guards standing nearby slapped Jesus across the face. "Is that the way to answer the high priest?" he demanded.

23 Jesus replied, "If I said anything wrong, you must prove it. But if I'm speaking the truth, why are you beating me?"

24 Then Annas bound Jesus and sent him to Caiaphas, the high priest.

Peter Denies Knowing Jesus
(227/Matthew 26:69-75; Mark 14:66-72; Luke 22:54-65)
25 Meanwhile, as Simon Peter was standing by the fire warming himself, they asked him again, "You're not one of his disciples, are you?"

He denied it, saying, "No, I am not."

THE SIX STAGES OF JESUS' TRIAL Although Jesus' trial lasted less than 18 hours, he was taken to six different hearings.			
	Before Jewish Authorities	Preliminary Hearing before Annas (John 18:12-24)	Because the office of high priest was for life, Annas was still the "official" high priest in the eyes of the Jews, even though the Romans had appointed another. Thus, Annas still carried much weight in the high council.
		Hearing before Caiaphas (Matthew 26:57-68)	Like the hearing before Annas, this hearing was conducted at night in secrecy. It was full of illegalities that made a mockery of justice (see the chart in Matthew 27, p. 1607).
	Before Roman Authorities	Trial before the High Council (Matthew 27:1, 2)	Just after daybreak, 70 members of the high council met to rubber-stamp their approval of the previous hearings to make them appear legal. The purpose of this trial was not to determine justice, but to justify their own preconceptions of Jesus' guilt.
		First Hearing before Pilate (Luke 23:1-5)	The religious leaders had condemned Jesus to death on religious grounds, but only the Roman government could grant the death penalty. Thus, they took Jesus to Pilate, the Roman governor, and accused him of treason and rebellion, crimes for which the Roman government gave the death penalty. Pilate saw at once that Jesus was innocent, but he was afraid about the uproar being caused by the religious leaders.
		Hearing before Herod (Luke 23:6-12)	Because Jesus' home was in the region of Galilee, Pilate sent Jesus to Herod Antipas, the ruler of Galilee, who was in Jerusalem for the Passover celebration. Herod was eager to see Jesus do a miracle, but when Jesus remained silent, Herod wanted nothing to do with him and sent him back to Pilate.
		Last Hearing before Pilate (Luke 23:13-25)	Pilate didn't like the religious leaders. He wasn't interested in condemning Jesus because he knew Jesus was innocent. However, he knew that another uprising in his district might cost him his job. First he tried to compromise with the religious leaders by having Jesus beaten, an illegal action in itself. But finally he gave in and handed Jesus over to be executed. Pilate's self-interest was stronger than his sense of justice.

(Mark 14:53-65). The religious leaders knew they had no grounds for charging Jesus, so they tried to build evidence against him by using false witnesses (Mark 14:55-59).

• **18:22-27** We can easily blame the high council for their injustice in condemning Jesus, but we must remember that Peter and the rest of the disciples also contributed to Jesus' pain by deserting and denying him (Matthew 26:56, 75). While most of us are not like the religious leaders, we are all like the disciples, for all of us have been guilty of denying that Christ is Lord in vital areas of our lives or of keeping secret our identity as believers in times of pressure. Don't excuse yourself by pointing at others whose sins seem worse than yours. Instead, come to Jesus for forgiveness and healing.

18:25 The other three Gospels say that Peter's three denials happened near a fire in the courtyard outside Caiaphas's palace. John places the first denial outside Annas's home and the other two denials outside Caiaphas's home. This was very likely the

same courtyard. The high priest's compound was large, and Annas and Caiaphas undoubtedly lived near each other.

18:25-27 Imagine standing outside while Jesus, your Lord and Master, is questioned. Imagine watching this man, whom you have come to believe is the long-awaited Messiah, being abused and beaten. Naturally Peter was confused and afraid. It is a serious sin to deny Christ, but Jesus forgave Peter (21:15-17). No sin is too great for Jesus to forgive if you are truly repentant. He will forgive even your worst sin if you turn from it and ask his pardon.

26 But one of the household slaves of the high priest, a relative of the man whose ear Peter had cut off, asked, "Didn't I see you out there in the olive grove with Jesus?" 27 Again Peter denied it. And immediately a rooster crowed.

18:27
John 13:38

Jesus Stands Trial before Pilate
(**230**/Matthew 27:11-14; Mark 15:2-5; Luke 23:1-5)

28 Jesus' trial before Caiaphas ended in the early hours of the morning. Then he was taken to the headquarters of the Roman governor.* His accusers didn't go inside because it would defile them, and they wouldn't be allowed to celebrate the Passover. 29 So Pilate, the governor, went out to them and asked, "What is your charge against this man?"

30 "We wouldn't have handed him over to you if he weren't a criminal!" they retorted.

31 "Then take him away and judge him by your own law," Pilate told them.

"Only the Romans are permitted to execute someone," the Jewish leaders replied. 32 (This fulfilled Jesus' prediction about the way he would die.*)

18:32
Matt 20:19
John 12:32

33 Then Pilate went back into his headquarters and called for Jesus to be brought to him. "Are you the king of the Jews?" he asked him.

18:33
Luke 23:3
John 19:9

34 Jesus replied, "Is this your own question, or did others tell you about me?"

35 "Am I a Jew?" Pilate retorted. "Your own people and their leading priests brought you to me for trial. Why? What have you done?"

36 Jesus answered, "My Kingdom is not an earthly kingdom. If it were, my followers would fight to keep me from being handed over to the Jewish leaders. But my Kingdom is not of this world."

18:36
Matt 26:53
Luke 17:21
John 6:15

18:28 Greek *to the Praetorium;* also in 18:33.   **18:32** See John 12:32-33.

18:27 This fulfilled Jesus' words to Peter after he promised he would never deny him (Mark 14:31; John 13:38).

18:28 By Jewish law, entering the house of a Gentile would cause a Jewish person to be ceremonially defiled. As a result, he could not take part in worship at the Temple or celebrate the festivals until he was restored to a state of "cleanness." Afraid of being

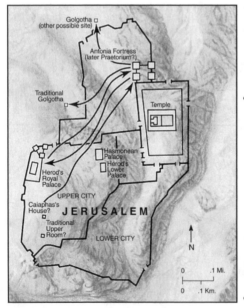

JESUS' TRIAL AND CRUCIFIXION Jesus was taken from trial before the Jewish high council to trial before the Roman governor, Pilate, in Pilate's palace. Pilate sent him to Herod (Luke 23:5-12), but Herod just returned Jesus to Pilate. Responding to threats from the mob, Pilate finally turned Jesus over to be crucified.

defiled, these men stayed outside the house where they had taken Jesus for trial. They kept the ceremonial requirements of their religion while harboring murder and treachery in their hearts.

18:29 This Roman governor, Pilate, was in charge of Judea (the region where Jerusalem was located) from A.D. 26 to 36. Pilate was unpopular with the Jews because he had raided the Temple treasuries for money to build an aqueduct. He did not like the Jews, but when Jesus, the King of the Jews, stood before him, Pilate found him innocent.

18:30 Pilate knew what was going on; he knew that the religious leaders hated Jesus, and he did not want to act as their executioner. They could not sentence him to death themselves—permission had to come from a Roman leader. But Pilate initially refused to sentence Jesus without sufficient evidence. Jesus' life became a pawn in a political power struggle.

• **18:31ff** Pilate made four attempts to deal with Jesus: (1) He tried to put the responsibility on someone else (18:31); (2) he tried to find a way of escape so he could release Jesus (18:39); (3) he tried to compromise by having Jesus flogged rather than handing him over to die (19:1-3); and (4) he tried a direct appeal to the sympathy of the accusers (19:15). Everyone has to decide what to do with Jesus. Pilate tried to let everyone else decide for him—and in the end, he lost.

18:32 This prediction is recorded in Matthew 20:19 and John 12:32, 35. Crucifixion was a common method of execution for criminals who were not Roman citizens.

18:34 If Pilate was asking this question in his role as the Roman governor, he would have been inquiring whether Jesus was setting up a rebel government. But the Jews were using the word *king* to mean their religious ruler, the Messiah. Israel was a captive nation, under the authority of the Roman Empire. A rival king might have threatened Rome; a Messiah could have been a purely religious leader.

• **18:36, 37** Pilate asked Jesus a straightforward question, and Jesus answered clearly. Jesus is a King, but one whose Kingdom is not of this world. There seems to have been no question in Pilate's mind that Jesus spoke the truth and was innocent of any crime. It also seems apparent that while recognizing the truth, Pilate chose to reject it. It is a tragedy when we fail to recognize the truth. It is a greater tragedy when we recognize the truth but fail to heed it.

18:37
John 8:47
1 Jn 4:6

³⁷Pilate said, "So you are a king?"

Jesus responded, "You say I am a king. Actually, I was born and came into the world to testify to the truth. All who love the truth recognize that what I say is true."

Pilate Hands Jesus Over to Be Crucified
(**232**/Matthew 27:15-26; Mark 15:6-15; Luke 23:13-25)

³⁸"What is truth?" Pilate asked. Then he went out again to the people and told them, "He is not guilty of any crime. ³⁹But you have a custom of asking me to release one prisoner each year at Passover. Would you like me to release this 'King of the Jews'?"

⁴⁰But they shouted back, "No! Not this man. We want Barabbas!" (Barabbas was a revolutionary.)

19:1
Isa 50:6; 53:5

19:3
John 18:22

19:4
Luke 23:4
John 18:38

19 Then Pilate had Jesus flogged with a lead-tipped whip. ²The soldiers wove a crown of thorns and put it on his head, and they put a purple robe on him. ³"Hail! King of the Jews!" they mocked, as they slapped him across the face.

⁴Pilate went outside again and said to the people, "I am going to bring him out to you now, but understand clearly that I find him not guilty." ⁵Then Jesus came out wearing the crown of thorns and the purple robe. And Pilate said, "Look, here is the man!"

19:6
John 18:31

⁶When they saw him, the leading priests and Temple guards began shouting, "Crucify him! Crucify him!"

"Take him yourselves and crucify him," Pilate said. "I find him not guilty."

19:7
Lev 24:16
Matt 26:63-66

⁷The Jewish leaders replied, "By our law he ought to die because he called himself the Son of God."

⁸When Pilate heard this, he was more frightened than ever. ⁹He took Jesus back into the headquarters* again and asked him, "Where are you from?" But Jesus gave no answer. ¹⁰"Why don't you talk to me?" Pilate demanded. "Don't you realize that I have the power to release you or crucify you?"

19:11
Rom 13:1

19:12
Luke 23:2
Acts 17:7

¹¹Then Jesus said, "You would have no power over me at all unless it were given to you from above. So the one who handed me over to you has the greater sin."

¹²Then Pilate tried to release him, but the Jewish leaders shouted, "If you release this

19:9 Greek *the Praetorium*.

18:38 Pilate was cynical; he thought that all truth was relative. To many government officials, truth was whatever the majority of people agreed with or whatever helped advance their own personal power and political goals. When there is no standard or acknowledgement of truth, there is no basis for moral right and wrong. Justice becomes whatever works or whatever helps those in power. In Jesus and his Word we have a standard for truth and for our moral behavior.

18:40 Barabbas was a rebel against Rome, and although he had committed murder, he was probably a hero among the Jews. The Jews hated being governed by Rome and paying taxes to the despised government. Barabbas, who had led a rebellion and failed, was released instead of Jesus, the only one who could truly help Israel. For more on Barabbas, see the note on Luke 23:18, 19.

19:1ff To grasp the full picture of Jesus' crucifixion, read John's perspective along with the other three accounts in Matthew 27, Mark 15, and Luke 23. Each writer adds meaningful details, but each has the same message—Jesus died on the cross, in fulfillment of Old Testament prophecy, so that we could be saved from our sins and be given eternal life.

19:1-3 Flogging could have killed Jesus. The usual procedure was to bare the upper half of the victim's body and tie his hands to a pillar before whipping him with a three-pronged whip, with pieces of lead in the prongs. The number of lashes was determined by the severity of the crime; up to 40 were permitted under Jewish law (Deuteronomy 25:3). After being flogged, Jesus also endured other agonies recorded here and in the other Gospels.

19:2-5 The soldiers went beyond their orders to whip Jesus—they also mocked his claim to royalty by placing a crown on his head and a royal robe on his shoulders.

19:7 The truth finally came out—the religious leaders had not brought Jesus to Pilate because he was causing rebellion against

Rome, but because they thought he had broken their religious laws. Blasphemy, one of the most serious crimes in Jewish law, deserved the death penalty. Accusing Jesus of blasphemy would give credibility to their case in the eyes of Jews; accusing Jesus of treason would give credibility to their case in the eyes of the Romans. They didn't care which accusation Pilate listened to, as long as he would cooperate with them in killing Jesus.

• **19:10** Throughout the trial we see that Jesus was in control, not Pilate or the religious leaders. Pilate vacillated, the Jewish leaders reacted out of hatred and anger, but Jesus remained composed. He knew the truth, he knew God's plan, and he knew the reason for his trial. Despite the pressure and persecution, Jesus remained unmoved. It was really Pilate and the religious leaders who were on trial, not Jesus. When you are questioned or ridiculed because of your faith, remember that while you may be on trial before your accusers, they are on trial before God.

19:11 When Jesus said the man who delivered him to Pilate was guiltier than Pilate, he was not excusing Pilate for reacting to the political pressure placed on him. Pilate was responsible for his decision about Jesus. Caiaphas and the other religious leaders were guilty of a greater sin because they premeditated Jesus' murder.

19:12, 13 This veiled threat by the Jewish leaders pressured Pilate into allowing Jesus to be crucified. As Roman governor of the area, Pilate was expected to keep the peace. Because Rome could not afford to keep large numbers of troops in the outlying regions, they maintained control by crushing rebellions immediately with brute force. Pilate was afraid that reports to Caesar of insurrection in his region would cost Pilate his job and perhaps even his life. When we face a tough decision, we can take the easy way out, or we can stand for what is right regardless of the cost. If we know the good we ought to do and don't do it, we sin (James 4:17).

man, you are no 'friend of Caesar.'* Anyone who declares himself a king is a rebel against
Caesar."

¹³When they said this, Pilate brought Jesus out to them again. Then Pilate sat down on the
judgment seat on the platform that is called the Stone Pavement (in Hebrew, *Gabbatha*). ¹⁴It
was now about noon on the day of preparation for the Passover. And Pilate said to the people,* "Look, here is your king!"

¹⁵"Away with him," they yelled. "Away with him! Crucify him!"

"What? Crucify your king?" Pilate asked.

"We have no king but Caesar," the leading priests shouted back.

¹⁶Then Pilate turned Jesus over to them to be crucified.

Jesus Is Led Away to Be Crucified
(**234**/Matthew 27:32-37; Mark 15:21-24; Luke 23:26-31)
So they took Jesus away. ¹⁷Carrying the cross by himself, he went to the place called Place of
the Skull (in Hebrew, *Golgotha*).

Jesus Is Placed on the Cross
(**235**/Matthew 27:35-44; Mark 15:25-32; Luke 23:32-43)
¹⁸There they nailed him to the cross. Two others were crucified with him, one on either side,
with Jesus between them. ¹⁹And Pilate posted a sign on the cross that read, "Jesus of Nazareth,* the King of the Jews." ²⁰The place where Jesus was crucified was near the city, and the
sign was written in Hebrew, Latin, and Greek, so that many people could read it.

²¹Then the leading priests objected and said to Pilate, "Change it from 'The King of the
Jews' to 'He said, I am King of the Jews.'"

²²Pilate replied, "No, what I have written, I have written."

²³When the soldiers had crucified Jesus, they divided his clothes among the four of
them. They also took his robe, but it was seamless, woven in one piece from top to bottom.
²⁴So they said, "Rather than tearing it apart, let's throw dice* for it." This fulfilled the Scripture that says, "They divided my garments among themselves and threw dice for my clothing."* So that is what they did.

²⁵Standing near the cross were Jesus' mother, and his mother's sister, Mary (the wife of
Clopas), and Mary Magdalene. ²⁶When Jesus saw his mother standing there beside the dis-
ciple he loved, he said to her, "Dear woman, here is your son." ²⁷And he said to this disciple,
"Here is your mother." And from then on this disciple took her into his home.

19:13 Matt 27:19
19:24 †Ps 22:18
19:25 Matt 27:55-56 Mark 15:40-41 Luke 8:2; 23:49
19:26 John 2:4; 13:23; 20:2; 21:7, 20

19:12 "Friend of Caesar" is a technical term that refers to an ally of the emperor.   **19:14** Greek *Jewish people;* also in 19:20.   **19:19** Or *Jesus the Nazarene.*   **19:24a** Greek *cast lots.*   **19:24b** Ps 22:18.

19:13 The Stone Pavement was part of the Tower of Antonia bordering the northwest corner of the Temple complex.

19:15 The Jewish leaders were so desperate to get rid of Jesus that, despite their intense hatred for Rome, they shouted, "We have no king but Caesar." How ironic that they feigned allegiance to Rome while rejecting their own Messiah! Their own words condemned them, for God was to be their only true King, and they had abandoned every trace of loyalty to him. The priests had truly lost their reason for existence—instead of turning people to God, they claimed allegiance to Rome in order to kill their Messiah.

19:17 The Place of the Skull was probably a hill outside Jerusalem along a main road. Many executions took place here so the Romans could use them as an example to the people.

• **19:18** Crucifixion was a Roman form of execution. The condemned man was forced to carry his cross along a main road to the execution site, as a warning to the people. Types of crosses and methods of crucifixion varied. Jesus was nailed to his cross; some people were tied with ropes. Death came by suffocation because the weight of the body made breathing difficult as the victim lost strength. Crucifixion was a hideously slow and painful death.

19:19 This sign was meant to be ironic. A king, stripped nearly naked and executed in public view, had obviously lost his kingdom forever. But Jesus, who turns the world's wisdom upside down,

was just coming into his Kingdom. His death and resurrection would strike the deathblow to Satan's rule and would establish Jesus' eternal authority over the earth. Few people reading the sign that bleak afternoon understood its real meaning, but the sign was absolutely true. All was not lost. Jesus was King of the Jews—and of the Gentiles, and of the whole universe.

19:20 The sign was written in three languages: Hebrew for the native Jews, Latin for the Roman occupation forces, and Greek for foreigners and Jews visiting from other lands. In a double irony, the multi-lingual sign declared that Jesus was Lord of all.

19:23, 24 Roman soldiers in charge of crucifixions customarily took for themselves the clothes of the condemned men. They divided Jesus' clothing, throwing dice to determine who would get his seamless garment, the most valuable piece of clothing. This fulfilled the prophecy in Psalm 22:18.

19:25-27 Even while dying on the cross, Jesus was concerned about his family. He instructed John to care for Mary, Jesus' mother. Our families are precious gifts from God, and we should value and care for them under all circumstances. Neither Christian work nor key responsibilities in any job or position excuse us from caring for our families. What can you do today to show your love to your family?

19:27 Jesus asked his close friend John, the writer of this Gospel, to care for Jesus' mother, Mary, whose husband, Joseph, must have been dead by this time. Why didn't Jesus assign this task to his brothers? As the oldest son, Jesus entrusted his mother to a person who stayed with him at the cross—and that was John.

Jesus Dies on the Cross (**236**/Matthew 27:45-56; Mark 15:33-41; Luke 23:44-49)

19:28
†Pss 22:15; 69:21

19:30
Job 19:26-27

19:31
Deut 21:22-23

[28]Jesus knew that his mission was now finished, and to fulfill Scripture he said, "I am thirsty."* [29]A jar of sour wine was sitting there, so they soaked a sponge in it, put it on a hyssop branch, and held it up to his lips. [30]When Jesus had tasted it, he said, "It is finished!" Then he bowed his head and released his spirit.

[31]It was the day of preparation, and the Jewish leaders didn't want the bodies hanging there the next day, which was the Sabbath (and a very special Sabbath, because it was the Passover). So they asked Pilate to hasten their deaths by ordering that their legs be broken.

19:28 See Pss 22:15; 69:21.

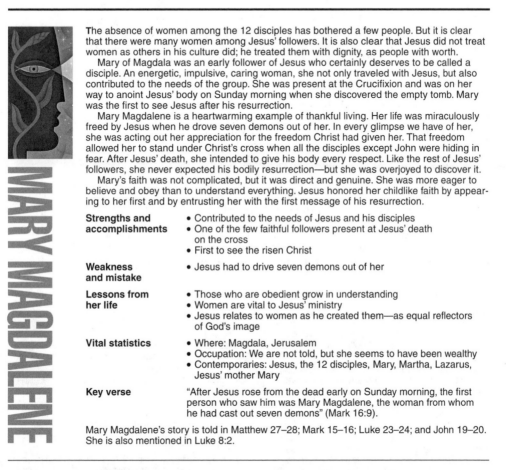

The absence of women among the 12 disciples has bothered a few people. But it is clear that there were many women among Jesus' followers. It is also clear that Jesus did not treat women as others in his culture did; he treated them with dignity, as people with worth.

Mary of Magdala was an early follower of Jesus who certainly deserves to be called a disciple. An energetic, impulsive, caring woman, she not only traveled with Jesus, but also contributed to the needs of the group. She was present at the Crucifixion and was on her way to anoint Jesus' body on Sunday morning when she discovered the empty tomb. Mary was the first to see Jesus after his resurrection.

Mary Magdalene is a heartwarming example of thankful living. Her life was miraculously freed by Jesus when he drove seven demons out of her. In every glimpse we have of her, she was acting out her appreciation for the freedom Christ had given her. That freedom allowed her to stand under Christ's cross when all the disciples except John were hiding in fear. After Jesus' death, she intended to give his body every respect. Like the rest of Jesus' followers, she never expected his bodily resurrection—but she was overjoyed to discover it.

Mary's faith was not complicated, but it was direct and genuine. She was more eager to believe and obey than to understand everything. Jesus honored her childlike faith by appearing to her first and by entrusting her with the first message of his resurrection.

MARY MAGDALENE

Strengths and accomplishments	• Contributed to the needs of Jesus and his disciples • One of the few faithful followers present at Jesus' death on the cross • First to see the risen Christ
Weakness and mistake	• Jesus had to drive seven demons out of her
Lessons from her life	• Those who are obedient grow in understanding • Women are vital to Jesus' ministry • Jesus relates to women as he created them—as equal reflectors of God's image
Vital statistics	• Where: Magdala, Jerusalem • Occupation: We are not told, but she seems to have been wealthy • Contemporaries: Jesus, the 12 disciples, Mary, Martha, Lazarus, Jesus' mother Mary
Key verse	"After Jesus rose from the dead early on Sunday morning, the first person who saw him was Mary Magdalene, the woman from whom he had cast out seven demons" (Mark 16:9).

Mary Magdalene's story is told in Matthew 27–28; Mark 15–16; Luke 23–24; and John 19–20. She is also mentioned in Luke 8:2.

19:29 This sour wine was a cheap wine that the Roman soldiers drank while waiting for those crucified to die.

19:30 Until this time, a complicated system of sacrifices had atoned for sins. Sin separates people from God, and only through the sacrifice of an animal, a substitute, could people be forgiven and become clean before God. But people sin continually, so frequent sacrifices were required. Jesus, however, became the final and ultimate sacrifice for sin. The word *finished* is the same as "paid in full." Jesus came to *finish* God's work of salvation (4:34; 17:4), to pay the full penalty for our sins. With his death, the complex sacrificial system ended because Jesus took all sin upon himself. Now we can freely approach God because of what Jesus did for us. Those who believe in Jesus' death and resurrection can live eternally with God and escape the penalty that comes from sin.

19:31 It was against God's law to leave the body of a dead person exposed overnight (Deuteronomy 21:23), and it was also against the law to work after sundown on Friday, when the Sabbath began. This is why the religious leaders urgently wanted to get Jesus' body off the cross and buried by sundown.

19:31-35 These Romans were experienced soldiers. They knew from many previous crucifixions whether a man was dead or alive. There was no question that Jesus was dead when they checked him, so they decided not to break his legs as they had done to the other victims. Piercing his side and seeing the sudden flow of blood and water (indicating that the sac surrounding the heart and the heart itself had been pierced) was further proof of his death. Some people say Jesus didn't really die, that he only passed out—and that's how he came back to life. But we have the witness of an impartial party, the Roman soldiers, that Jesus died on the cross (see Mark 15:44, 45).

Then their bodies could be taken down. [32]So the soldiers came and broke the legs of the two men crucified with Jesus. [33]But when they came to Jesus, they saw that he was already dead, so they didn't break his legs. [34]One of the soldiers, however, pierced his side with a spear, and immediately blood and water flowed out. [35](This report is from an eyewitness giving an accurate account. He speaks the truth so that you also can believe.*) [36]These things happened in fulfillment of the Scriptures that say, "Not one of his bones will be broken,"* [37]and "They will look on the one they pierced."*

19:35
John 20:30-31;
21:24
1 Jn 1:1

19:36
†Exod 12:46
Num 9:12
†Ps 34:20

19:37
†Zech 12:10
Rev 1:7

Jesus Is Laid in the Tomb (**237**/Matthew 27:56-61; Mark 15:42-47; Luke 23:50-56)
[38]Afterward Joseph of Arimathea, who had been a secret disciple of Jesus (because he feared the Jewish leaders), asked Pilate for permission to take down Jesus' body. When Pilate gave permission, Joseph came and took the body away. [39]With him came Nicodemus, the man who had come to Jesus at night. He brought about seventy-five pounds* of perfumed ointment made from myrrh and aloes. [40]Following Jewish burial custom, they wrapped Jesus' body with the spices in long sheets of linen cloth. [41]The place of crucifixion was near a garden, where there was a new tomb, never used before. [42]And so, because it was the day of preparation for the Jewish Passover* and since the tomb was close at hand, they laid Jesus there.

19:39
John 3:1-2; 7:50

19:40
Luke 24:12
John 20:5-7

Jesus Rises from the Dead (**239**/Matthew 28:1-7; Mark 16:1-8; Luke 24:1-12)
20 Early on Sunday morning,* while it was still dark, Mary Magdalene came to the tomb and found that the stone had been rolled away from the entrance. [2]She ran and found Simon Peter and the other disciple, the one whom Jesus loved. She said, "They have taken the Lord's body out of the tomb, and we don't know where they have put him!"
[3]Peter and the other disciple started out for the tomb. [4]They were both running, but the other disciple outran Peter and reached the tomb first. [5]He stooped and looked in and saw the linen wrappings lying there, but he didn't go in. [6]Then Simon Peter arrived and went inside. He also noticed the linen wrappings lying there, [7]while the cloth that had covered Jesus' head was folded up and lying apart from the other wrappings. [8]Then the disciple who had reached the tomb first also went in, and he saw and believed—[9]for until then they still hadn't understood the Scriptures that said Jesus must rise from the dead. [10]Then they went home.

20:2
John 13:23

20:3
Luke 24:12

20:5
John 19:40

20:7
John 11:44

20:9
John 2:22

19:35 Some manuscripts read *can continue to believe.* **19:36** Exod 12:46; Num 9:12; Ps 34:20. **19:37** Zech 12:10. **19:39** Greek *100 litras* [32.7 kilograms]. **19:42** Greek *because of the Jewish day of preparation.* **20:1** Greek *On the first day of the week.*

19:32 The Roman soldiers would break victims' legs to hasten the death process. When a person hung on a cross, death came by suffocation, but the victim could push against the cross with his legs to hold up his body and keep breathing. With broken legs, he would suffocate almost immediately.

19:34, 35 The graphic details of Jesus' death are especially important in John's record because he was an eyewitness.

19:36, 37 Jesus died as the lambs for the Passover meal were being slain. Not a bone was to be broken in these sacrificial lambs (Exodus 12:46; Numbers 9:12). Jesus, the Lamb of God, was the perfect sacrifice for the sins of the world (1 Corinthians 5:7).

19:38, 39 Four people were changed in the process of Jesus' death. The criminal, dying on the cross beside Jesus, asked Jesus to include him in his Kingdom (Luke 23:39-43). The Roman officer proclaimed that Jesus was surely the Son of God (Mark 15:39). Joseph and Nicodemus, members of the Jewish high council and secret followers of Jesus (7:50-52), came out of hiding. These men were changed more by Jesus' death than by his life. They realized who Jesus was, and that realization brought out their belief, proclamation, and action. When confronted with Jesus and his death, we should be changed—to believe, proclaim, and act.

• **19:38-42** Joseph of Arimathea and Nicodemus were secret followers of Jesus. They were afraid to make this allegiance known because of their positions in the Jewish community. Joseph was a leader and honored member of the Jewish high council. Nicodemus, also a member of the high council, had come to Jesus by night (3:1) and later tried to defend him before the other religious leaders (7:50-52). Yet they risked their reputations to provide for Jesus' burial. Are you a secret believer? Do you hide your faith from your friends and fellow workers? This is an appropriate time to step out of hiding and let others know whom you follow.

19:42 As they buried Jesus, Nicodemus and Joseph had to hurry to avoid working on the Sabbath, which began Friday evening at sundown. This tomb was probably a cave carved out of the stone hillside. It was large enough for a person to walk into, so Joseph and Nicodemus carried Jesus' body into it. A large stone was rolled in front of the entrance.

20:1 Other women came to the tomb along with Mary Magdalene. The other Gospel accounts give their names. For more information on Mary Magdalene, see her Profile on page 1797.

20:1 The stone was not rolled away from the entrance to the tomb so Jesus could get out. He could have left easily without moving the stone. It was rolled away so others could get *in* and see that Jesus was gone.

• **20:1ff** People who hear about the Resurrection for the first time may need time before they can comprehend this amazing story. Like Mary and the disciples, they may pass through four stages of belief. (1) At first, they may think the story is a fabrication, impossible to believe (20:2). (2) Like Peter, they may check out the facts and still be puzzled about what happened (20:6). (3) Only when they encounter Jesus personally are they able to accept the fact of the Resurrection (20:16). (4) Then, as they commit themselves to the risen Lord and devote their lives to serving him, they begin to understand fully the reality of his presence with them (20:28).

20:6, 7 The linen wrappings were left as if Jesus' body had simply vacated them. The cloth that covered Jesus' head was still rolled up in the shape of a head, and it was at about the right distance from the wrappings that had enveloped Jesus' body. A grave robber couldn't possibly have made off with Jesus' body and left the linens as if they were still shaped around it.

20:9 As further proof that the disciples did not fabricate this story, we find that Peter and John were surprised that Jesus was

Jesus Appears to Mary Magdalene (240/Mark 16:9-11)

20:11-18
Mark 16:9-11

20:12
Mark 16:5
Luke 24:4

20:14
Mark 16:9
Luke 24:16
John 21:4

¹¹Mary was standing outside the tomb crying, and as she wept, she stooped and looked in. ¹²She saw two white-robed angels, one sitting at the head and the other at the foot of the place where the body of Jesus had been lying. ¹³"Dear woman, why are you crying?" the angels asked her.

"Because they have taken away my Lord," she replied, "and I don't know where they have put him."

¹⁴She turned to leave and saw someone standing there. It was Jesus, but she didn't recognize him. ¹⁵"Dear woman, why are you crying?" Jesus asked her. "Who are you looking for?"

She thought he was the gardener. "Sir," she said, "if you have taken him away, tell me where you have put him, and I will go and get him."

¹⁶"Mary!" Jesus said.

She turned to him and cried out, "Rabboni!" (which is Hebrew for "Teacher").

THOMAS

Thomas, so often remembered as "Doubting Thomas," deserves to be respected for his faith. He was a doubter, but his doubts had a purpose—he wanted to know the truth. Thomas did not idolize his doubts; he gladly believed when given reasons to do so. He expressed his doubts fully and had them answered completely. Doubting was only his way of responding, not his way of life.

Although our glimpses of Thomas are brief, his character comes through with consistency. He struggled to be faithful to what he knew, despite what he felt. At one point, when it was plain to everyone that Jesus' life was in danger, only Thomas put into words what most were feeling, "Let's go, too—and die with Jesus" (John 11:16). He didn't hesitate to follow Jesus.

We don't know why Thomas was absent the first time Jesus appeared to the disciples after the Resurrection, but he was reluctant to believe their witness to Christ's resurrection. Not even 10 friends could change his mind!

We can doubt without having to live a doubting way of life. Doubt encourages rethinking. Its purpose is more to sharpen the mind than to change it. Doubt can be used to pose the question, get an answer, and push for a decision. But doubt was never meant to be a permanent condition. Doubt is one foot lifted, poised to step forward or backward. There is no motion until the foot comes down.

When you experience doubt, take encouragement from Thomas. He didn't stay in his doubt but allowed Jesus to bring him to belief. Take encouragement also from the fact that countless other followers of Christ have struggled with doubts. The answers God gave them may help you, too. Don't settle into doubts, but move on from them to decision and belief. Find another believer with whom you can share your doubts. Silent doubts rarely find answers.

Strengths and accomplishments	• One of Jesus' 12 disciples • Intense both in doubt and belief • A loyal and honest man
Weaknesses and mistakes	• Along with the others, abandoned Jesus at his arrest • Refused to believe the others' claims to have seen Christ and demanded proof • Struggled with a pessimistic outlook
Lessons from his life	• Jesus does not reject doubts that are honest and directed toward belief • Better to doubt out loud than to disbelieve in silence
Vital statistics	• Where: Galilee, Judea, Samaria • Occupation: Disciple of Jesus • Contemporaries: Jesus, other disciples, Herod, Pilate
Key verses	"Then he said to Thomas, 'Put your finger here and look at my hands. Put your hand into the wound in my side. Don't be faithless any longer. Believe!' 'My Lord and my God!' Thomas exclaimed" (John 20:27-28).

Thomas's story is told in the Gospels. He is also mentioned in Acts 1:13.

---

not in the tomb. When John saw the linen wrappings looking like an empty cocoon from which Jesus had emerged, he believed that Jesus had risen. It wasn't until after they had seen the empty tomb that they remembered what the Scriptures and Jesus had said—he would die, but he would also rise again!

20:9 Jesus' resurrection is the key to the Christian faith. Why? (1) Just as he said, Jesus rose from the dead. We can be confident, therefore, that he will accomplish all he has promised.

(2) Jesus' bodily resurrection shows us that the living Christ, not a false prophet or imposter, is ruler of God's eternal Kingdom. (3) We can be certain of our own resurrection because Jesus was resurrected. Death is not the end—there is future life. (4) The divine power that brought Jesus back to life is now available to us to bring our spiritually dead selves back to life. (5) The Resurrection is the basis for the church's witness to the world.

¹⁷"Don't cling to me," Jesus said, "for I haven't yet ascended to the Father. But go find my brothers and tell them, 'I am ascending to my Father and your Father, to my God and your God.'"

¹⁸Mary Magdalene found the disciples and told them, "I have seen the Lord!" Then she gave them his message.

20:17
Matt 28:10
John 16:28
Rom 8:29
Col 1:18
Heb 2:11

Jesus Appears to His Disciples (**244**/Luke 24:36-43)

¹⁹That Sunday evening* the disciples were meeting behind locked doors because they were afraid of the Jewish leaders. Suddenly, Jesus was standing there among them! "Peace be with you," he said. ²⁰As he spoke, he showed them the wounds in his hands and his side. They were filled with joy when they saw the Lord! ²¹Again he said, "Peace be with you. As the Father has sent me, so I am sending you." ²²Then he breathed on them and said, "Receive the Holy Spirit. ²³If you forgive anyone's sins, they are forgiven. If you do not forgive them, they are not forgiven."

20:19-23
Matt 28:16-20
Luke 24:36-49
20:20
John 16:20-22
20:21
Matt 28:19
John 17:18
20:22
John 7:37-39;
14:16-18, 26

Jesus Appears to Thomas (**245**/Mark 16:14)

²⁴One of the twelve disciples, Thomas (nicknamed the Twin),* was not with the others when Jesus came. ²⁵They told him, "We have seen the Lord!"

But he replied, "I won't believe it unless I see the nail wounds in his hands, put my fingers into them, and place my hand into the wound in his side."

20:24
John 11:16

²⁶Eight days later the disciples were together again, and this time Thomas was with them. The doors were locked; but suddenly, as before, Jesus was standing among them. "Peace be with you," he said. ²⁷Then he said to Thomas, "Put your finger here, and look at my hands. Put your hand into the wound in my side. Don't be faithless any longer. Believe!"

²⁸"My Lord and my God!" Thomas exclaimed.

²⁹Then Jesus told him, "You believe because you have seen me. Blessed are those who believe without seeing me."

20:28
John 1:1, 18;
10:30; 14:9
Col 2:9
Titus 2:13
2 Pet 1:1
1 Jn 5:20
20:29
1 Pet 1:8

20:19 Greek *In the evening of that day, the first day of the week.*   **20:24** Greek *Thomas, who was called Didymus.*

20:17 Mary did not want to lose Jesus again. She had not yet understood the Resurrection. Perhaps she thought this was his promised second coming (14:3). But Jesus did not want to be detained at the tomb. If he did not ascend to heaven, the Holy Spirit could not come. Both he and Mary had important work to do.

• **20:18** Mary didn't recognize Jesus at first. Her grief had blinded her; she couldn't see him because she didn't expect to see him. Then he spoke her name, and immediately she recognized him. Imagine the love that flooded her heart when she heard her Savior saying her name. Jesus is near you, and he is calling your name. Can you, like Mary, regard him as your Lord?

20:18 Mary did not meet the risen Christ until she had discovered the empty tomb. She responded with joy and obedience by going to tell the disciples. We cannot meet Christ until we discover that he is indeed alive, that his tomb is empty. Are you filled with joy by this good news, and do you share it with others?

• **20:21** Jesus again identified himself with his Father. He told the disciples by whose authority he did his work. Then he passed the job to his disciples of spreading the Good News of salvation around the world. Whatever God has asked you to do, remember: (1) Your authority comes from God, and (2) Jesus has demonstrated by words and actions how to accomplish the job he has given you. As the Father sent Jesus, Jesus sends his followers . . . and you.

20:22 This may have been a special filling of the Holy Spirit for the disciples, a foretaste of what all believers would experience from the time of Pentecost (Acts 2) and forever after. To do God's work, we need the guidance and power of the Holy Spirit. We must avoid trying to do his work in our own strength.

20:22 There is life in the breath of God. Man was created but did not come alive until God breathed into him the breath of life (Genesis 2:7). God's first breath made man different from all other forms of creation. Now, through the breath of Jesus, God imparted eternal, spiritual life. With this inbreathing came the power to do God's will on earth.

20:23 Jesus was giving the disciples their Spirit-powered and Spirit-guided mission—to preach the Good News about Jesus so people's sins might be forgiven. The disciples did not have the power to forgive sins (only God can forgive sins), but Jesus gave them the privilege of telling new believers that their sins *have been* forgiven because they have accepted Jesus' message (see the note on Matthew 16:19). All believers have this same privilege. We can announce forgiveness of sins with certainty when we ourselves have found repentance and faith.

• **20:24-29** Have you ever wished you could actually see Jesus, touch him, and hear his words? Are there times you want to sit down with him and get his advice? Thomas wanted Jesus' physical presence. But God's plan is wiser. He has not limited himself to one physical body; he wants to be present with you at all times. Even now he is with you in the form of the Holy Spirit. You can talk to him, and you can find his words to you in the pages of the Bible. He can be as real to you as he was to Thomas.

• **20:25-28** Jesus wasn't hard on Thomas for his doubts. Despite his skepticism, Thomas was still loyal to the believers and to Jesus himself. Some people need to doubt before they believe. If doubt leads to questions, and questions lead to answers, and if the answers are accepted, then doubt has done good work. It is when doubt becomes stubbornness and stubbornness becomes a prideful lifestyle that doubt harms faith. When you doubt, don't stop there. Let your doubt deepen your faith as you continue to search for the answer.

20:27 Jesus' resurrected body was unique. It was not the same kind of flesh and blood Lazarus had when he came back to life. Jesus' body was no longer subject to the same laws of nature as before his death. He could appear in a locked room; yet he was not a ghost or apparition because he could be touched and could eat. Jesus' resurrection was *literal* and *physical*—he was not a disembodied spirit.

20:29 Some people think they would believe in Jesus if they could see a definite sign or miracle. But Jesus says we are blessed if we can believe without seeing. We have all the proof we need in

20:30
John 21:25

20:31
John 3:15; 19:35
1 Jn 5:13

30The disciples saw Jesus do many other miraculous signs in addition to the ones recorded in this book. 31But these are written so that you may continue to believe* that Jesus is the Messiah, the Son of God, and that by believing in him you will have life by the power of his name.

Jesus Appears to Seven Disciples (246)

21:2
John 1:45-51;
11:16; 20:24

21:3
Luke 5:5

21 Later, Jesus appeared again to the disciples beside the Sea of Galilee.* This is how it happened. 2Several of the disciples were there—Simon Peter, Thomas (nicknamed the Twin),* Nathanael from Cana in Galilee, the sons of Zebedee, and two other disciples.

3Simon Peter said, "I'm going fishing."

"We'll come, too," they all said. So they went out in the boat, but they caught nothing all night.

21:4
Luke 24:16
John 20:14

4At dawn Jesus was standing on the beach, but the disciples couldn't see who he was. 5He called out, "Fellows,* have you caught any fish?"

"No," they replied.

21:6
Luke 5:4-7

21:7
John 13:23

6Then he said, "Throw out your net on the right-hand side of the boat, and you'll get some!" So they did, and they couldn't haul in the net because there were so many fish in it.

7Then the disciple Jesus loved said to Peter, "It's the Lord!" When Simon Peter heard that it was the Lord, he put on his tunic (for he had stripped for work), jumped into the water, and headed to shore. 8The others stayed with the boat and pulled the loaded net to the shore, for they were only about a hundred yards* from shore. 9When they got there, they found breakfast waiting for them—fish cooking over a charcoal fire, and some bread.

21:9
John 18:18

10"Bring some of the fish you've just caught," Jesus said. 11So Simon Peter went aboard and dragged the net to the shore. There were 153 large fish, and yet the net hadn't torn.

12"Now come and have some breakfast!" Jesus said. None of the disciples dared to ask him, "Who are you?" They knew it was the Lord. 13Then Jesus served them the bread and the fish. 14This was the third time Jesus had appeared to his disciples since he had been raised from the dead.

21:14
John 20:19, 26

20:31 Some manuscripts read *that you may believe.* **21:1** Greek *Sea of Tiberias,* another name for the Sea of Galilee. **21:2** Greek *Thomas, who was called Didymus.* **21:5** Greek *Children.* **21:8** Greek *200 cubits* [90 meters].

**JESUS'
APPEARANCES
AFTER HIS
RESURRECTION**

Mary Magdalene	Mark 16:9-11; John 20:11-18
The other women at the tomb	Matthew 28:8-10
Peter in Jerusalem	Luke 24:34; 1 Corinthians 15:5
The two travelers on the road	Mark 16:12, 13; Luke 24:13-35
Ten disciples behind closed doors	Mark 16:14; Luke 24:36-43; John 20:19-25
All the disciples, with Thomas (excluding Judas Iscariot)	John 20:26-31; 1 Corinthians 15:5
Seven disciples while fishing	John 21:1-14
Eleven disciples on the mountain	Matthew 28:16-20
A crowd of 500	1 Corinthians 15:6
Jesus' brother James	1 Corinthians 15:7
Those who watched Jesus ascend into heaven	Luke 24:44-49; Acts 1:3-8

The truth of Christianity rests heavily on the Resurrection. If Jesus rose from the grave, who saw him? How trustworthy were the witnesses? Those who claimed to have seen the risen Jesus went on to turn the world upside down. Most of them also died for being followers of Christ. People rarely die for halfhearted belief. These are the people who saw Jesus risen from the grave.

---

the words of the Bible and the testimony of believers. A physical appearance would not make Jesus any more real to us than he is now.

20:30, 31 To understand the life and mission of Jesus more fully, all we need to do is study the Gospels. John tells us that his Gospel records only a few of the many events in Jesus' life on earth. But the Good News includes everything we need to know to believe that Jesus is the Messiah, the Son of God, through whom we receive eternal life.

21:1ff This chapter tells how Jesus commissioned Peter. Perhaps Peter needed special encouragement after his denial—he may have felt completely worthless. Verses 1-14 set the scene for Jesus' conversation with Peter.

21:7 Only John ("the disciple Jesus loved") recognized Jesus in the dim morning light, undoubtedly because Jesus had performed a similar miracle earlier (Luke 5:1-11).

Jesus Challenges Peter (**247**)

15After breakfast Jesus asked Simon Peter, "Simon son of John, do you love me more than these?*"

21:15
Matt 26:33

"Yes, Lord," Peter replied, "you know I love you."

"Then feed my lambs," Jesus told him.

16Jesus repeated the question: "Simon son of John, do you love me?"

21:16
Acts 20:28
Heb 13:20-21
1 Pet 5:2-3

"Yes, Lord," Peter said, "you know I love you."

"Then take care of my sheep," Jesus said.

17A third time he asked him, "Simon son of John, do you love me?"

21:17
John 13:38; 16:30

Peter was hurt that Jesus asked the question a third time. He said, "Lord, you know everything. You know that I love you."

Jesus said, "Then feed my sheep.

18"I tell you the truth, when you were young, you were able to do as you liked; you dressed yourself and went wherever you wanted to go. But when you are old, you will stretch out your hands, and others* will dress you and take you where you don't want to go." 19Jesus said this to let him know by what kind of death he would glorify God. Then Jesus told him, "Follow me."

21:19
John 13:36
2 Pet 1:14

20Peter turned around and saw behind them the disciple Jesus loved—the one who had leaned over to Jesus during supper and asked, "Lord, who will betray you?" 21Peter asked Jesus, "What about him, Lord?"

21:20
John 13:23, 25

22Jesus replied, "If I want him to remain alive until I return, what is that to you? As for you, follow me." 23So the rumor spread among the community of believers* that this disciple wouldn't die. But that isn't what Jesus said at all. He only said, "If I want him to remain alive until I return, what is that to you?"

21:22
Matt 16:27

24This disciple is the one who testifies to these events and has recorded them here. And we know that his account of these things is accurate.

21:24
John 15:27; 19:35
1 Jn 1:1-3
3 Jn 1:12

25Jesus also did many other things. If they were all written down, I suppose the whole world could not contain the books that would be written.

21:25
John 20:30

21:15 Or *more than these others do?*   **21:18** Some manuscripts read *and another one.*   **21:23** Greek *the brothers.*

21:15-17 In this beach scene, Jesus led Peter through an experience that would remove the cloud of his denial. Peter had denied Jesus three times. Three times Jesus asked Peter if he loved him. When Peter answered yes, Jesus told him to feed his sheep. It is one thing to say you love Jesus, but the real test is willingness to serve him. Peter had repented, and here Jesus was asking him to commit his life. Peter's life changed when he finally realized who Jesus was. His occupation changed from fisherman to evangelist; his identity changed from impetuous to "rock"; and his relationship to Jesus changed—he was forgiven, and he finally understood the significance of Jesus' words about his death and resurrection.

• **21:15-17** Jesus asked Peter three times if he loved him. The first time Jesus said, "Do you love (Greek *agape:* volitional, self-sacrificial love) me more than these?" The second time, Jesus focused on Peter alone and still used the word translated into Greek, *agape.* The third time, Jesus used the word translated into Greek, *phileo* (signifying affection, affinity, or brotherly love) and asked, in effect, "Are you even my friend?" Each time Peter responded with the word translated into Greek as *phileo.* Jesus doesn't settle for quick, superficial answers. He has a way of getting to the heart of the matter. Peter had to face his true feelings and motives when Jesus confronted him. How would you respond if Jesus asked you, "Do you love me? Do you really love me? Are you even my friend?"

21:18, 19 This was a prediction of Peter's death by crucifixion. Tradition indicates that Peter was crucified for his faith—upside down because he did not feel worthy of dying as his Lord did. Despite what Peter's future held, Jesus told him to follow him. We may be uncertain and fearful about our future. But if we know God is in control, we can confidently follow Christ.

21:21, 22 Peter asked Jesus how John would die. Jesus replied that Peter should not concern himself with that. We tend to compare our lives to others, whether to rationalize our own level of devotion to Christ or to question God's justice. Jesus responds to us as he did to Peter: "What is that to you? As for you, follow me."

21:23 Early church history reports that after John spent several years as an exile on the island of Patmos, he returned to Ephesus where he died as an old man, near the end of the first century.

• **21:25** John's stated purpose for writing his Gospel was to show that Jesus was the Son of God (20:31). He clearly and systematically presented the evidence for Jesus' claims. When evidence is presented in the courtroom, those who hear it must make a choice. Those who read the Gospel of John must also make a choice—is Jesus the Son of God, or isn't he? You are the jury. The evidence has been clearly presented. You must decide. Read John's Gospel and believe!

STUDY QUESTIONS

Thirteen lessons for individual or group study

It's always exciting to get more than you expect. And that's what you'll find in this Bible study guide—much more than you expect. Our goal was to write thoughtful, practical, dependable, and application-oriented studies of God's word.

This study guide contains the complete text of the selected Bible book. The commentary is accurate, complete, and loaded with unique charts, maps, and profiles of Bible people.

With the Bible text, extensive notes and helps, and questions to guide discussion, Life Application Bible Studies have everything you need in one place.

The lessons in this Bible study guide will work for large classes as well as small-group studies. To get everyone involved in your discussions, encourage participants to answer the questions before each meeting.

Each lesson is divided into five easy-to-lead sections. The section called "Reflect" introduces you and the members of your group to a specific area of life touched by the lesson. "Read" shows which chapters to read and which notes and other features to use. Additional questions help you understand the passage. "Realize" brings into focus the biblical principle to be learned with questions, a special insight, or both. "Respond" helps you make connections with your own situation and personal needs. The questions are designed to help you find areas in your life where you can apply the biblical truths. "Resolve" helps you map out action plans for that day.

Begin and end each lesson with prayer, asking for the Holy Spirit's guidance, direction, and wisdom.

Recommended time allotments for each section of a lesson are as follows:

Segment	60 minutes	90 minutes
Reflect on your life	*5 minutes*	*10 minutes*
Read the passage	*10 minutes*	*15 minutes*
Realize the principle	*15 minutes*	*20 minutes*
Respond to the message	*20 minutes*	*30 minutes*
Resolve to take action	*10 minutes*	*15 minutes*

All five sections work together to help a person learn the lessons, live out the principles, and obey the commands taught in the Bible.

Also, at the end of each lesson, there is a section entitled "More for studying other themes in this section." These questions will help you lead the group in studying other parts of each section not covered in depth by the main lesson.

But don't just listen to God's word. You must do what it says. Otherwise, you are only fooling yourselves. For if you listen to the word and don't obey, it is like glancing at your face in a mirror. You see yourself, walk away, and forget what you look like. But if you look carefully into the perfect law that sets you free, and if you do what it says and don't forget what you heard, then God will bless you for doing it (James 1:22-25).

LESSON 1
ENOUGH EVIDENCE TO BELIEVE
JOHN INTRODUCTION

REFLECT
on your life

1 What gives you confidence in someone?

_____

_____

_____

2 What makes you lose confidence in someone?

_____

_____

_____

READ
the passage

Read the three pages of introductory material to John. Note the Key Verses under Vital Statistics. Become familiar with the land of Israel by tracing the travels of Jesus on the map.

3 What was John's purpose for writing this Gospel?

_____

_____

_____

4 What evidence do people need in order to be convinced that Jesus is God's Son?

_____

_____

_____

_____

5 What evidence does John give that Jesus is God's Son?

_____

_____

_____

_____

6 What evidence for Jesus' deity could you present to someone if asked?

_____   REALIZE
                                                        the principle
_____

_____

_____

John was one of the disciples closest to Jesus. He saw everything Jesus did and heard everything Jesus said. John wrote his Gospel to present eyewitness evidence of Jesus' deity so that we may believe and have eternal life. If you are unsure of your faith or of the claims of Christ, this Gospel will give you the evidence you need to decide for Christ. If you are already a believer, this study will boost your confidence.

7 List some questions about God, Jesus, the Bible, or the Christian faith that you always wanted to ask but didn't know whom to ask.

_____   RESPOND
                                                        to the message
_____

_____

_____

_____

_____

_____

8 How might this study of John help answer those questions?

_____

_____

_____

_____

9 Which of your questions is most important to have answered? Why?

_____

_____

_____

RESOLVE
to take action

10 List one or two questions from above that you will begin searching for an answer to this week.

_____

_____

_____

11 To whom can you talk or what can you read this week to find an answer to your question(s)?

_____

_____

_____

_____

MORE
for studying
other themes
in this section

A What do you hope to gain from this study of John? How would you like your life to be different after studying and applying the truths in this book?

B If someone accused you in a court of law of being a Christian, what evidence could they use to prove their claim?

C If your home were dug up one thousand years from now, what would the evidence say about you?

D What is eternal life? How can someone receive eternal life? What difference does it make now to have life after death?

E How does a person receive the Holy Spirit? What does the Holy Spirit do in the world? in your life? How can you live in the power of the Spirit?

LESSON 2
WHAT IS GOD LIKE?
JOHN 1:1-34

REFLECT
on your life

1 Describe yourself without referring to your appearance, career, or accomplishments.

_____

_____

_____

_____

2 How would you describe God to a person who has never been to church?

_____

_____

_____

_____

READ
the passage

Read John 1:1-34 and the following notes:

❐ 1:1   ❐ 1:3-5   ❐ 1:4, 5   ❐ 1:8   ❐ 1:14   ❐ 1:18   ❐ 1:29

3 What are some of the words John (the Gospel writer) uses to describe Christ?

_____

_____

_____

_____

4 What did people know about God before Jesus came?

_____

_____

_____

_____

_____

Communication is difficult without having common experiences or under-standing. Ideas may be interesting, but they must be fleshed out to be mean-ingful. God became flesh in Jesus Christ. No longer do we have to guess what God is like or just discuss him as a concept. Jesus is God come to earth to take away our sins and to give us new life. If God cares that much about us, we can trust him with our daily concerns. Because Jesus is God, we know that what he says is true; we know that his death on the cross really was for sin; and we know that we should obey him and imitate his life.

5 How are Jesus' words and life unique?

_____

_____

_____

_____

6 How are his words and life common to all human beings?

_____

_____

_____

_____

7 What does Jesus' life tell you about God?

_____

_____

_____

_____

_____

8 How does the fact that God's Son came to earth as a human being affect your faith in him?

_____

_____

_____

_____

9 What evidence for Jesus' deity does John appeal to in these verses?

_____

_____

_____

10 How is your faith impacted by the fact that Jesus is God?

_____

_____

_____

RESOLVE
to take action

11 As you encounter the frustrations and difficulties of daily life, remind yourself that Jesus became fully human and experienced frustrations and feelings similar to yours. What will remind you of this fact this week?

_____

_____

_____

MORE
for studying
other themes
in this section

A What does it mean to live in the light of Christ?

B What characteristics of God can others recognize in your life?

C In what areas of life are you stumbling around in darkness?

D What was John the Baptist's mission in life? What qualities of John the Baptist do you admire? How do you need to be open to God so that he will develop these qualities in you?

E According to 1:29, Jesus came to take away the world's sin. In 1:1-34, how does this happen?

F What is new in the life of a person who has been reborn?

LESSON 3
RESPONSES MAKE A DIFFERENCE
JOHN 1:35–2:25

*R*EFLECT
on your life

1 If Jesus were calling twelve disciples today, where would he go? What types of people would he choose?

_____

_____

_____

_____

*R*EAD
the passage

Read John 1:35–2:25 and the following notes:

❏ 1:35ff ❏ 1:37 ❏ 1:46 ❏ 2:5 ❏ 2:14 ❏ 2:14-16 ❏ 2:15, 16 ❏ 2:23-25

2 How did the disciples respond to Jesus? Why did they follow him?

_____

_____

_____

_____

3 Why did Mary respond to Jesus the way she did?

_____

_____

_____

4 How did the Temple leaders respond to Jesus?

_____

_____

_____

5 How does Jesus call disciples today? Why did you decide to follow him?

_____

_____

_____

_____

_____

6 How did John the Baptist respond to Jesus?

_____

_____

_____

_____

7 Give at least one modern example of each kind of response to Jesus.

Response	Biblical example	Modern example
Submission	Mary	_____
Obedience	disciples	_____
Defiance	Temple leaders	_____
Superficiality	people at Passover	_____

The way we respond to Jesus is critical because it can make the difference between life and death—eternally. It can affect our sense of joy and fulfillment as believers. When Andrew, John, Philip, and Nathanael responded, they became disciples—close, intimate companions of Jesus during his three years of public ministry. Belief is not the only criterion of faithfulness to God, but it is the first correct response. What you believe about Christ is fundamental. The Jewish leaders blindly practiced traditional religious rituals and at the same time conducted lucrative business in the Temple. Their defensive rather than repentant response to Jesus revealed the true nature of their heart and faith.

8 What in your life could show disrespect for God?

_____

_____

_____

_____

_____

9 What in your life shows respect for God?

_____

_____

_____

_____

_____

_____

10 What makes it difficult to follow Jesus?

RESPOND
to the message

_____

_____

_____

_____

_____

_____

11 If you sensed God wanted you to give up your lifelong career and serve him in another way, what questions or reservations would you have?

_____

_____

_____

_____

_____

_____

RESOLVE
to take action

12 What response do you need to make in obedience to God this week? What do you know you should do that you have been putting off?

_____

_____

_____

_____

_____

A Why did John the Baptist's disciples follow Jesus? Why did John the Baptist give up these followers?

MORE
for studying
other themes
in this section

B How did Peter come to Christ? Who introduced you to Christ? Who have you introduced to him?

C What does the wedding incident tell us about Jesus? Why did this miracle convince the disciples that Jesus was the Messiah? What would it take to convince you?

D Why did Jesus clear out the Temple? Who or what would he clear out of your church?

E What do Jesus' actions teach us about anger? What makes you angry?

F Why didn't Jesus trust the people at the Passover feast (2:23-24)?

G What evidence for Jesus' deity does John appeal to in these verses?

LESSON 4
POINTING THE WAY
JOHN 3:1–4:42

REFLECT
on your life

1 When was the last time you had to convince someone of something?

_____

_____

_____

2 What was your approach?

_____

_____

_____

READ
the passage

Read John 3:1–4:42, the personality profile of Nicodemus, and the following notes:

❏ 3:1   ❏ 3:3   ❏ 3:16   ❏ 3:19-21   ❏ 3:25ff   ❏ 3:26   ❏ 4:4   ❏ 4:5-7

❏ 4:35   ❏ 4:39

3 What do we learn about Nicodemus from this passage?

_____

_____

_____

4 What do we learn about John the Baptist?

_____

_____

_____

5 What do we learn about the Samaritan woman?

_____

_____

_____

6 Compare Jesus' discussion with Nicodemus with his discussion with the Samaritan woman.

REALIZE
the principle

_____

_____

_____

_____

_____

7 Summarize the gospel message as found in this section.

_____

_____

_____

_____

_____

_____

John the Baptist pointed his disciples to Jesus. Understanding the role God had called him to play in the Kingdom, John gave his complete loyalty and support to Jesus. John is an excellent example of humility and single-minded devotion. Jesus pointed his disciples to a ripe harvest. For a group of men who were at that time thinking only about food, Jesus' call to reach a lost world had to be convicting. Jesus modeled what he said by pointing both Nicodemus and the Samaritan woman to faith in God. The Scriptures still point us, as Christ's disciples today, to reach a lost world.

8 What individuals come to mind when you read Jesus' words "already ripe for harvest" (4:35)?

RESPOND
to the message

_____

_____

_____

9 What happens to a person who dies without Christ?

_____

_____

_____

_____

10 How is the daily life of a nonbeliever different from that of a believer?

_____

_____

_____

_____

_____

11 What difference does knowing Christ make in your life?

_____

_____

_____

_____

_____

12 What slows you down or stops you from sharing your faith with others?

_____

_____

_____

_____

_____

RESOLVE
to take action

13 Whom will you pray for this week about his or her need to find Christ?

_____

_____

_____

_____

14 List two or three steps you can take this week to begin pointing this person to Christ.

_____

_____

_____

_____

A What evidence for Jesus' deity does John appeal to in these verses?

B How does a person become born again? How would you explain this event to your friends?

C How do we know that God loves us? How can we show his love to others? How can we sow for Christ? How can we reap?

D Why did Christ come to earth?

E What happened as a result of Jesus' talking with the Samaritan woman?

MORE
for studying
other themes
in this section

LESSON 5
MAKING A CLAIM
JOHN 4:43–5:47

REFLECT
on your life

1 Think of a friend or acquaintance who has a crippling physical problem. How did this happen to him or her? How has that person adjusted to life?

_____

_____

_____

_____

_____

_____

READ
the passage

Read John 4:43–5:47, the chart "The Claims of Christ," and the following notes:

❑ 4:46-49   ❑ 4:50   ❑ 4:51   ❑ 5:10   ❑ 5:17ff   ❑ 5:31ff   ❑ 5:39, 40   ❑ 5:45

2 What are the similarities between the healing of the official's son and the healing of the man by the pool?

_____

_____

_____

3 What are the differences?

_____

_____

_____

4 What four witnesses of his deity does Jesus appeal to in John 5:33-47?

_____

_____

_____

_____

5 If Jesus were not God, why would he make that claim?

_____

_____

_____

REALIZE
the principle

Some say that Jesus never said he was God, but John quotes Jesus' claim to deity several times. Jesus not only claimed to be God, but he also provided miraculous evidence to prove it. Knowing Jesus is God gives us great confidence when we pray and when we follow his teachings. And having a written record of his life on earth gives real answers to the question "What is God like?" Anyone who wants to know about God has only to look at Jesus.

6 Give some examples of how people try to explain away Jesus' deity.

_____

_____

_____

_____

RESPOND
to the message

7 What would it take to convince people that Jesus is God?

_____

_____

_____

8 If a person really believes that Jesus is God, what difference should this make in his or her life?

_____

_____

_____

_____

9 What changes might you make in your life to reflect more clearly Christ's divine authority over your life?

_____

_____

_____

_____

_____

10 What Bible verse can you memorize or carry with you this week that affirms Jesus' deity in your own mind and that you can use with others?

_____

_____

_____

MORE
for studying
other themes
in this section

A Explain the statement "A prophet is honored everywhere except in his own hometown and among his own family" (Matt 13:57). How does it relate to your attempts to share the gospel?

B What evidence is there in these verses that Jesus came for all people?

C What was the problem with healing the lame man on the Sabbath? When have you let rules or procedures get in the way of helping people? What religious rules not found in the Bible do people follow today?

D Why did Jesus heal these people? How do you think Jesus would respond to your request for help?

E Describe Jesus' relationship with his Father.

LESSON 6
GOING FOR THE WRONG REASONS
JOHN 6:1-71

REFLECT
on your life

1 What are some right and wrong reasons for going to church?

_____

_____

_____

_____

_____

2 Why do people give up on religion or stop attending church?

_____

_____

_____

READ
the passage

Read John 6:1-71 and the following notes:

❒ 6:5-7   ❒ 6:13   ❒ 6:26   ❒ 6:28, 29   ❒ 6:41   ❒ 6:66   ❒ 6:67, 68   ❒ 6:70

3 At this time in Jesus' ministry, why were people following him?

_____

_____

_____

4 What two sayings of Jesus troubled the Jews?

_____

_____

_____

5 Why did many of Jesus' disciples desert him (6:66)? What was so shocking about Jesus' statement in 6:65?

_____

_____

_____

_____

6 How has God tested your faith?

_____

_____

_____

_____

_____

REALIZE
the principle

7 When has God provided for your needs in a dramatic or miraculous way? How did that affect your faith?

_____

_____

_____

_____

_____

8 What is it about Jesus that people find difficult to understand or believe today?

_____

_____

_____

_____

_____

Often people followed Jesus for the wrong reasons (e.g., to see a show, to get food, to be healed, etc.). Like the people in John 6, sometimes we also come to him only for what we can get. Jesus asks us to come believing in him, with no strings attached. Many of the people had only defensive responses to Jesus' statements. When God's word steps on our toes, our best response is humble repentance, not a proud defense. Seeking God with a whole heart, a pure heart, is what pleases him most.

9 What strings do you find easy to attach to your faith in Christ?

_____

_____

_____

_____

10 In what ways do you follow Christ for what he can do for you rather than for what you can do for him?

_____

_____

_____

_____

11 How can you begin to follow him more wholeheartedly?

_____

_____

_____

12 Complete this statement and make it your prayer: "Lord, I will trust in you and follow you, even if I don't get _____."

MORE
for studying
other themes
in this section

A What evidence for Jesus' deity does John appeal to in these verses?

B How did Jesus test Philip? Did Philip pass or fail?

C What part did the disciples play in feeding the five thousand? Who else played a part in this miracle? Why do you think Jesus involved other people in this miracle?

D What did the people think about Jesus after he fed the five thousand? What did the disciples think about Jesus after seeing him in action?

E What do you have to offer Jesus that he can use to make a miracle?

F What needs in your life has God met for which you can be thankful?

LESSON 7
RELIGIOUS BUT FAR FROM GOD
JOHN 7:1–8:59

REFLECT
on your life

1 What famous people have you met?

_____

_____

_____

2 When were you near someone important or famous but didn't realize it (you learned about it later)?

_____

_____

_____

READ
the passage

Read John 7:1–8:59 and the following notes:

❏ 7:3-5   ❏ 7:13   ❏ 7:19   ❏ 7:26   ❏ 7:46-49   ❏ 7:50-52   ❏ 7:51

❏ 8:32   ❏ 8:34, 35

3 What clues can you find that indicate the following people were religious but far from faith in God: the brothers of Jesus, the crowd in Jerusalem, the Pharisees and other Jewish leaders?

_____

_____

_____

_____

4 What doubts did the crowds have about Jesus?

_____

_____

_____

5 What do you think was happening spiritually with Nicodemus?

_____

_____

_____

6 Some people believed in Jesus but were afraid to speak up. What reasons do people give today for not speaking up for Christ?

_____

_____

_____

REALIZE
the principle

7 How are people religious today yet still far from God?

_____

_____

_____

The Jewish leaders were very religious but not very spiritual. They focused on sin and missed forgiveness, focused on the Sabbath and missed the Lord of the Sabbath, focused on their earthly heritage and missed their heavenly heritage, focused on Jesus' words and missed his message. These people thought they were close to God himself, but they missed him. It is easy for us to do the same. We can be busy about many church activities, even read the Scriptures and pray daily, and still have hearts far from God. We can be close to Jesus and yet miss him completely.

8 What keeps you busy at home? at work? at church?

_____

_____

_____

_____

RESPOND
to the message

9 Which, if any, of these activities can absorb so much of your attention that it can cause you to miss Christ?

_____

_____

_____

_____

10 What can you do to be more aware of Christ?

_____

_____

_____

_____

11 How can too much religious activity dull you spiritually?

_____

_____

_____

_____

_____

12 What can you do to avoid developing a callous, religious mind-set?

_____

_____

_____

_____

RESOLVE
to take action

13 What do you need to do this week to let Jesus renew your mind, heart, and spirit? What will help you get close to him again?

_____

_____

_____

_____

14 What can you do in church this Sunday to see Jesus clearly?

_____

_____

_____

A What evidence for Jesus' deity does John appeal to in these verses?

MORE
for studying
other themes
in this section

B Why did the world hate Jesus? How does the world respond to you?

C If you were to ask your neighbors, "Who is Jesus Christ?" what responses would you get? How can you tell them of Christ's true identity?

D Where did Jesus come from? Where did people think he came from? How did this affect how they felt about him?

E What does it mean to be spiritually thirsty? How has the Holy Spirit quenched your spiritual thirst?

F What do you think Jesus wrote in the dirt when he confronted the accusers of the adulterous woman? Why did the older men leave first? How did Jesus respond to the woman and her sin? With whom do you identify in the story?

G How is Jesus the light of your life?

H How has Jesus set you free?

I What was so important about being Abraham's descendants? Who are Abraham's true descendants?

J Why did the Jews want to stone Jesus?

LESSON 8
EYES THAT WILL NOT SEE
JOHN 9:1–10:42

REFLECT
on your life

1 Close your eyes and imagine what it would be like to be totally blind. How would your blindness affect your work and your family life?

_____

_____

_____

2 Now imagine that you were blind and all alone in the world with no means of support. What would you do? How would you live? How would you feel?

_____

_____

_____

READ
the passage

Read John 9:1–10:42 and the following notes:

❏ 9:2, 3 ❏ 9:13-17 ❏ 9:25 ❏ 9:28, 34 ❏ 10:1 ❏ 10:11, 12
❏ 10:16 ❏ 10:24

3 What were the doubts of the neighbors?

_____

_____

_____

4 What were the doubts of the Pharisees?

_____

_____

_____

5 How did each of these groups respond to their doubts?

_____

_____

_____

_____

6 How did the formerly blind man describe Jesus?

_____

_____

_____

_____

7 How did the Pharisees respond to this description of Jesus and his questions?

_____

_____

_____

_____

8 How did the man who had been healed of blindness respond when he saw Jesus?

_____

_____

_____

9 In what ways were the Pharisees blind?

_____

_____

_____

Physical blindness is considered a handicap. It is a world of darkness that many have learned to overcome. Spiritual blindness is a darkness of another kind. It is caused by unbelief. A person can receive spiritual sight just as the blind man received his physical sight—through faith and obedience. He believed the words of Jesus and obeyed him. He went to the pool of Siloam and washed his eyes. Then, hearing that Jesus was the Messiah, he readily believed and worshiped. You and I can receive spiritual sight by hearing the words of Jesus, believing, and responding in obedience. Listen carefully to his words. They are light and sight to the one who hears and obeys.

REALIZE
the principle

10 How can we be spiritually blind?

_____

_____

_____

_____

RESPOND
to the message

11 What part does doubt play in spiritual blindness? How has Jesus been a light to you?

_____

_____

_____

_____

12 What unanswered questions or doubts are hindering you from fully trusting the words of Jesus?

_____

_____

_____

_____

13 How has God opened your eyes? What spiritual insights about yourself has God helped you clearly see?

_____

_____

_____

_____

14 What are some areas of spiritual blindness in your life that friends or family have pointed out to you?

_____

_____

_____

_____

15 Pray this week that God would show you one area of your life where you have been blind to his teaching. (This could be a relationship, a habit, or a thought pattern.) Write it here and describe how you believe God wants you to deal with that blindness.

RESOLVE
to take action

_____

_____

_____

16 What will you do this week to begin to resolve your doubts?

_____

_____

_____

_____

A What evidence for Jesus' deity does John appeal to in these verses?

MORE
for studying
other themes
in this section

B Why was the man born blind? What are some of the reasons God allows suffering and pain in the world? How do you respond to an illness or difficult situation? How could a difficult experience in your life bring glory to God?

C How was the formerly blind man's faith tested? How has your faith been tested? What can you do to be ready to pass these tests?

D Which name of Jesus means the most to you and why?

E What is the difference between a shepherd and a hired hand? Why does Jesus call himself "the good shepherd"? How can you have "a rich and satisfying life"?

F Who are the "other sheep" in 10:16? Who are the "other sheep" you know who are waiting to hear?

G Why did the people find it so difficult to accept the proof for Jesus' divinity? What would it take to convince people today that Jesus is God?

H Why did the Pharisees want to kill Jesus?

LESSON 9
A RESURRECTION OF HOPE
JOHN 11:1–12:50

1 How do people in our society deny mortality—the fact that death is inevitable for everyone?

_____

_____

_____

_____

_____

2 How would you explain death to a six-year-old child?

_____

_____

_____

_____

Read John 11:1–12:50 and the following notes:

❐ 11:5-7   ❐ 11:14, 15   ❐ 11:33-37   ❐ 12:13   ❐ 12:16   ❐ 12:23-25
❐ 12:27   ❐ 12:31

3 What reason did Jesus give for waiting to go to Lazarus?

_____

_____

_____

4 How did Martha and Mary respond when they saw Jesus?

_____

_____

_____

5 Why did Jesus raise Lazarus from the dead? How did people respond to this?

_____

_____

_____

6 How did Jesus face the prospect of his own death?

_____

_____

_____

7 What can we learn from Martha's conversations with Jesus in 11:21-27, 39-40?

_____

_____

_____

_____

REALIZE
the principle

The stark reality is that every person has to die. Many look at death with a sense of fear: "What lies ahead? . . . Is this life all there is?" Sometimes we react by holding on to this life, afraid to lose it and afraid to face the next. But the message of Jesus Christ is hope. Though we die, we will be raised again and live forever with Christ. He is preparing a place for us in heaven and coming back for us. Instead of fearing death, we can live with confidence. Our confidence is in his promise and in his demonstration of power over death. Knowing that he is able to raise the dead and that he experienced death himself, we can take comfort in knowing that he understands our deepest fears.

8 How do people love their life today (12:25)?

_____

_____

_____

_____

9 How can the story of Jesus and Lazarus give us hope?

_____

_____

_____

_____

10 What frightens you most about death and dying?

_____

_____

_____

_____

11 How can this story of Jesus and Lazarus help you prepare for death?

_____

_____

_____

_____

12 What in this life are you holding on to that you need to let go of and lose?

_____

_____

_____

_____

13 Make two lists, one of your fears and the other of those things that tend to take priority over Christ in your life. Pray through these lists daily, asking God to remove your fears and giving him anything that stands in the way of total devotion to Christ.

Fears   _Misplaced priorities_

_____   _____

_____   _____

_____   _____

_____   _____

A What evidence for Jesus' deity does John appeal to in these verses?

B Why did Mary and Martha ask Jesus for help? How do you need his help?

MORE
for studying
other themes
in this section

C How can troubles be opportunities for honoring Christ?

D What does the story of Jesus and Lazarus teach us about God's timing? When have you tried to hurry God?

E Why did the disciples try to talk Jesus out of going to Jerusalem?

F Why did Jesus cry? What causes his sorrow today?

G Why didn't Lazarus's resurrection convince everyone of Jesus' divinity?

H How did Mary change from chapter 11 to chapter 12? How can you be more like Mary?

I What kind of person was Judas? Why did Jesus allow him to be a disciple?

J Why did the Jews want to kill Lazarus?

K What were the people expecting when they greeted Jesus at the gates of Jerusalem with such enthusiasm? What misconceptions do people have about Jesus today?

L Why was Jesus troubled (12:27)?

M What is implied concerning evangelism today in Jesus' statement, "When I am lifted up from the earth, I will draw everyone to myself" (12:32)?

N What did Jesus mean when he told the disciples, "Walk in the light while you can" (12:35)? How can we become children of light?

O To whom are you afraid to declare your faith? Of what are you afraid in declaring your faith?

LESSON 10
BEING A SERVANT OF ALL
JOHN 13:1–14:14

REFLECT
on your life

1 What is the dirtiest or most distasteful job you have ever had to do?

_____

_____

_____

2 Describe a time when you saw a leader, a parent, or someone in authority do a similar kind of work.

_____

_____

_____

READ
the passage

Read John 13:1–14:14, the personality profile of John, and the following notes:

❑ 13:1ff   ❑ 13:1-17   ❑ 13:6, 7   ❑ 13:12ff   ❑ 13:34   ❑ 13:34, 35

3 Why was Peter shocked at Jesus' actions?

_____

_____

_____

_____

4 From what you know about the other disciples, how do you think they felt?

_____

_____

_____

_____

5 What reason did Jesus give for washing the disciples' feet?

_____

_____

_____

6 What does it mean to serve others?

_____

_____

_____

_____

REALIZE
the principle

Jesus not only taught his disciples to be servants, but he also continually demonstrated servanthood by his actions. In humility, he became a man, served everyone around him, and willingly gave up his life for us. Jesus loves and serves each of us, even though he knows the secret motives of our hearts. Jesus told the disciples, and us, to follow his example and serve others. This is what it means to be his true disciple.

7 How does Jesus' statement in 13:34-35 relate to his example of washing the disciples' feet?

_____

_____

_____

8 Describe a true Christian servant you know.

_____

_____

_____

9 When are you like Peter in this story? When are you like Jesus?

_____

_____

_____

_____

_____

RESPOND
to the message

10 Why is it more difficult to serve some people than others?

_____

_____

_____

_____

11 Whom is it difficult for you to serve?

_____

_____

_____

12 How can you demonstrate the servant attitude of Jesus in your home? at work? at school? in your church?

_____

_____

_____

_____

_____

_____

RESOLVE
to take action

13 Select one or two specific persons whom you will try to serve better this week.

_____

_____

_____

_____

14 What are you going to do to serve them? What is required of you? How could you go above or beyond? What could you do that they would never ask for?

_____

_____

_____

_____

_____

A What evidence for Jesus' deity does John appeal to in these verses?

B What did Jesus know about his disciples (e.g., Peter, Judas, John)? How did that knowledge affect his actions toward them? How would you treat someone you knew would betray, deny, or desert you?

C How did Jesus respond to Thomas and Philip in chapter 14?

D What hope from chapter 14 could you share at a funeral?

E What does it mean that Jesus is the way? the truth? the life? How can someone come to the Father through Christ?

F If seeing Jesus is seeing the Father, what have you learned about the characteristics of God the Father through Jesus?

G What have you asked God for in the name of Jesus recently?

MORE
for studying
other themes
in this section

LESSON 11
A CLOSE RELATIONSHIP WITH CHRIST
JOHN 14:15–17:26

REFLECT
on your life

1 Be very quiet for a moment or two. Listen carefully and write down everything you hear.

_____

_____

_____

_____

2 What's the difference between casual and careful listening? Who listens carefully to you?

_____

_____

_____

READ
the passage

Read John 14:15–17:26 and the following notes:

❏ 14:16   ❏ 14:17ff   ❏ 15:1ff   ❏ 15:2, 3   ❏ 15:5, 6   ❏ 15:5-8   ❏ 15:16
❏ 15:26   ❏ 16:1-16   ❏ 17:1ff   ❏ 17:11   ❏ 17:20

3 What does the Holy Spirit do for us?

_____

_____

_____

_____

4 What does it mean to remain in Jesus? What are the results of remaining in him?

_____

_____

_____

_____

5 What kinds of problems and difficulties does Jesus predict for his followers?

_____

_____

_____

_____

6 What resources does Jesus offer us in the face of adversity?

_____

_____

_____

REALIZE
the principle

7 What comes to your mind when you hear the world *counselor?* In what ways is the Holy Spirit our Counselor and Comforter?

_____

_____

_____

8 How is prayer a resource?

_____

_____

_____

_____

9 What are the results of praying in Jesus' name?

_____

_____

_____

Jesus expressed concern for his disciples and encouraged them the night before he was arrested and crucified. His parting words placed strong emphasis on the close relationship offered to everyone who would follow him. Through the work of the Holy Spirit (our Counselor) and our obedience, we can live close to God in a relationship that is compared to the living unity of a grapevine and its branches. Through prayer each one of us is able to approach God directly and tell him the deepest, innermost thoughts of our heart. With great love and under-standing, God answers when we pray in the name of Jesus.

RESPOND
to the message

10 What can we do to stay close to Jesus, like a branch to the vine?

_____

_____

_____

_____

11 What does the Holy Spirit do to nurture our vine–branch relationship with Jesus?

_____

_____

_____

_____

12 In what ways does God prune a fruitful believer? What kind of pruning experiences have you had over the past few months?

_____

_____

_____

_____

13 What new insights has the Holy Spirit revealed to you about God in the past few months? How have those insights affected the way you live?

_____

_____

_____

_____

_____

_____

14 What can you do this week to improve your relationship with Christ?

_____

_____

_____

_____

15 What one request will you make in prayer this week, expecting God to answer?

_____

_____

A What evidence for Jesus' deity does John appeal to in these verses?

B What kind of peace does the world offer us? How does God's peace differ?

C What does it mean to "produce much fruit" for Christ (15:5)? How can we produce fruit for him?

D How has God shown love for you? How can you love others as he has loved you?

E What are the differences between being someone's servant and being his or her friend? What are the advantages of being God's friend?

F What difference does it make to you that Jesus chose you?

G Why would the world hate Jesus' followers? In what ways have you experienced this hatred? How do the world's values differ from yours?

H How is prayer like a battleground? How should you improve your prayer life?

I How can Christians have joy?

J How can a person receive eternal life?

K Why does Jesus want his followers to be in the world? How can we change the world for him?

L In what ways can believers "be one" (17:21)?

MORE
for studying
other themes
in this section

LESSON 12
REJECTING THE SON OF GOD
JOHN 18:1–19:42

REFLECT
on your life

1 What public figures have issued denials recently?

_____

_____

_____

2 As a child, when did you deny the truth, lying to protect yourself?

_____

_____

_____

READ
the passage

Read John 18:1–19:42 and the following notes:

❐ 18:10, 11   ❐ 18:11   ❐ 18:13   ❐ 18:22-27   ❐ 18:31ff   ❐ 18:36, 37
❐ 19:10   ❐ 19:18   ❐ 19:38-42

3 In chapters 18 and 19, what people or groups of people rejected Jesus?

_____

_____

_____

4 To what three different people did Peter deny knowing Jesus? Why did Peter deny Jesus?

_____

_____

_____

5 In what ways do people reject Jesus today?

_____

_____

_____

_____

_____

6 How do we deny Jesus today?

_____

_____

_____

_____

_____

7 Who would want to condemn Jesus today?

_____

_____

_____

_____

Everyone around Jesus, including his closest friends, turned their back on him. Judas betrayed him. Peter denied him. The Jewish leaders condemned him. Pilate merely accommodated him. And the crowd rejected him. Jesus—the Son of God, the worker of miracles, the proclaimer of truth, the man of compassion—was clearly rejected by all. Jesus had to face the cross utterly alone. Jesus subjected himself to unmerciful punishment to pay the penalty we deserve for our sin. He did not accuse, fight back, or fight for his life. He knew that his purpose was to die for us, in our place. Those who ignore him today reject both his life and his death. Receive his sacrifice and forgiveness. Don't continue to reject him.

8 What kinds of pressure make it difficult for you to identify with Jesus?

_____

_____

_____

_____

_____

RESPOND
to the message

9 Why do Christians hesitate to identify themselves with Jesus?

_____

_____

_____

_____

_____

10 How might Christians become more bold, develop more courage, and be more consistent in what they profess?

_____

_____

_____

_____

11 How can Christians support and encourage a brother or sister who has faced rejection because of his or her faith?

_____

_____

_____

_____

_____

RESOLVE
to take action

12 What are you going to do this week to build your confidence in being a consistent witness for Christ?

_____

_____

_____

_____

MORE
for studying
other themes
in this section

A What evidence for Jesus' deity does John appeal to in these verses?

B Why did Judas betray Jesus? What misconceptions about Jesus do people have today? How can we tell them the truth about Christ?

C What kinds of punishment did Jesus endure?

D What were Jesus' responses to Pilate's questions? Why do you think he answered that way?

E Why did Pilate ask, "What is truth?" How would you answer him? Why did he worry about being Caesar's friend? How did this affect Pilate's actions?

F How is Jesus the King? Where are his subjects and kingdom?

G Who crucified Jesus? Why did Jesus die on the cross? With which person(s) in the story can you identify most (John, Peter, Judas, the soldiers, Pilate, Mary, the crowd, Nicodemus, Joseph, Barabbas, or others)?

H How do we know that Jesus really died on the cross? What difference does that make to your faith?

I In the story, whose lives were changed most by Jesus' death? How has your life been changed by Christ?

LESSON 13
DOUBT RESOLVED . . . I BELIEVE!
JOHN 20:1–21:25

REFLECT
on your life

1 Think back to a time when you said something you knew to be true but no one believed you. How did you respond to their doubts?

_____

_____

_____

_____

READ
the passage

Read John 20:1–21:25, the personality profiles of Mary Magdalene and Thomas, and the following notes:

❐ 20:1ff ❐ 20:18 ❐ 20:21 ❐ 20:24-29 ❐ 20:25-28 ❐ 21:15-17 ❐ 21:25

2 How did Mary Magdalene react when she found the stone rolled away?

_____

_____

_____

3 How did the disciples first respond when they found the tomb empty?

_____

_____

_____

4 How did Thomas respond to the report that Jesus was alive? What did it take for him to believe?

_____

_____

_____

5 What evidence for the Resurrection does John present?

_____

_____

_____

6 What doubts did you once have about Jesus?

_____ REALIZE
the principle
_____

_____

_____

7 What doubts do you still have about Jesus?

_____

_____

_____

8 For what reason did John write his Gospel (20:31)?

_____

_____

We have all faced doubts about God, the Bible, another person's testimony, and even ourselves. The critical question is, what do we do about our doubts? We can casually ignore God's claims, continually question them, stubbornly resist them, flatly deny them—or look for answers. God tells us to believe and to have faith. But he does not ask us to believe without careful consideration of clear evidence. John has provided us with ample evidence for a reasonable faith in Jesus Christ. What kind of evidence would you accept? Believe him and find life. "Blessed are those who believe without seeing me" (John 20:29).

9 What evidence is most convincing to you that Jesus is God's Son and that you need to believe in him?

_____ RESPOND
to the message
_____

_____

_____

_____

10 What evidence that Jesus is alive do you see in other people's lives?

_____

_____

_____

_____

11 What kinds of situations or circumstances tend to make your faith falter?

_____

_____

_____

_____

_____

12 What lingering doubts do you have that cause you concern?

_____

_____

_____

_____

13 What would it take for you to resolve those doubts and believe?

_____

_____

_____

_____

R
RESOLVE
to take action

14 Rather than deny your doubts, embrace them, try to understand them, and search out the evidence to answer them. With which doubt can you begin? What kind of evidence of God's faithfulness do you need?

_____

_____

_____

_____

_____

A What evidence for Jesus' deity does John appeal to in these verses?

B How is your life different since you first believed? How can you spread the news about the risen Christ?

C What doubts do your unbelieving friends have? What could you do to help them work through their doubts?

D How does the Bible bring life (20:31)? How can you improve your Bible study?

E What have you learned about Jesus' love from his relationship with Peter? What would your response be if Jesus asked you the questions he asked Peter?

F How did Peter respond to Jesus' questions? What are the "these" that Jesus asked Peter about in 21:15?

G How would you respond to Jesus' question, "Do you love me?"

H Why do we tend to compare our life with other people's lives? How does Jesus' answer to Peter in 21:22 relate to that tendency?

I If the Jews worshiped on Saturday, the Sabbath, what reason would the believers in Christ have for worshiping on Sunday, the first day of the week?

MORE
for studying
other themes
in this section

Take Your Bible Study to the **Next Level**

The ***Life Application Study Bible*** helps you apply truths in God's Word to everyday life. It's packed with nearly 10,000 notes and features that make it today's #1–selling study Bible.

Life Application Notes: Thousands of Life Application notes help explain God's Word and challenge you to apply the truth of Scripture to your life.

Personality Profiles: You can benefit from the life experiences of over a hundred Bible figures.

Book Introductions: These provide vital statistics, an overview, and a timeline to help you quickly understand the message of each book.

Maps: Over 200 maps next to the Bible text highlight important Bible places and events.

Christian Worker's Resource: Enhance your ministry effectiveness with this practical supplement.

Charts: Over 260 charts help explain difficult concepts and relationships.

Harmony of the Gospels: Using a unique numbering system, the events from all four Gospels are harmonized into one chronological account.

Daily Reading Plan: This reading plan is your guide to reading through the entire Bible in one unforgettable year.

Topical Index: A master index provides instant access to Bible passages and features that address the topics on your mind.

Dictionary/Concordance: With entries for many of the important words in the Bible, this is an excellent starting place for studying the Bible text.

Available in the New Living Translation, New International Version, King James Version, and New King James Version. Take an interactive tour of the *Life Application Study Bible* at
www.NewLivingTranslation.com/LASB

CP0271